Mathematical Methods and Operation Research in Logistics, Project Planning, and Scheduling, 2nd Edition

Mathematical Methods and Operation Research in Logistics, Project Planning, and Scheduling, 2nd Edition

Guest Editors

Zsolt Tibor Kosztyán
Zoltán Kovács

MDPI

Basel • Beijing • Wuhan • Barcelona • Belgrade • Novi Sad • Cluj • Manchester

Guest Editors

Zsolt Tibor Kosztyán
Department of Quantitative Methods
University of Pannonia
Veszprém
Hungary

Zoltán Kovács
Department of Supply Chain Management
University of Pannonia
Veszprém
Hungary

Editorial Office
MDPI AG
Grosspeteranlage 5
4052 Basel, Switzerland

This is a reprint of the Special Issue, published open access by the journal *Mathematics* (ISSN 2227-7390), freely accessible at: https://www.mdpi.com/si/mathematics/Operation_Research_II.

For citation purposes, cite each article independently as indicated on the article page online and as indicated below:

Lastname, A.A.; Lastname, B.B. Article Title. *Journal Name* **Year**, *Volume Number*, Page Range.

ISBN 978-3-7258-4367-1 (Hbk)
ISBN 978-3-7258-4368-8 (PDF)
https://doi.org/10.3390/books978-3-7258-4368-8

Contents

About the Editors

Zsolt Tibor Kosztyán

Zsolt Tibor Kosztyán is a full professor and head of the Department of Quantitative Methods, University of Pannonia. His research interest is the development of methodologies to manage complex management problems and systems relating to mathematical models and algorithms of project management, production, maintenance, and network science. This research area is on the frontier between Management Science and Applied Informatics and Applied Network Science. He obtained an MSc in Information Technology from the University of Pannonia in 2002, and received his PhD also from the University of Pannonia in 2006. He has been awarded 15 National and 2 International Scholarships. He has more than a hundred cumulative impact factors.

Zoltán Kovács

Zoltán Kovács is a full professor at the Department of Supply Chain Management, University of Pannonia, the former dean of the Faculty of Business and Economics. Zoltán received his MSc in Industrial Engineering from the University of Pannonia in 1980, and received his PhD from the Budapest University of Technology and Economics. He was awarded a six-month Fulbright Scholarship in 1993–1994 in the USA. Zoltán started his career in the meat industry as the head of quality control lab and later worked for a coal mining company as IT associate. In SCM, he has special interest in production and service management, logistics, and maintenance. He extensively uses statistical methods and Monte Carlo simulation. Zoltán is the author of books 'Operations Management' and 'Logistics' and co-authored—among others—'Reliability and Maintenance'.

mathematics

MDPI

Editorial

Preface to the Special Issue on "Mathematical Methods and Operation Research in Logistics, Project Planning, and Scheduling, 2nd Edition"

Zsolt Tibor Kosztyán [1,2,*] and Zoltán Kovács [3,*]

1 Department of Quantitative Methods, Institute of Management, Faculty of Business Administration and Economics, University of Pannonia, 8200 Veszprem, Hungary
2 Research Fellow, Institute of Advanced Studies Kőszeg (iASK), 9730 Kőszeg, Hungary
3 Department of Supply Chain Management, Institute of Management, Faculty of Business Administration and Economics, University of Pannonia, 8200 Veszprem, Hungary
* Correspondence: kosztyan.zsolt@gtk.uni-pannon.hu (Z.T.K.); kovacs.zoltan@gtk.uni-pannon.hu (Z.K.)

In the last decade, the Fourth Industrial Revolution (Industry 4.0) brought to the fore flexible supply chains and flexible design projects. More recently, the COVID-19 pandemic, the economic problems that accompanied it, and the resulting supply issues have further increased the role of logistics and supply chains. Therefore, planning and scheduling procedures that can respond flexibly to changing circumstances have become more valuable in both logistics and projects.

There are already several competing criteria in project and logistics process planning and scheduling that need to be reconciled. Additionally, the pandemic has shown that even more emphasis needs to be placed on taking potential risks into account. Flexibility and resilience are emphasized in all decision-making processes, including the scheduling of logistics processes, activities, and projects.

The aim of this Special Issue was to gather novel, original publications that offer new methods and approaches in the field of planning and scheduling in logistics and project planning that are able to respond to the challenges of a dynamic environment.

The present Special Issue of the MDPI journal *Mathematics*, titled "Mathematical Methods and Operation Research in Logistics, Project Planning, and Scheduling, 2nd Edition", contains a total of eight articles that cover a wide range of topics related to the theory, models, and applications of project planning, project scheduling, and operation research problems in logistics. These topics include, among others, scheduling problems, research allocation problems in project planning, routing and warehousing problems in logistics, and risk aggregation problems in risk assessments.

In Contribution 1, Wang et al. develop a resilient supply chain optimization model that considers both proactive and reactive defense strategies to address disruptions caused by events like the COVID-19 pandemic. The model aims to maximize the expected profit by determining optimal raw material inventory, temporary distribution center locations, and product design changes in response to supply disruptions and distribution center failures. The study contributes to logistics and operations research by providing a comprehensive approach to improving supply chain resilience, demonstrating how combining strategies like inventory mitigation, temporary facility locations, and product redesign can significantly reduce losses during major disruptions.

In Contribution 2, Zhang et al. present a multi-objective Q-learning-based brain storm optimization (MQBSO) algorithm to solve an integrated distributed flow shop and distribution scheduling problem. The proposed MQBSO outperforms other metaheuristics in obtaining promising solutions, as demonstrated through extensive numerical experiments and statistical tests. The study contributes to operations research, particularly scheduling problems, by addressing a novel integrated production and distribution problem in a distributed manufacturing environment and introducing an effective solution method that combines reinforcement learning with metaheuristics.

In Contribution 3, Xu et al. propose a novel shared bicycle demand prediction method based on station clustering and a deep learning model called GCN-GRU-AM. This approach outperforms other models in predicting bicycle demand across different regions and time periods. The study contributes to logistics and transportation research by improving resource allocation and bicycle management in shared bicycle systems, while also advancing machine learning applications through the development of a hybrid deep learning model that effectively captures spatial–temporal patterns in bicycle usage data.

In Contribution 4, Nirenjan et al. analyze a complex queueing system with multiple control policies, including two-phase bulk service, active Bernoulli feedback, server breakdowns, and vacations. The authors derive a probability-generating function for queue size and various performance measures using supplementary variable techniques. The model has practical applications in optimizing power efficiency in LTE-A networks using the Discontinuous Reception (DRX) mechanism, contributing to the research fields of telecommunications and operations.

In Contribution 5, Leon et al. propose a two-step methodology combining heuristic algorithms and simulation techniques to optimize task sequencing for Automated Guided Vehicles (AGVs) in manufacturing environments. The developed heuristic algorithms, particularly MLRF/LPTF, consistently outperform the NEH-based approach in minimizing makespan, with improvements ranging from 16.82% to 19.49% on average across various instances. The study contributes to the field of operations and logistics research by addressing the complex challenge of AGV task sequencing with resource sharing and dynamic queues, offering a scalable solution that can handle large instances and potentially be extended to stochastic settings.

In Contribution 6, Mihalcz and Kosztyán describe how incorporating additional factors beyond the traditional three used in FMEA (Severity, Occurrence, and Detection) can lead to a more comprehensive risk assessment in supply chains. Specifically, their study demonstrates that adding Cost and Control as factors and using a fuzzy logic approach results in a more accurate identification of significant risks. The proposed framework, TREF (Total Risk Evaluation Framework), offers supply chain managers a practical tool to evaluate their processes, regardless of the mathematical foundations or the variety of variables utilized in risk assessment.

In Contribution 7, Ni et al. investigate a two-machine group scheduling problem with sequence-independent setup times and round-trip transportation times, derived from steel manufacturing requirements. The authors develop a mixed-integer programming model to minimize makespan and propose a two-stage heuristic algorithm for an NP-hard case of a single transporter, which achieves solutions within 1.38% of lower bounds for large problem instances. The study contributes to the fields of both scheduling and transportation by incorporating round-trip transportation times and limited transportation capacity constraints into the group scheduling problem, advancing our understanding of coordinated scheduling decisions with restricted material flows in multi-stage manufacturing settings.

Finally, in Contribution 8, Souse et al. propose a novel approach to the fuzzy multi-item newsvendor problem for inventory management applications. The main contributions of their study include a new credibility estimation to explore impactful demand scenarios, a simulation procedure for comparing different fuzzy MINP approaches, and a modified genetic algorithm to enhance solution generation and evaluation. The proposed hybrid algorithm significantly outperformed previous fuzzy approaches, improving profit by up to 55% in low-budget scenarios, and slightly outperformed classical approaches in complex cases.

Collectively, these eight studies enhance our theoretical understanding and provide practical methodologies that may be immediately implemented and modified across various sectors. This collection successfully addresses the complex issues encountered by contemporary logistics and scheduling systems by integrating heuristic approaches, stochastic optimization, and real-world supply chain scenarios.

This volume will serve as a vital reference for researchers, practitioners, and decision-makers aiming to create and operate efficient, robust, and flexible logistics and scheduling systems.

As Guest Editors of this Special Issue, we are grateful to all authors who contributed their articles. We would also like to express our gratitude to all reviewers for their valuable comments on improving the submitted papers. The goal of this Special Issue was to attract quality and novel papers in the field of "Mathematical Methods and Operation Research in Logistics, Project Planning, and Scheduling". We hope that the international scientific community finds the included research papers impactful, and that these contributions will motivate further operations research on solving complex problems in various disciplines and application fields.

Conflicts of Interest: The authors declare no conflicts of interest.

List of Contributions:

1. Wang, N.; Chen, J.; Wang, H. Resilient supply chain optimization considering alternative supplier selection and temporary distribution center location. *Mathematics* **2023**, *11*, 3955.
2. Zhang, S.; Xu, J.; Qiao, Y. Multi-Objective Q-Learning-Based Brain Storm Optimization for Integrated Distributed Flow Shop and Distribution Scheduling Problems. *Mathematics* **2023**, *11*, 4306.
3. Xu, J.Y.; Qian, Y.; Zhang, S.; Wu, C.C. Demand Prediction of Shared Bicycles Based on Graph Convolutional Network-Gated Recurrent Unit-Attention Mechanism. *Mathematics* **2023**, *11*, 4994.
4. Niranjan, S.P.; Devi Latha, S.; Mahdal, M.; Karthik, K. Multiple control policy in unreliable two-phase bulk queueing system with active Bernoulli feedback and vacation. *Mathematics* **2024**, *12*, 75.
5. Leon, J.F.; Peyman, M.; Martin, X.A.; Juan, A.A. Simulation of Heuristics for Automated Guided Vehicle Task Sequencing with Resource Sharing and Dynamic Queues. *Mathematics* **2024**, *12*, 271.
6. Mihálcz, I.; Kosztyán, Z.T. REFS-A Risk Evaluation Framework on Supply Chain. *Mathematics* **2024**, *12*, 841.
7. Ni, Y.; Dai, S.; Yuan, S.; Wang, B.; Zhang, Z. Model and Algorithm for a Two-Machine Group Scheduling Problem with Setup and Transportation Time. *Mathematics* **2024**, *12*, 888.
8. Sousa, J.M.; Luís, R.; Santos, R.M.; Mendonça, L.; Vieira, S.M. Fuzzy multi-item newsvendor problem: An application to inventory management. *Mathematics* **2024**, *12*, 1652.

mathematics

MDPI

Article

Resilient Supply Chain Optimization Considering Alternative Supplier Selection and Temporary Distribution Center Location

Na Wang [1], Jingze Chen [2] and Hongfeng Wang [2,*]

[1] Department of Basic Computing and Mathematics, Shenyang Normal University, Shenyang 110034, China; nawang@synu.edu.cn
[2] College of Information Science and Engineering, Northeastern University, Shenyang 110819, China; 2110328@stu.neu.edu.cn
* Correspondence: hfwang@mail.neu.edu.cn

Abstract: The global supply chain is facing huge uncertainties due to potential emergencies, and the disruption of any link may threaten the security of the supply chain. This paper considers a disruption scenario in which supply disruption and distribution center failure occur simultaneously from the point of view of the manufacturer. A resilient supply chain optimization model is developed based on a combination of proactive and reactive defense strategies, including manufacturer's raw material mitigation inventory, preference for temporary distribution center locations, and product design changes, with the objective of obtaining maximum expected profit. The proposed stochastic planning model with demand uncertainty is approximated as a mixed integer linear programming model using Latin hypercube sampling (LHS), sample average approximation (SAA), and scenario reduction (SR) methods. In addition, an improved genetic algorithm (GA) is also developed to determine the approximate optimal solution. The algorithm ensures the feasibility of the solution and improves the solving efficiency through specific heuristic repair strategies. Numerical experiments are conducted to verify the application and advantages of the proposed disruption recovery model and approach. The experimental results show that the proposed resilient supply chain optimization model can effectively reduce the recovery cost of manufacturers after disruption, and the proposed approach performs well in dealing with related problems.

Keywords: resilient supply chain; disruption recovery; heuristic; genetic algorithm

MSC: 90B06

1. Introduction

In recent years, the COVID-19 pandemic has caused an unprecedented impact on the global supply chain [1]. Unlike limited-scale shocks to supply chains caused by natural disasters such as earthquakes, hurricanes, and floods in the past, the modern global supply chain faces the risk of disruption on a much larger scale than ever before [2].

With the process of globalization and the increased geographic concentration of industries, disruptions at one or a few nodes can affect almost all the nodes and links in the supply chain [3]. Prior to the pandemic, the disruptions discussed in the literature were usually local or regional, they rarely affected the supply chain structure, they were of limited duration, and they mostly occurred after predictable risks [4]. However, disruptions caused by the COVID-19 pandemic can occur simultaneously or sequentially at various points in the supply chain, including suppliers, manufacturers, facilities, and markets, and can propagate forward and backward through material flows, ultimately affecting the entire supply chain network [5,6]. In addition, as companies in the manufacturing supply chain become more connected, disruptions caused by the pandemic would be even more disruptive to assembly manufacturing industries that rely on upstream suppliers [7]. Semiconductor shortages during the pandemic have impacted nearly all global auto manufacturers, causing production capacity losses and order backlogs [8]. The household appliance and electronics industries were similarly plagued by supply shortages and surges in production and orders during the pandemic [9].

To ensure the normal operation of the supply chain, it is necessary to improve the resilience of the supply chain network [10,11]. Strategies for resilient systems can be classified according to their characteristics as proactive defenses and reactive defenses [12]. Proactive strategies focus on taking action before a disruption takes place by adding redundancy. In the case of uncertain demand or supply disruption, companies can use inventory and reserve capacity to mitigate the risk of supply chain disruption [13,14]. The planning and location of back-up facilities can mitigate the impact on the supply chain after a facility failure. In the case of disruption of existing facilities due to a pandemic, the pandemic prevention policies and the extent of the pandemic in different countries and regions will influence the manufacturers' location decisions. In addition, global logistics and distribution centers have been proposed to be constructed along the Belt and Road to improve distribution efficiency, and local policies may also influence manufacturers' location decisions [15,16]. Some scholars have introduced a resilience theory to enhance the ability of ports and shipping systems to withstand various risks [17,18]. This reactive strategy is to adopt the appropriate mitigation strategy after a disruption. It is critical to develop the appropriate recovery strategy for supply chain resilience after disruptions [19,20]. Hishamuddin et al. [21] developed a disruption recovery method to obtain a production revision plan with a minimum expected total cost by determining the optimal manufacturing lot size and optimal recovery time for production runs within the recovery time window. Paul et al. [22] developed a reactive mitigation approach to manage sudden supply disruptions in the supply chain.

This paper considers a manufacturing supply chain in which supply disruption and distribution center failure may occur simultaneously. Therefore, the challenges of this study are twofold. On the one hand, there are disruptions originating on the supply side that can lead to shortages of raw materials, which in turn affect production. On the other hand, disruptions also originate from the existing distribution centers, which can lead to disruptions in the distribution and transportation of products. In addition, the uncertainty of demand also needs to be considered, which makes decisions more challenging in practice. For supply disruptions, considering the long-term nature and uncertainty of disruptions in the context of a pandemic, this paper adopts a design change strategy for multiple products based on the work of Chen et al. [23]. The key issue is how to determine the change plan and alternative supplier selection, and thus reconfigure the supply network and determine a new production plan. For distribution center failure due to the pandemic, the key issue is to determine a location for a temporary distribution center considering the manufacturer's selection preference and the impact of the pandemic, as well as the handling capacity and construction cost. The contributions of this work are as follows:

- This work considers the disruption scenario in which supply disruption and distribution center failure occur simultaneously. A two-stage stochastic programming model based on a combination of proactive and reactive defense strategies is developed to improve supply chain resilience in manufacturing companies.
- The two-stage stochastic programming model is transformed into a mixed integer linear programming (MILP) model using Latin hypercubic sampling (LHS), sample average approximation (SAA), and scenario reduction (SR) to deal with continuous demand scenarios and discrete disruptions scenarios, respectively.
- For the model characteristics, this work develops an improved genetic algorithm combined with a heuristic algorithm to increase the efficiency of solving large-scale problems. A specific heuristic repair strategy is designed to ensure the feasibility of the solution.

- By analyzing the results, we verify the superiority of the proposed resilient strategy and algorithm in settling the supply chain disruption problem.

The remainder of this paper is organized as follows: Section 2 provides an overview of the relevant literature. The problem definition and the underlying assumptions are given in Section 3. Section 4 presents the notations and the mathematical model. Section 5 states the transformation method of the model and the proposed improved genetic algorithm. Numerical experiments and a discussion of the results are given in Section 6. Section 7 summarizes the paper and provides directions for future research.

2. Literature Review

The complexity of products, globally dispersed design, production activities, and extensive supply chains under globalization processes pose challenges for today's enterprises. These challenges affect companies' management of their supply chain networks and have been exacerbated by the disruptions to global supply chains caused by the COVID-19 pandemic. This situation is unprecedented, and previous studies have rarely addressed this issue directly [24].

Over the past few decades, there has been significant research on the theoretical background and key strategies of resilient supply chains to address disruption risks that may occur [25]. The literature on strategies to enhance resilience can be divided into two main aspects. One aspect is a proactive defense strategy to mitigate supply chain risks through multiple sourcing, maintaining inventory and contracting with backup suppliers [26]. Pal et al. [27] developed a three-stage supply chain model consisting of a supplier, manufacturer, and retailer to increase inventory by purchasing raw materials in advance, allowing for rapid production resumption in the event of a supply disruption. Jabbarzadeh et al. [28] proposed a stochastic bi-objective optimization model in which the two objectives were to minimize total expected costs and maximize sustainability performance. Additional production capacity, multi-source sourcing, and selection of alternate suppliers are considered in their model. Namdar et al. [29] investigated the impact of purchasing strategies such as backup supplier contracts and spot purchasing on supply chain resilience. It was found that the buyer's early warning ability plays an important role in improving supply chain resilience. Shahed et al. [30] considered the simultaneous existence of supplier disruptions and demand uncertainty and developed a mathematical model to maximize profits by adopting an appropriate inventory policy to cope with possible disruptions in the supply chain network. Vali-Siar and Roghanian [31] proposed a multi-objective optimization model under uncertainty using multiple sourcing, enhanced infrastructure, redundant capacity, and dual-channel distribution strategies to improve supply chain resilience.

Another aspect is a reactive defense strategy to enable the supply chain to recover quickly from disruptions by developing an appropriate recovery strategy. Sawik [32] proposed a two-period modeling approach for the selection of recovery suppliers and recovery assembly plants and the decisions implemented during and after the disruption, comparing it with a multi-period approach. Paul et al. [33] considered three types of uncertain disruptions in the manufacturing supply chain: demand fluctuation, production disruption, and supply disruption, developing a quantitative model to generate a recovery plan after disruption. Khalilabadi et al. [34] developed a multi-stage stochastic planning model that uses a product substitution strategy to mitigate uncertain demand fluctuations in a multi-product supply chain. Chen et al. [35] investigated a disruption recovery strategy from a product design change and life cycle perspective and proposed a mixed integer linear programming model to solve the supply chain disruption recovery problem.

In the past, few scholars have combined proactive and reactive strategies in the design of resilient supply chains. Elluru et al. [36] proposed a location routing model that combine proactive and reactive approaches, taking into account supply chain disruptions caused by disasters. The proactive approach considered the risk factors of the facility prior to the disruption, and the reactive approach considered recovery strategies and the associated penalties. However, the long duration of the pandemic and the uncertainty about the timing and magnitude of disruptions make it necessary for enterprises to consider both pre-disruption defense strategies and post-disruption recovery strategies.

Recently, supply chain disruption recovery strategies for the pandemic have focused on the impact of disruptions on supply, production, and demand fluctuation [37]. Paul et al. [20] developed a recovery model to help enterprises for high-demand products make decisions when designing revised production schedules after supply disruptions. Nagurney et al. [38] considered the uncertainty of product demand and the impact of the COVID-19 pandemic on the workforce and developed a supply chain network optimization model to cope with supply chain disruptions. Taking into account the supply disruptions and demand fluctuations caused by the pandemic, Sawik [39] proposed a multi-portfolio approach and a scenario-based stochastic MIP model to optimize supply chain operations under ripple effects using risk mitigation inventory and alternate supplier procurement strategies. Paul et al. [40] developed a stochastic mathematical model to optimize the recovery of a three-stage supply chain with demand, supply, and capacity uncertainties due to the multi-dimensional impact of the COVID-19 pandemic.

Most existing studies have ignored the possible impact of the pandemic on facilities such as distribution centers. Distribution centers may be at risk of failing to close or not being able to meet uncertain demands. Manufacturers should consider planning backup facilities in advance or constructing temporary distribution centers if existing facilities fail. By properly locating distribution centers, the total cost of the supply chain can be reduced, and the order allocation and transportation efficiency can be improved [41,42]. Amin and Baki [43] developed a multi-objective mixed integer linear programming model for a supply chain network including multiple plants, distribution centers, demand, and products to select the best supplier and distribution center sites considering the uncertainty of demand. Jakubovskis et al. [44] proposed a robust optimization modeling method for facility location and capacity planning under uncertain demand and determined which capabilities can contribute to solution robustness through experiments. Ortiz-Astorquiza [45] conducted a review of multi-level facility location problems that extend several classical facility location problems and identified three different categories of multi-level facility location problems based on the types of decisions made in the optimization process. Saragih et al. [46] developed a heuristic method for solving the location–inventory–routing problem in a three-level supply chain system with uncertain demand. Fu et al. [47] developed a simulation-based optimization approach to the facility location and capacity planning problem under the Belt and Road initiative by considering both policy preference and customer demand uncertainties.

Table 1 summarizes the differences between this paper and related studies in the literature in terms of the types of disruptions considered and the resilience strategies employed, providing additional details to distinguish studies based on resilient supply chain optimization.

Table 1. Comparison between this paper and relevant studies in the literature in terms of encountered disruption and methodology.

Articles	Type of Disruption	Strategy of Resilience		Methodology	
		Proactive	Reactive	Deterministic	Stochastic
Pal et al. [27]	Sd	√		√	
Jabbarzadeh et al. [28]	Sd	√			√
Namdar et al. [29]	Sd	√		√	
Shahed et al. [30]	Sd, Df	√			√
Vali-Siar and Roghanian [31]	Sd, Df	√			√
Sawik [32]	Sd, Pd		√	√	
Paul et al. [33]	Sd, Pcu, Df		√	√	
Khalilabadi et al. [34]	Df		√		√

Table 1. *Cont.*

Articles	Type of Disruption	Strategy of Resilience		Methodology	
		Proactive	Reactive	Deterministic	Stochastic
Chen et al. [35]	Sd		√	√	
Elluru et al. [36]	Dnf	√	√	√	
Paul et al. [20]	Sd		√	√	
Nagurney et al. [38]	La		√		√
Paul et al. [40]	Su, Pcu, Df		√		√
Sawik [39]	Sd, Df	√			√
This paper	Sd, Dnf, Df	√	√		√

Sd: supply disruption, Su: supply uncertainty, Pd: production disruption, Pcu: production capacity uncertainty, La: labor availability, Dnf: distribution network failure, Df: demand fluctuation.

3. Problem Description and Assumptions

3.1. Problem Statement

This paper considers a four-tier supply chain network consisting of suppliers, manufacturers, distribution centers, and customers, where the distribution centers are established by the manufacturer based on the region, the number of orders, and the level of transport logistics. Nodes have a hierarchical relationship between the upstream and downstream components of the supply chain. Each layer of nodes can only be connected to its neighboring layer of nodes, and the layers of nodes are independent of each other. The supply chain network structure is shown in Figure 1. Manufacturers produce a variety of products, and each product requires a variety of parts. Different products may require the same parts, and each part is provided by one supplier. The products are first transported by the manufacturer to the distribution centers, each of which has a maximum capacity, and are then transported by the distribution center to the appropriate customers within its coverage area. Each customer's demand for each product is uncertain.

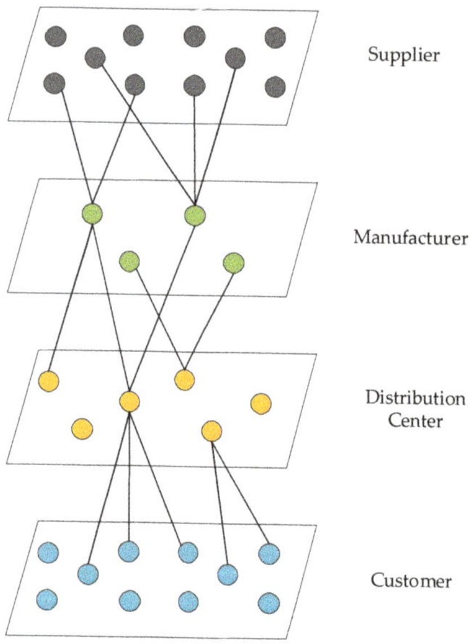

Figure 1. Hierarchical supply chain network.

Due to the COVID-19 pandemic, disruptions may occur in any link of the supply chain, and multiple facilities in the supply chain network may fail at the same time or one after another. Considering the ripple effect, after a disruption occurs at a certain point in the supply chain, it can spread upstream or downstream along the supply chain, leading to more large-scale failures. The propagation of disruptions in the supply chain network is shown in Figure 2, where green indicates that a node is functioning normally, yellow indicates that a node is partially disabled, red indicates that a node is completely disabled, and blue indicates that a node is affected. Here, (a) demonstrates a healthy supply chain network and (b) demonstrates disruptions occurring simultaneously at the suppliers and distribution centers, where S2 and D2 partially fail and S4 and D3 completely fail. Additionally, (c) demonstrates the supply chain network after disruption, where the productions of P1 and P2 are affected due to the failure of suppliers S2 and S4. Due to the partial failure of distribution center D2, the demands of customers C2 and C4 cannot be met. The complete failure of D3 results in an inability to handle the C5 demand, and the link between the nodes is disconnected. (d) denotes the supply chain network after considering the propagation of the disruption ripple effect. Due to the supply disruption, the production capacity of product P1 decreases and the production of product P2 is stopped. Customer C1-C4 orders for P1 may be backordered, and orders for P2 must be cancelled. All the orders for customer C5 were cancelled due to the failure of the upstream distribution center.

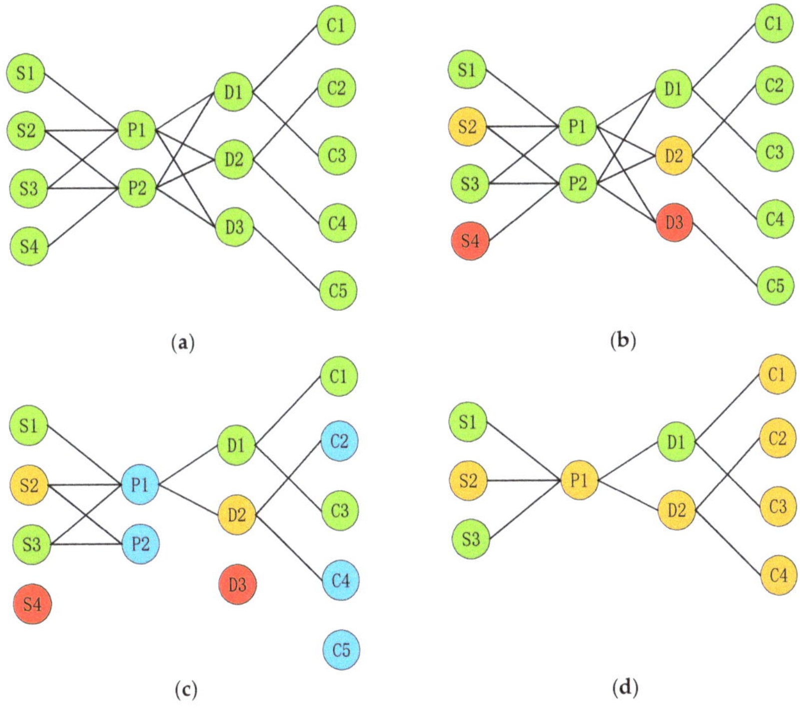

Figure 2. Process of disruption propagation. (**a**) A healthy supply chain network; (**b**) disruptions occurring simultaneously at the suppliers and distribution centers; (**c**) the supply chain network after disruption; (**d**) the supply chain network after the propagation of the disruption ripple effect.

In order to establish a resilient supply chain network, this paper considers a combination of proactive and reactive defense strategies. The manufacturer develops appropriate raw material inventory plans and locates and constructs temporary distribution centers before disruptions occur. The objective is to determine the inventory quantities for each raw material, as well as to find a subset of temporary distribution center locations under conditions that simultaneously satisfy selection preferences, warehouse capacity, and transportation capacity constraints in order to minimize raw material inventory costs and temporary distribution center fixed costs. Considering the uncertainty of the duration of supply disruptions, the manufacturer can make design changes and partially reconfigure suppliers that cannot continue production due to supply shortages, resuming production as soon as possible. After the failure of some distribution centers, the manufacturer selects which distribution centers to open from the constructed temporary distribution centers and reconfigures the distribution network. The reconfigured supply chain network after the adoption of the recovery strategy is shown in Figure 3, where TD1 and TD2 represent the selected temporary distribution centers. When the manufacturer holds a certain amount of raw material inventory and adds AS2 as the substitute supplier for S2, P1 can fully resume production and P2 can resume partial production. In addition, NS1 is the new supplier of the new product NP1 after the design change.

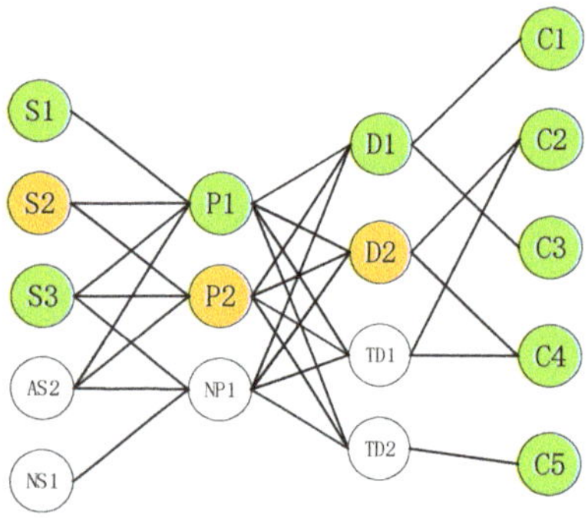

Figure 3. Reconfigured supply chain network after adoption of the recovery strategy.

This paper considers three types of disturbances that can occur in a manufacturing supply chain, namely supply disruptions, distribution center failures, and demand uncertainty, where the magnitude of supply disruptions and distribution center failures is also uncertain. These three disturbances can occur individually or simultaneously. It is difficult to obtain an accurate picture of the probability of disruption to suppliers and distribution centers as well as demand fluctuations. Manufactures can only obtain estimates from historical data. Therefore, manufacturers need to consider the following three important questions before/after disruptions:

- How to determine the inventory quantity of each raw material before disruptions;
- How to locate the temporary distribution center;
- How to choose the product change option and alternative suppliers.

3.2. Assumptions

In order to make the study more relevant and feasible, the following basic assumptions are made:

- The disruption of each supplier and distribution center is independent of each other, and the disruption may cause partial or complete failure of the facility.
- Emergency procurement needs are taken into account to consider the additional procurement cost, but the production delay caused by emergency procurement is not considered, and there is a procurement cost difference between the backup supplier and the original supplier.
- Product design changes require consideration of product design costs and new raw material procurement costs.
- The manufacturer's preference weight coefficient for the location of the new distribution center is determined by the triangular fuzzy number $M(l,\ m,u)$;
- The demand of each customer for each product satisfies the normal distribution $N \sim (\mu,\sigma^2)$, and each customer's demand is independent of the others. When the

demand of customers cannot be met due to supply shortage, the cost of sales loss will be incurred.

- Products are shipped immediately after production, regardless of storage at the manufacturer, and there are inventory capacity limitations at the distribution center.

4. Model Formulation

4.1. Notations and Decision Variables

In order to build a mathematical model, some notations are defined and listed as follows:

List of indices:

i	Index for original suppliers
j	Index for alternative suppliers
p	Index for products
l	Index for original distribution centers
m	Index for temporary distribution centers
n	Index for customers
s	Index for disruption scenarios

List of decision variables:

x_{ij}^{s}	1 if the part from the ith original supplier is changed to the raw material from the jth alternative supplier for the sth disruption scenario, else 0
k_m	1 if the mth temporary distribution center is built, else 0
y_m^s	1 if the mth temporary distribution center is used for the sth disruption scenario, else 0
X_{ij}^{s}	Quantity to be procured for the sth disruption scenario from the jth alternative supplier of the ith original supplier
I_i	Inventory of raw materials supplied by the ith original supplier
Z_{pl}^{s}	Quantity of the pth product transported from the manufacturer to the lth original distribution center for the sth disruption scenario
Z_{pm}^{s}	Quantity of the pth product transported from the manufacturer to the mth temporary distribution center for the sth disruption scenario
Z_{pln}^{s}	Quantity of the pth product transported from the lth original distribution center to the nth customer for the sth disruption scenario
Z_{pmn}^{s}	Quantity of the pth product transported from the mth temporary distribution center to the nth customer for the sth disruption scenario

List of parameters:

u_i^s	1 if the ith original supplier for the sth disruption scenario has not been disrupted, else 0
v_l^s	1 if the lth original distributor center for the sth disruption scenario has not been disrupted, else 0
P_s	Probability of the sth disruption scenario
w_{ip}	1 if the ith supplier supplies raw material for the pth product, else 0
X_i	Quantity to be procured from the ith original supplier
γ	Inventory as a percentage of supply
C_i	Unit procurement cost of raw materials from the ith supplier
C_{ij}	Unit procurement cost of raw materials from the jth alternative supplier of the ith supplier
Q_{ij}	Fixed change cost for the jth alternative supplier of the ith supplier
Qc_{ij}	Unit production cost of changing the raw material for the product from the ith supplier to the jth alternative supplier
Pc_p	Unit production cost of the pth product
Is_i	Minimum safety stock of raw materials supplied by the ith original supplier
I_{max}	Maximum raw material inventory capacity of the manufacturer
μ	Minimum percentage of inventory held by the manufacturer
CI_i	Unit inventory cost of the raw materials supplied by the ith original supplier
E_l	Unit transportation cost from the manufacturer to the lth original distribution center
E_m	Unit transportation cost from the manufacturer to the mth temporary distribution center
E_{ln}	Unit transportation cost from the lth original distribution center to the nth customer
E_{mn}	Unit transportation cost from the mth temporary distribution center to the nth customer
F_{np}	Unit out-of-stock loss cost of the pth product order for the nth customer
K_m	Fixed cost for the mth temporary distribution center

K'_m	Operating cost for the mth temporary distribution center
A_{ij}	Maximum capacity of the jth alternative supplier of the ith original supplier
G_l	Maximum capacity of the lth original distribution center
H_m	Maximum capacity of the mth temporary distribution center
$\tilde{D}_{np}$	Quantity demanded by the nth customer for the pth product, which satisfies a normal distribution
$\tilde{\alpha}_l$	Capacity failure coefficient of the lth original distribution center after a disruption
β_m	Preference weight coefficient for the manufacturer's preference for the mth candidate temporary distribution center
θ	Expectation for manufacturer preference of selected locations

4.2. Model Development

It is difficult to accurately predict the probability of disruption to suppliers and distribution centers as well as demand fluctuations. For modeling and experimentation, as we assume that any supplier disruption and distribution center failure event is random, we generate disruption scenarios to determine characteristics such as the disruption size and duration. To describe disruption scenarios, A is the set consisting of all the suppliers and distribution centers, and A_S is the set of all the disrupted suppliers and failure distribution centers under the disruption scenario s. If the probability of disruption of element a in the set A_S is p_a and the elements are independent of each other, then the probability P_s of the occurrence of scenario s can be calculated by the following equation [48]:

$$P_s = \prod\nolimits_{a \in A_S} p_a \prod\nolimits_{a \in A \backslash A_S} (1 - p_a) \tag{1}$$

In order to characterize the manufacturer's preference for candidate locations, each location is associated with a preference factor, including factors such as local policy orientation, regional epidemic levels, and transportation levels, which indicate the degree of manufacturer preference for building a distribution center in that location It is difficult to know the exact selection preferences, and manufactures can only obtain estimates from managers and experts. Since the manufacturer's preference weight coefficient $\tilde{\beta}_m$ for the temporary distribution center location is somewhat fuzzy, triangular fuzzy numbers can represent the pessimistic, most likely, and optimistic values of the expert opinion. Therefore, they can be used to evaluate the manufacturer's preference for temporary distribution centers. This paper determines the triangular fuzzy number $M(l,\ m,\ u)$ for all alternative locations through expert scoring, where m denotes the most likely preference weight coefficient for the alternative location, l and u denote the upper and lower bounds of the preference weight coefficient for the alternative location, respectively, and the graded mean integration method is used to represent the triangular fuzzy number, which transforms the manufacturer's preference weight coefficient β_m from a fuzzy number to a definite value. This can be expressed as follows:

$$\begin{aligned} G\left(\tilde{\beta}_m(\alpha)\right) &= \frac{\int_0^1 \left(\frac{\alpha}{2}\right)\left[L^{-1}(\alpha)+R^{-1}(\alpha)\right]d\alpha}{\int_0^1 \alpha d\alpha} = \int_0^1 \alpha\left[L^{-1}(\alpha) + R^{-1}(\alpha)\right]d\alpha \\ &= \tfrac{1}{6}(l + 4m + u) \end{aligned} \tag{2}$$

where $L^{-1}(\alpha)$ and $R^{-1}(\alpha)$ are the inverse functions of $L(\alpha)$ and $R(\alpha)$ (left and right function of the triangular fuzzy number), respectively, and the values of $L^{-1}(\alpha)$ and $R^{-1}(\alpha)$ are $l + (m - l)\alpha$ and $u - (u - m)\alpha$, respectively.

In order to establish a resilient supply chain network, it is necessary to not only determine the inventory plan and the construction of temporary facilities before the disruption, but also to decide the recovery plan based on the disruption scenario and the identified supply chain network. Therefore, considering both proactive and reactive defense strategies, a two-stage stochastic planning model is developed in this section. The first stage is to decide on the manufacturer's inventory plan for each raw material and the location of the temporary distribution centers considering the manufacturer's preference before the disruption. The second stage is to make decisions about product design changes, which temporary distribution centers will be used and their processing capacity, and delivery plans for order requirements after the disruption.

The objective function of the first stage is to maximize the total profit, which includes the cost of raw material inventory planning, the cost of temporary distribution center location construction, and the expected profit associated with disruption scenarios and stochastic demand. The first-stage model is established as follows:

$$max\ E_{\xi}R(x,y,X,Z,S,\xi) - \sum_{i\in I} CI_i I_i - \sum_{m\in M} K_m k_m \tag{3}$$

s.t.

$$I_i \le \gamma X_i,\ \forall i \in I \tag{4}$$

$$I_i \ge Is_i,\ \forall i \in I \tag{5}$$

$$\sum_{i\in I} I_i \ge \mu I_{max} \tag{6}$$

$$\sum_{i\in I} I_i \le I_{max} \tag{7}$$

$$\sum_{m\in M} \beta_m k_m \ge \theta \tag{8}$$

$$k_m \in \{0,1\},\ \forall m \in M \tag{9}$$

$$I_i\ are\ positive\ integers,\ \forall i \in I \tag{10}$$

where $R(x,y,X,Z,S,\xi)$ denotes the expected profit associated with disruption scenarios and stochastic demand, which can be determined by the second-stage model. Constraints (4)–(7) constrain the inventory capacity of each raw material. Constraint (8) ensures the manufacturer's preference for the selected locations for the temporary distribution centers. Constraints (9) and (10) define the range of decision variables.

The objective function of the second stage is to maximize the expected profit associated with the disruption scenario and stochastic demand, including the manufacturer's product revenue, the manufacturer's procurement cost from the original supplier, the product change cost, the production cost, the transportation cost from the manufacturer to the distribution centers and from the distribution centers to the customers, and the cost of lost sales. The second-stage model is established as follows:

$$\begin{gathered} R(x,y,X,Z,S,\xi) = \\ max \sum_{s\in S} P_s\{\sum_{p\in P} R_p\left(\sum_{l\in L} Z^s_{pl} + \sum_{m\in M} Z^s_{pm}\right) - [\sum_{i\in I} u^s_i X_i C_i + \sum_{i\in I}\sum_{j\in J}(x^s_{ij} Q_{ij} + \\ X^s_{ij} C_{ij} + X^s_{ij} Qc_{ij}) + \sum_{p\in P} Pc_p\left(\sum_{l\in L} Z^s_{pl} + \sum_{m\in M} Z^s_{pm}\right) + \sum_{m\in M} K'_m y^s_m + \sum_{p\in P}(\sum_{l\in L} E_l Z^s_{pl} + \\ \sum_{m\in M} E_m Z^s_{pm}) + \sum_{n\in N}\sum_{p\in P}\left(\sum_{l\in L} E_{ln} Z^s_{pln} + \sum_{m\in M} E_{mn} Z^s_{pmn}\right) + \sum_{n\in N}\sum_{p\in P} F_{np}(\widetilde{D}_{np} - \\ \sum_{l\in L} Z^s_{pln} - \sum_{m\in M} Z^s_{pmn})]\} \end{gathered} \tag{11}$$

s.t.

$$X^s_{ij} \le (1-u^s_i) x^s_{ij} A_{ij},\ \forall i \in I, j \in J, s \in S \tag{12}$$

$$\sum_{j\in J} x^s_{ij} = 1 - u^s_i,\ \forall i \in I, s \in S \tag{13}$$

$$u^s_i X_i + \sum_{j\in J} X^s_{ij} + (1-u^s_i) I_i \ge \sum_{p\in P} w_{ip}\left(\sum_{l\in L} Z^s_{pl} + \sum_{m\in M} Z^s_{pm}\right),\ \forall i \in I, s \in S \tag{14}$$

$$u^s_i X_i + \sum_{j\in J} X^s_{ij} + (1-u^s_i) I_i \le \sum_{n\in N}\sum_{p\in P} w_{ip}\widetilde{D}_{np}, \forall i \in I,\ s \in S \tag{15}$$

$$y_m^s \le k_m,\ \forall m \in M, s \in S \tag{16}$$

$$\sum_{m\in M} y_m^s \ge 1 - v_l^s,\ \forall s \in S,\ l \in L \tag{17}$$

$$\sum_{m\in M} y_m^s \le \sum_{l\in L} (1 - v_l^s),\ \forall s \in S \tag{18}$$

$$\sum_{p\in P} Z_{pl}^s \le v_l^s G_l + (1 - \widetilde{\alpha}_l)(1 - v_l^s) G_l,\ \forall l \in L, s \in S \tag{19}$$

$$\sum_{p\in P} Z_{pm}^s \le y_m^s H_m,\ \forall m \in M, s \in S \tag{20}$$

$$\sum_{n\in N} Z_{pln}^s = Z_{pl}^s,\ \forall p \in P, l \in L, s \in S \tag{21}$$

$$\sum_{n\in N} Z_{pmn}^s = Z_{pm}^s,\ \forall p \in P, m \in M, s \in S \tag{22}$$

$$\sum_{l\in L} Z_{pln}^s + \sum_{m\in M} Z_{pmn}^s \le \widetilde{D}_{np},\ \forall p \in P, n \in N, s \in S \tag{23}$$

$$x_{ij}^s,\ y_m^s \in \{0,1\},\ \forall i \in I, j \in J, m \in M, s \in S \tag{24}$$

$$X_{ij}^s,\ Z_{pl}^s,\ Z_{pm}^s,\ Z_{pln}^s,\ Z_{pmn}^s \text{ are positive integers},\ \forall i \in I, j \in J, p \in P, l \in L, m \in M, n \in N, s \in S \tag{25}$$

where (12) indicates that the supply of the alternative suppliers must be equal to or less than their maximum supply capacity. Constraint (13) indicates that, at most, one of the alternative suppliers of the disrupted supplier has been selected. Constraints (14) and (15) ensure that the quantity of product produced by the manufacturer exceeds the amount shipped to the distribution center, but does not exceed the demand. Constraints (16)–(18) constrain which of the constructed temporary distribution centers are used. Constraints (19) and (20) indicate that the quantity of product transported from the manufacturer to the original distribution center and to the new distribution center does not exceed the handling capacity of the distribution center. Constraints (21) and (22) ensure that the quantity of each product shipped from the distribution center to the customer equals the quantity shipped by the manufacturer to the distribution center. Constraint (23) ensures that the supply of products from all the distribution centers to the customer cannot exceed the demand of this customer. Constraint (24) constrains the binary nature of the decision variables x_{ij}^s, y_m^s. Finally, (25) defines the other decision variables as positive integers.

5. Solution Approach

5.1. SAA and SR Method

The model developed in this paper contains fuzzy and random numbers. For the fuzzy number n, the fuzzy preference weight coefficients are transformed into a deterministic value by using the graded mean integration method to defuzzify the triangular fuzzy number in Section 4.2 through Equation (1). Since the proposed model contains uncertain demands, this paper considers Latin hypercube sampling (LHS) to obtain samples. Then, the SAA method is used to handle the uncertain demand from discrete samples rather than continuous distribution functions to approximate the expected cost [49]. Assume that $\gamma_1, \gamma_2, \ldots, \gamma_K$ are K uncertain demand scenarios and k is the set of demand scenarios of size K, since disruptions are difficult to describe using continuous probability distribution functions and the probability of each disruption scenario is different. Therefore, for discrete disrupted scenarios, the scenario reduction (SR) method can be adopted to reduce the number of disruption scenarios [50]. The main idea of the SR method is to select a subset from the full set of scenarios, reduce the number of scenarios, and minimize the difference between the optimal objective function value of the full scenario problem and the optimal objective function value of the reduced scenario problem. Using the SAA and SR method, the two-stage stochastic planning model can be rewritten as a deterministic MILP model as follows:

$$max\ \frac{1}{K}\sum_{k\in K}\{\sum_{s\in\hat{S}}\hat{p}_s[\sum_{p\in P}R_p(\sum_{l\in L}Z^s_{plk}+\sum_{m\in M}Z^s_{pmk})-\sum_{i\in I}u^s_iX_iC_i-\sum_{i\in I}\sum_{j\in J}(x^s_{ijk}Q_{ij}+X^s_{ijk}C_{ij}+X^s_{ijk}Qc_{ij})-\sum_{p\in P}Pc_p(\sum_{l\in L}Z^s_{plk}+\sum_{m\in M}Z^s_{pmk})-\sum_{m\in M}K'_my^s_{mk}-\sum_{p\in P}(\sum_{l\in L}E_lZ^s_{plk}+\sum_{m\in M}E_mZ^s_{pmk})-\sum_{n\in N}\sum_{p\in P}(\sum_{l\in L}E_{ln}Z^s_{plnk}+\sum_{m\in M}E_{mn}Z^s_{pmnk})-\sum_{n\in N}\sum_{p\in P}F_{np}(D_{npk}-\sum_{l\in L}Z^s_{plnk}-\sum_{m\in M}Z^s_{pmnk})]\}-\sum_{i\in I}CI_iI_i-\sum_{m\in M}K_mk_m \tag{26}$$

s.t.

$$X^s_{ijk}\le(1-u^s_i)x^s_{ijk}A_{ij},\ \forall i\in I,j\in J,s\in S,\ k\in K \tag{27}$$

$$\sum_{j\in J}x^s_{ijk}=1-u^s_i,\ \forall i\in I,s\in S,k\in K \tag{28}$$

$$I_i\le\gamma X_i,\ \forall i\in I \tag{29}$$

$$I_i\ge Is_i,\ \forall i\in I \tag{30}$$

$$\sum_{i\in I}I_i\ge\mu I_{max} \tag{31}$$

$$\sum_{i\in I}I_i\le I_{max} \tag{32}$$

$$u^s_iX_i+\sum_{j\in J}X^s_{ijk}+(1-u^s_i)I_i\ge\sum_{p\in P}w_{ip}\left(\sum_{l\in L}Z^s_{plk}+\sum_{m\in M}Z^s_{pmk}\right),\ \forall i\in I,s\in S,\ k\in K \tag{33}$$

$$u^s_iX_i+\sum_{j\in J}X^s_{ijk}+(1-u^s_i)I_i\le\sum_{n\in N}\sum_{p\in P}w_{ip}D_{npk},\forall i\in I,\ s\in S,\ k\in K \tag{34}$$

$$\sum_{m\in M}\beta_mk_m\ge\theta \tag{35}$$

$$y^s_{mk}\le k_m,\ \forall m\in M,s\in S,k\in K \tag{36}$$

$$\sum_{m\in M}y^s_{mk}\ge 1-v^s_l,\ \forall s\in S,\ l\in L,k\in K \tag{37}$$

$$\sum_{m\in M}y^s_{mk}\le\sum_{l\in L}(1-v^s_l),\ \forall s\in S,k\in K \tag{38}$$

$$\sum_{p\in P}Z^s_{plk}\le v^s_lG_l+\left(1-\tilde{\alpha}_l\right)(1-v^s_l)G_l,\ \forall l\in L,s\in S,\ k\in K \tag{39}$$

$$\sum_{p\in P}Z^s_{pmk}\le y^s_mH_m,\ \forall m\in M,s\in S,\ k\in K \tag{40}$$

$$\sum_{n\in N}Z^s_{plnk}=Z^s_{plk},\ \forall p\in P,l\in L,s\in S,\ k\in K \tag{41}$$

$$\sum_{n\in N}Z^s_{pmnk}=Z^s_{pmk},\ \forall p\in P,m\in M,s\in S,\ k\in K \tag{42}$$

$$\sum_{l\in L}Z^s_{plnk}+\sum_{m\in M}Z^s_{pmnk}\le D_{npk},\ \forall p\in P,n\in N,s\in S,\ k\in K \tag{43}$$

$$k_m,x^s_{ijk},\ y^s_{mk}\in\{0,1\},\ \forall i\in I,j\in J,m\in M,s\in S,k\in K \tag{44}$$

$$I_i\ ,X^s_{ijk},\ Z^s_{plk},\ Z^s_{pmk},\ Z^s_{plnk},\ Z^s_{pmnk}\ are\ positive\ integers,\ \forall i\in I,j\in J,p\in P,l\in L,m\in M,n\in N,s\in S,\ k\in K \tag{45}$$

where $\hat{S}$ and $\hat{p}_s$ denote the set of new disruption scenarios and the corresponding probability of disruption occurrence after descending the disruption scenario.

5.2. Improved Genetic Algorithm

The proposed problem of alternative supplier selection and temporary distribution center location is very complex, which is NP-hard by nature. Various optimization tools have been widely used to solve similar small- and medium-sized problems, although there are limitations in terms of long solution times and the size of the solutions. This requires the development of an efficient and effective optimization algorithm to find the optimal or approximate optimal solution [51]. Genetic algorithms are stochastic global search optimization methods whose computational mechanisms are derived from natural selection and natural adaptation processes. Therefore, considering that the model processed using the SAA and SR methods is MILP with constraints, an improved genetic algorithm is developed in this paper as a solution to determine the optimal value. The algorithm adopts a number of effective strategies to solve the problem by targeting the repair heuristics for the specific problem of the proposed model to improve the solving power of the algorithm.

The components of a chromosome are encoded in segments. The first part determines the selection options for alternative suppliers after product design changes for each disruption scenario using integer coding. The second part indicates the quantity of each raw material in stock using integer coding. The third part determines the location of the temporary distribution center and is binary coded.

Since it is not easy to randomly generate raw material inventory quantities that satisfy the manufacturer's inventory capacity constraints and demand constraints as feasible chromosomes, a specific repair heuristic is developed to ensure the feasibility of the solution represented by the chromosome. The repair heuristic is presented as follows:
Step 1: Calculate the sum of the inventory of each raw material. If it exceeds the manufacturer's maximum inventory capacity, proceed to step 2, otherwise proceed to step 3. Step 2: Count the number b_i of disruptions for each supplier in all the disruption situations S and calculate the maximum inventory of each raw material as $B_i = I_{max} \times (b_i / \sum_{i \in I} b_i)$. If the inventory of the ith raw material exceeds B_i, it will be changed to B_i, otherwise it will remain unchanged. Step 3: If the total inventory of raw materials is less than μI_{max}, first calculate $b_i / \sum_{i \in I} b_i$ to sort from largest to smallest, and then increase the inventory of each raw material in order until the requirement is satisfied, otherwise it will remain unchanged.

After generating the alternative supplier solution x_{ij}^{s} after the product change and the original raw material inventory I_i by chromosome, a heuristic strategy is designed to obtain the procurement quantity of each alternative raw material according to the customer's demand for each product under a disruption scenario. The heuristic strategy is presented as follows:

Step 1: Determine the current disruption scenario s, if $u_i = 0$ and $x_{ij} = 1$, calculate $X_{ij} = \sum_{n \in N} \sum_{p \in P} w_{ip} D_{npk} - I_i$, otherwise $X_{ij} = 0$.

Step 2: In order to avoid the calculated X_{ij} violating the supply capacity limit A_{ij} of the selected alternative supplier, if $X_{ij} > A_{ij}$, $X_{ij} = A_{ij}$, otherwise X_{ij} remains unchanged.

In the evaluation process, the objective function of maximizing the manufacturer's profit is used as the fitness function. The part of the function related to the decision variables contained in the generated chromosome can be calculated directly. The remaining part of the function is related to the quantity of raw materials purchased by the manufacturer, and the allocation of orders between the manufacturer, distribution centers, and retailers can be formulated as an integer programming problem determined through optimization using Gurobi. The procedures of the improved genetic algorithm are presented in Figure 4.

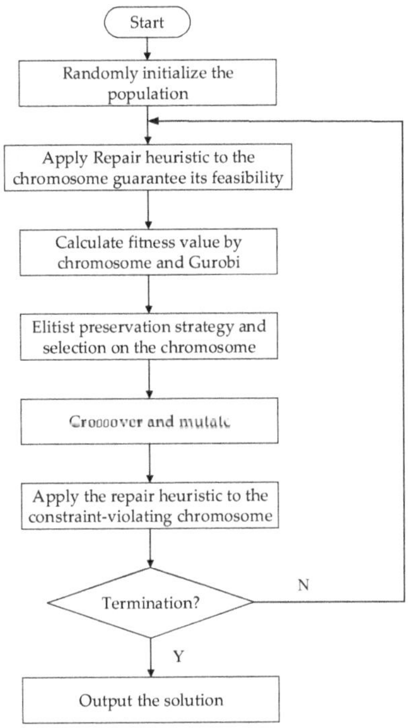

Figure 4. Flowchart of the improved genetic algorithm.

6. Numerical Experiments

This section verifies the feasibility of the proposed model and the validity of the proposed genetic algorithm through numerous examples. The parameters are determined based on the assumptions made for the model, and values are assigned to each parameter through a randomly generated data set. In addition, we perform a sensitivity analysis on the different parameters to characterize the effect of their changes on the results.

6.1. Computational Results

It is assumed that eight suppliers provide raw materials for the manufacturer, and the manufacturer produces three products, each of which requires a different combination of raw materials. The products will first be shipped from the manufacturer to the distribution center and then distributed to the customers according to their orders. There are five distribution centers that deliver orders to ten customers, and the distribution areas can overlap. After the supply disruption, five alternative suppliers are available for each raw material that needs to be changed, and their maximum supply capacity is required to meet the raw material quantity required for the production of the product. There are six temporary distribution center locations to be selected, taking into account the manufacturer's selection preferences and the new distribution center capacity constraints. The parameters of each part of the supply chain are determined based on the assumptions made for the model and are generated randomly within the range of values. Table 2 presents the range of values for the parameter information of the alternative suppliers.

Table 2. Supplier parameters.

Supplier	Alternative Supplier	B_{ij}	Q_{ij}	C_{ij}
S1	AS1–AS5	(19,500, 21,500)	(10,000, 13,500)	(3, 5)
S2	AS6–AS10	(20,000, 21,500)	(12,500, 15,000)	(2, 4)
S3	AS11–AS15	(9100, 9350)	(10,000, 13,000)	(4, 5)
S4	AS16–AS20	(19,500, 21,500)	(12,500, 14,500)	(3, 5)
S5	AS21–AS25	(19,500, 21,000)	(10,500, 12,000)	(2, 3)
S6	AS26–AS30	(20,500, 22,000)	(11,500, 13,500)	(3, 4)
S7	AS31–AS35	(10,500, 12,000)	(10,000, 11,500)	(4, 5)
S8	AS36–AS40	(9100, 9350)	(11,000, 13,500)	(2, 4)

The range of values for the parameters related to manufacturer selection preference, capacity, and fixed cost of the temporary distribution centers are shown in Table 3. Table 4 presents the parameter information of the customers' demand.

Table 3. Temporary distribution center parameters.

Distribution Center	K_m	H_m	Selection Preference
TD1	15,000	5900	(0.25, 0.30, 0.35)
TD2	16,000	6250	(0.2, 0.32, 0.56)
TD3	14,000	6000	(0.06, 0.1, 0.2)
TD4	12,500	6400	(0.04, 0.2, 0.3)
TD5	15,500	6150	(0.25, 0.45, 0.65)
TD6	17,000	6000	(0.16, 0.24, 0.28)

Table 4. Customer parameters.

Product	P1		P2		P3	
Customer	μ_{n1}	σ^2_{n1}	μ_{n2}	σ^2_{n2}	μ_{n3}	σ^2_{n3}
C1–C10	(800, 1000)	(60, 100)	(900, 1100)	(80, 120)	(900,1200)	(70, 150)

The numerical experiments assume different supplier disruptions as well as distribution center failures to demonstrate the validity of the proposed model of alternative supplier selection considering product design changes, as well as temporary distribution center location considering manufacturer selection preferences. In each disruption scenario, the combination of disrupted suppliers and failed distribution centers is different, and the disrupted suppliers and failed distribution centers are independent of each other. Considering the huge number of disruption scenarios generated by different supplier and distribution center combinations, we use the SR method to reduce the number of disruption scenarios and select typical samples of disruption scenarios to test the results of the problem to validate the proposed model and the improved genetic algorithm.

The disruption scenarios after the scenario reduction are shown in Table 5. Based on the results in Table 5, we can determine that the 8192 disruption scenarios are reduced to 6 scenarios, which demonstrates that the SR method is effective.

Table 5. Disruption scenarios after the SR.

Supplier	Distribution Center	Disruption Scenarios	Disruption Scenario after SR Method
8	5	8192	(1,1,1,1,1,1,1,1 ǀ 1,1,1,1,1), (0,0,0,0,0,0,0,0 ǀ 0,0,0,0,0), (0,0,1,0,1,0,1,1 ǀ 0,0,1,0,1), (0,0,1,0,0,0,0,1 ǀ 0,0,1,0,0), (1,1,1,0,1,1,1,1 ǀ 0,0,1,0,1), (1,1,1,0,1,1,1,1 ǀ 1,1,1,0,1)

Table 6 shows the manufacturer's total profit when the supply chain is functioning normally, the expected profit of the manufacturer in the presence of disruption without considering the resilient strategy, and the results of the manufacturer's solution using holding inventory before disruption, establishing temporary distribution centers, and using a product design change strategy after disruption. The optimization results show that by formulating a reasonable inventory plan, determining the location of the temporary distribution centers before disruptions, and selecting a reasonable product change plan for the raw materials when disruptions occur, the supply chain resilience can be improved, and the losses caused by disruptions to the supply chain can be reduced.

Table 6. The results under different supply chain states.

State of Supply Chain	Total Profit	Temporary Distribution Center
Normal operation	548,798	—
Without any measure	186,624	—
Proposed resilient strategy	315,161	TD1, TD4, TD5

Table 7 shows the manufacturer's maximum profit under different disruption scenarios and disruption recovery plans after adopting a proactive defense strategy, developing an inventory plan, and identifying temporary distribution center locations.

Table 7. Optimization results under different disruption scenarios.

Case	Disruption Scenario	Total Profit	Alternative Supplier Options	Distribution Center Options
1	(1,1,1,1,1,1,1,1 | 1,1,1,1,1)	388,122	—	—
2	(0,0,0,0,0,0,0,0 | 0,0,0,0,0)	−71,626	AS5, AS9, AS15, AS19, AS24, AS28, AS33, AS37	TD1, TD4, TD5
3	(0,0,1,0,1,0,1,1 | 0,0,1,0,1)	224,590	AS5, AS9, AS19, AS28	TD1, TD4
4	(0,0,1,0,0,0,0,1 | 0,0,1,0,0)	163,221	AS5, AS9, AS19, AS24, AS28, AS33,	TD1, TD4, TD5
5	(1,1,1,0,1,1,1,1 | 0,0,1,0,1)	409,376	AS19	TD1, TD4
6	(1,1,1,0,1,1,1,1 | 1,1,1,0,1)	418,586	AS19	TD4

Figure 5 gives the results of the supply chain reconfiguration optimization in the disruption scenario of Case 3. The original suppliers S1, S2, S4, and S6 were disrupted, and the production of products P1, P2, P3 are affected. By incorporating design changes for the disrupted raw materials, AS5, AS9, AS19, and AS28 are selected as new suppliers and a new supply network is established. Considering the manufacturer's selection preference as well as the handling capacity and construction cost of the temporary distribution center, TD1, TD4, and TD5 are identified as temporary distribution centers. Due to the pandemic, the original distribution centers D1, D2 and D4 failed at the same time. Considering the failure situation and customer demands, the temporary distribution centers TD1 and TD4 are opened. Taking the maximum total profit as the objective, the production, transportation, and distribution plans of the reconstructed supply chain network are determined.

In order to validate the performance of the proposed improved genetic algorithm, we conducted extensive numerical experiments on test problems with randomly generated data for different sizes of suppliers, product types, distribution centers, and customers. For small-scale problems, the proposed genetic algorithm has similar performance in terms of the approximate optimal solutions obtained compared to Gurobi, and high-quality solutions can be found for small-scale problems. When the problem size is larger, although the quality of the solution obtained by the proposed genetic algorithm decreases, it is still within the acceptable range of error. In addition, for the proposed stochastic programming model, Gurobi is unable to find a solution to the problem after running for a long time, as the disruption scenario and the sampling samples have increased. In Table 8, the optimality gap between the optimal solution obtained using the proposed algorithm and the optimal solution obtained using Gurobi is illustrated.

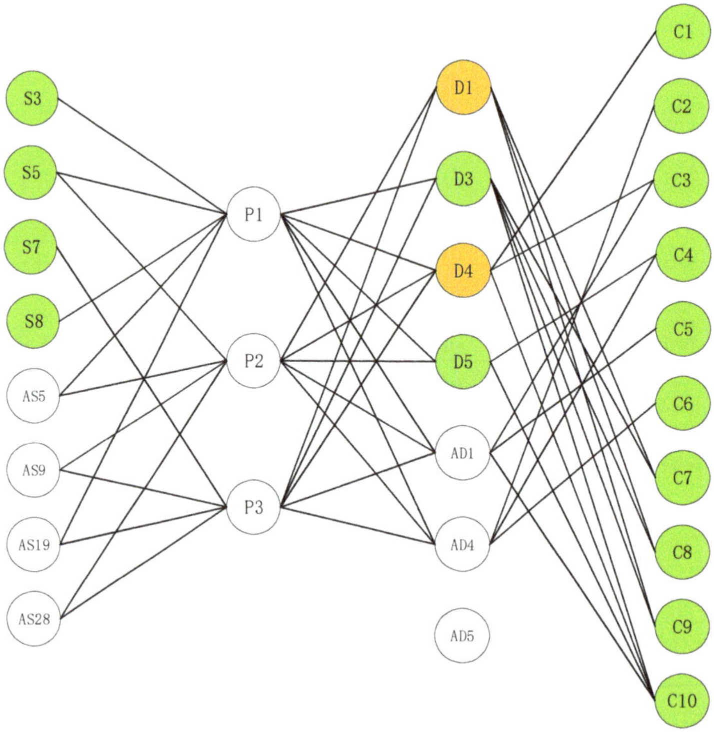

Figure 5. Optimal solution to the illustrative case 3.

Table 8. Results of Gurobi and the proposed genetic algorithm.

Instance	Supplier	Distribution Center	Customer	Disruption Scenario	Sample	$\frac{TC_{GA}-TC_{Gurobi}}{TC_{Gurobi}}$
1	8	5	10	6	10	0.023
2					30	0.021
3					50	0.025
4		10	25	8	10	0.032
5					30	0.036
6					50	0.038
7	12	5	10	8	10	0.045
8					30	0.05
9					50	0.048
10		10	25	9	10	0.054
11					30	0.049
12					50	*
13	16	5	10	9	10	0.076
14					30	0.072
15					50	*
16		10	25	10	10	0.082
17					30	*
18					50	*

* Gurobi cannot locate the solution to the problem after running for a long time.

6.2. Sensitivity Analysis

The manufacturer's total profit varies with different parameters. In this section, a sensitivity analysis is performed to illustrate the effects of various parameters on the expected profit of the proposed resilient supply chain. I_{max} and H_m are important parameters in the formulation of a proactive defense strategy, and Q_{ij} is an important parameter for determining the raw material change plan and selecting alternative suppliers after disruption. We examine the sensitivity of the objective function value with respect to changing these pricing parameters. To characterize the impact, a sensitivity analysis is performed for different parameters. Only one parameter is changed for each analysis, and the remainder are kept the same as in Section 6.1. We change the parameters to −50%, −25%, +25%, +50%, and +75% of the original value to solve for the result.

Figure 6 shows the variation in the manufacturer's expected total profit with the maximum raw material inventory capacity. It can be seen that as the maximum inventory capacity increases, the expected profit also increases. However, when the capacity increases to a certain value, profits no longer change. As the capacity continues to increase, the profit decreases due to redundancy.

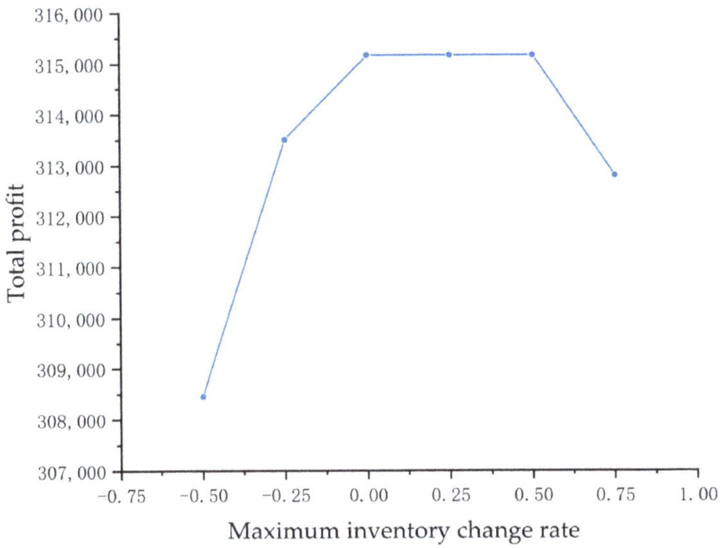

Figure 6. Sensitivity of the optimal objective value to I_{max}.

Figure 7 shows the variation in the manufacturer's total profit with the capacity of the temporary distribution center. When the other parameters are fixed, the expected profit of the manufacturer increases as the capacity of the temporary distribution center increases. The manufacturer's expected profit is more sensitive to the capacity of the temporary distribution center, and small changes in the parameter values can quickly change the resultant values. When it increases to a certain value, the profit tends to be constant. Therefore, it is necessary to plan the capacity of the temporary distribution center when selecting its location. Figure 8 shows the variation in the manufacturer's total profit with the cost of product change. It can be seen that the total profit decreases as the product change cost increases.

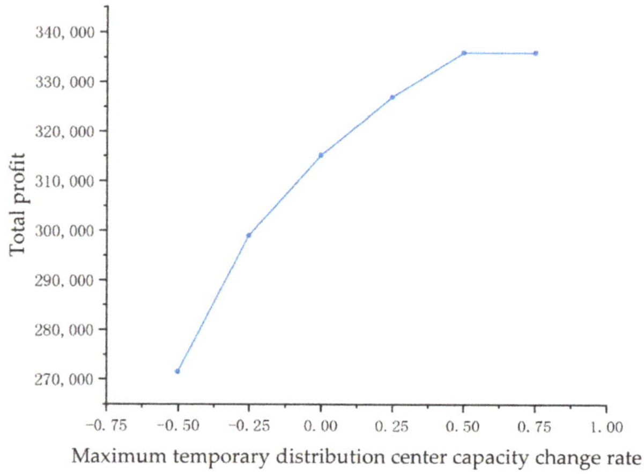

Figure 7. Sensitivity of the optimal objective value to H_m.

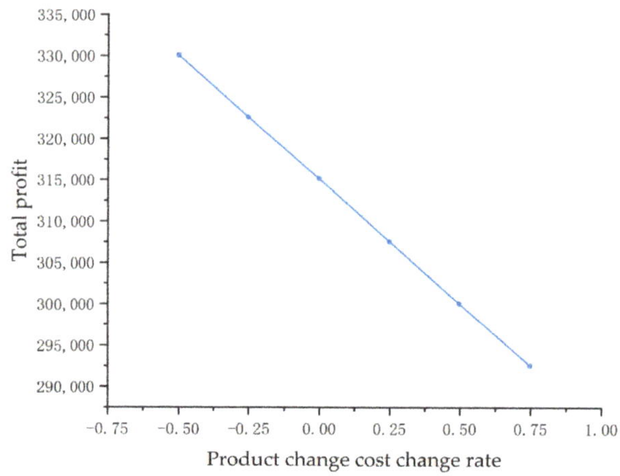

Figure 8. Sensitivity of the optimal objective value to Q_{ij}.

6.3. Managerial Insights

This paper considers a four-tier supply chain with uncertain demand. When the supply chain faces supply disruptions and the distribution center failures due to the pandemic, the manufacturer adopts a combination of proactive and reactive strategies. Mitigation and recovery decisions to improve supply chain resilience include raw material mitigation inventories and temporary distribution center locations before disruptions, as well as emergency sourcing and product changes after disruptions. This work can be used in a wide range of manufacturing industries to effectively reduce losses in the manufacturing supply chain in the event of supply disruptions and distribution center failures. This work is also applicable to changes in product and distribution networks caused by changes in demand. Our research can provide managers with the following insights:

- The computational results show that a combination of proactive and reactive resilience strategies can significantly improve expected profits under pandemic disruptions and ripple effects. The proposed model can help managers consider factors such as market demand, distribution center capacity, and the supply situation in the decision process of designing a resilient supply chain to cope with unexpected disruptions similar to those caused by a pandemic.

- The first stage of the model can help manufacturers effectively set mitigation inventory and the location of temporary distribution centers to compensate for possible supply shortages and existing distribution center failures in the event of pandemic disruptions, avoiding greater losses. To reduce the cost of redundancy, managers should reasonably plan inventory capacity and temporary distribution center capacity.
- The second-stage model can help managers make decisions about the product design change plan and the selection of alternative suppliers, as well as product transportation and delivery plans, taking into account the cost of product change and the sale loss caused by it, as well as the compensation cost for failing to deliver to customers on time and other factors.
- The improved genetic algorithm developed in this paper can help decision-makers to quickly assess the impact of different measures in response to the risk of a potential pandemic disruptions under different disruption scenarios in the future.

7. Conclusions

This paper investigates a resilient supply chain disruption recovery problem with the context of the COVID-19 pandemic, which considers a supply chain network with supply disruptions and distribution center failure risks, as well as the presence of demand fluctuations, adopting a make-to-order approach. A mathematical model is developed based on raw material inventory management and temporary distribution center location before disruption, and a product design change strategy is developed after the disruption with the objective of maximizing the manufacturer's profit. The two-stage stochastic programming model with demand uncertainty is approximated as an MILP model using SAA and LHS methods. To overcome the impact of a large number of disruption scenarios on the solution of the MILP model, SR is used to select representative disruption scenarios among them. First, a small-scale numerical example is given to illustrate the problem of selecting alternative suppliers, developing an integrated production plan and locating temporary distribution centers in the disruption scenario. The numerical experiment shows that the proposed model is effective in reducing the manufacturer's losses in the case of supply chain disruption. In addition, to efficiently solve large-sized problems, an improved genetic algorithm is proposed. Then, extensive numerical experiments are conducted using randomly generated test problems of different sizes. The results show that the proposed genetic algorithm has similar performance to Gurobi in finding the approximate optimal solution and can obtain a high-quality solution within the acceptable error range.

There are still issues in this paper that deserve further research and discussion. Firstly, we will consider a more realistic multi-product supply chain network and consider the impact of third-party distribution centers. Secondly, this work can be extended to multi-stage stochastic programming and the design of algorithms to obtain high quality solutions. Thirdly, considering the influence of the relationships between each link of the supply chain and the optimization results can be another research direction in the future.

Author Contributions: Conceptualization, N.W. and J.C.; methodology, N.W.; software, J.C.; validation, N.W. and J.C.; formal analysis, N.W. and J.C.; investigation, N.W.; resources, H.W.; data curation, J.C.; writing—original draft preparation, N.W. and J.C.; writing—review and editing, N.W., J.C. and H.W.; visualization, J.C.; supervision, H.W.; project administration, H.W.; funding acquisition, H.W. All authors have read and agreed to the published version of the manuscript.

Funding: This work is supported partly by National Key Research and Development Program of China under Grant No. 2020YFB1708200, National Nature Science Foundation of China (NSFC) under Grant No. 62173076 and Fundamental Scientific Research Project of Liaoning Provincial Department of Education under Grant No. LNKMZ20221468.

Data Availability Statement: The data presented in this study are available from the corresponding author upon request. The data are not publicly available due to privacy restrictions.

Conflicts of Interest: The authors declare no conflict of interest.

References

1. Chowdhury, M.T.; Sarkar, A.; Paul, S.K.; Moktadir, M.A. COVID-19 pandemic related supply chain studies: A systematic review. *Transp. Res. Logist. Transp. Rev.* **2021**, *148*, 102271. [CrossRef] [PubMed]
2. Salama, M.R.; McGarvey, R.G. Resilient supply chain to a global pandemic. *Int. J. Prod. Res.* **2023**, *61*, 2563–2593. [CrossRef]
3. Kim, S.H.; Tomlin, B. Guilt by association: Strategic failure prevention and recovery capacity investments. *Manag. Sci.* **2013**, *59*, 1631–1649. [CrossRef]
4. Ozdemir, D.; Sharma, M.; Dhir, A.; Daim, T. Supply chain resilience during the COVID-19 pandemic. *Technol. Soc.* **2022**, *68*, 101847.
5. Ivanov, D. Predicting the impacts of epidemic outbreaks on global supply chains: A simulation-based analysis on the coronavirus outbreak (COVID-19/SARS-CoV-2) case. *Transp. Res. Logist. Transp. Rev.* **2020**, *136*, 101922. [CrossRef] [PubMed]
6. Ivanov, D.; Sokolov, B.; Dolgui, A. The ripple effect in supply chains: Trade-off 'efficiency-flexibility-resilience' in disruption management. *Int. J. Prod. Res.* **2014**, *52*, 2154–2172. [CrossRef]
7. Li, Y.; Chen, K.; Collignon, S.; Collignon, S.; Ivanov, D. Ripple effect in the supply chain network: Forward and backward disruption propagation, network health and firm vulnerability. *Eur. J. Oper. Res.* **2021**, *291*, 1117–1131. [CrossRef]
8. Ramani, V.; Ghosh, D.; Sodhi, M.S. Understanding systemic disruption from the COVID-19-induced semiconductor shortage for the auto industry. *Omega* **2022**, *113*, 102720. [CrossRef]
9. Paul, S.K.; Chowdhury, P.; Chowdhury, M.T.; Chakrabortty, R.K.; Moktadir, M.A. Operational challenges during a pandemic: An investigation in the electronics industry. *Int. J. Logist. Manag.* **2023**, *34*, 336–362. [CrossRef]
10. Rajesh, R. Flexible business strategies to enhance resilience in manufacturing supply chains: An empirical study. *J. Manuf. Syst.* **2021**, *60*, 903–919.
11. El, B.J.; Ruel, S. Can supply chain risk management practices mitigate the disruption impacts on supply chains' resilience and robustness? Evidence from an empirical survey in a COVID-19 outbreak era. *Int. J. Prod. Econ.* **2021**, *233*, 2–51.
12. Wang, J.W.; Muddada, R.R.; Wang, H.F.; Ding, J.L.; Lin, Y.Z.; Liu, C.L.; Zhang, W.J. Toward a resilient holistic supply chain network system: Concept, review and future direction. *IEEE Syst. J.* **2016**, *10*, 410–421. [CrossRef]
13. Lucker, F.; Seifert, R.W.; Bicer, I. Roles of inventory and reserve capacity in mitigating supply chain disruption risk. *Int. J. Prod. Res.* **2019**, *57*, 1238–1249. [CrossRef]
14. Feng, X.H.; He, Y.C.; Kim, K.H. Space planning considering congestion in container terminal yards. *Transp. Res. Methodol.* **2022**, *158*, 52–77. [CrossRef]
15. Yang, D.; Pan, K.; Wang, S. On service network improvement for shipping lines under the one belt one road initiative of China. *Transp. Res. Logist. Transp. Rev.* **2018**, *117*, 82–95. [CrossRef]
16. Lee, P.T.W.; Hu, Z.H.; Lee, S.; Feng, X.H.; Notteboom, T. Strategic locations for logistics distribution centers along the Belt and Road: Explorative analysis and research agenda. *Transp. Policy* **2022**, *116*, 24–47. [CrossRef]
17. Liu, Y.; Ma, X.X.; Qiao, W.L.; Han, B. A methodology to model the evolution of system resilience for Arctic shipping from the perspective of complexity. *Marit. Policy Manag.* 2023. [CrossRef]
18. Panahi, R.; Afenyo, M.; Ng, A.K.Y. Developing a resilience index for safer and more resilient arctic shipping. *Marit. Policy Manag.* **2023**, *50*, 861–875. [CrossRef]
19. Ivanov, D.; Dolgui, A.; Sokolov, B.; Ivanova, M. Literature review on disruption recovery in the supply chain. *Int. J. Prod. Res.* **2017**, *55*, 6158–6174. [CrossRef]
20. Paul, S.K.; Chowdhury, P. A production recovery plan in manufacturing supply chains for a high-demand item during COVID-19. *Int. J. Phys. Distrib. Logist. Manag.* **2021**, *51*, 104–125. [CrossRef]
21. Hishamuddin, H.; Sarker, R.; Essam, D. A disruption recovery model for a single stage production inventory system. *Eur. J. Oper. Res.* **2012**, *222*, 464–473. [CrossRef]
22. Paul, S.K.; Sarker, R.; Essam, D. A reactive mitigation approach for managing supply disruption in a three-tier supply chain. *J. Intel. Manuf.* **2018**, *29*, 1581–1597. [CrossRef]
23. Chen, J.Z.; Wang, H.F.; Zhong, R.Y. A supply chain disruption recovery strategy considering product change under COVID-19. *J. Manuf. Syst.* **2021**, *60*, 920–927. [CrossRef]
24. Ivanov, D. Viable supply chain model: Integrating agility, resilience and sustainability perspectives-lessons from and thinking beyond the COVID-19 pandemic. *Ann. Oper. Res.* 2020. [CrossRef]
25. Tukamuhabwa, B.R.; Stevenson, M.; Busby, J.; Zorzini, M. Supply Chain Resilience: Definition, Review and Theoretical Foundations for Further Study. *Int. J. Prod. Res.* **2015**, *53*, 5592–5623. [CrossRef]
26. Torabi, S.A.; Baghersad, M.; Mansouri, S.A. Resilient Supplier Selection and Order Allocation Under Operational and Disruption Risks. *Transp. Res. Part E Logist. Transp. Rev.* **2015**, *79*, 22–48. [CrossRef]
27. Pal, B.; Sana, S.S.; Chaudhuri, K. A multi-echelon production–inventory system with supply disruption. *J. Manuf. Syst.* **2014**, *33*, 262–276. [CrossRef]
28. Jabbarzadeh, A.; Fahimnia, B.; Sabouhi, F. Resilient and sustainable supply chain design: Sustainability analysis under disruption risks. *Int. J. Prod. Res.* **2018**, *56*, 5945–5968. [CrossRef]
29. Namdar, J.; Li, X.P.; Sawhney, R.; Pradhan, N. Supply chain resilience for single and multiple sourcing in the presence of disruption risks. *Int. J. Prod. Res.* **2018**, *56*, 2339–2360. [CrossRef]

30. Shahed, K.S.; Azeem, A.; Ali, S.M.; Moktadir, M.A. A supply chain disruption risk mitigation model to manage COVID-19 pandemic risk. *Environ. Sci. Pollut. Res.* **2021**. [CrossRef]
31. Vali-Siar, M.M.; Roghanian, E. Sustainable, resilient and responsive mixed supply chain network design under hybrid uncertainty with considering COVID-19 pandemic disruption. *Sustain. Prod. Consump.* **2022**, *30*, 278–300. [CrossRef] [PubMed]
32. Sawik, T. Two-period vs. multi-period model for supply chain disruption management. *Int. J. Prod. Res.* **2018**, *57*, 4502–4518. [CrossRef]
33. Paul, S.K.; Sarker, R.; Essam, D.; Lee, P.T.W. A mathematical modelling approach for managing sudden disturbances in a three-tier manufacturing supply chain. *Ann. Oper. Res.* **2019**, *280*, 299–335. [CrossRef]
34. Khalilabadi, S.M.G.; Zegordi, S.H.; Nikbakhsh, E. A multi-stage stochastic programming approach for supply chain risk mitigation via product substitution. *Comput. Ind. Eng.* **2020**, *149*, 106786. [CrossRef]
35. Chen, J.Z.; Wang, H.F.; Fu, Y.P. A multi-stage supply chain disruption mitigation strategy considering product life cycle during COVID-19. *Environ. Sci. Pollut. Res.* **2022**. [CrossRef] [PubMed]
36. Elluru, S.; Gupta, H.; Kaur, H.; Singh, S.P. Proactive and reactive models for disaster resilient supply chain. *Ann. Oper. Res.* **2019**, *283*, 199–224. [CrossRef]
37. Li, Z.; Sheng, Y.Y.; Meng, Q.F.; Hu, X. Sustainable supply chain operation under COVID-19: Influences and response strategies. *Int. J. Logist. Res. Appl.* **2022**. [CrossRef]
38. Nagurney, A. Optimization of supply chain networks with inclusion of labor: Applications to COVID-19 pandemic disruptions. *Int. J. Prod. Econ.* **2021**, *235*, 108080. [CrossRef]
39. Sawik, T. Stochastic optimization of supply chain resilience under ripple effect: A COVID-19 pandemic related study. *Omega* **2022**, *109*, 102596. [CrossRef]
40. Paul, S.K.; Chowdhury, P.; Chakrabortty, R.K.; Ivanov, D.; Sallam, K. A mathematical model for managing the multi-dimensional impacts of the COVID-19 pandemic in supply chain of a high-demand item. *Ann. Oper. Res.* **2022**, 1–46. [CrossRef]
41. Diabat, A.; Dehghani, E.; Jabbarzadeh, A. Incorporating location and inventory decisions into a supply chain design problem with uncertain demands and lead times. *J. Manuf. Syst.* **2017**, *43*, 139–149. [CrossRef]
42. Shavandi, H.; Bozorgi, B. Developing a Location Inventory Model under Fuzzy Environment. *Int. J. Adv. Manuf. Tech.* **2012**, *63*, 191–200. [CrossRef]
43. Amin, S.H.; Baki, F. A facility location model for global closed-loop supply chain network design. *Appl. Math. Model.* **2017**, *41*, 316–330. [CrossRef]
44. Jakubovskis, A. Strategic facility location, capacity acquisition, and technology choice decisions under demand uncertainty: Robust vs. non-robust optimization approaches. *Eur. J. Oper. Res.* **2017**, *260*, 1095–1104. [CrossRef]
45. Ortiz-Astorquiza, C.; Contreras, I.; Laporte, G. Multi-level facility location problems. *Eur. J. Oper. Res.* **2018**, *267*, 791–805. [CrossRef]
46. Saragih, N.I.; Bahagia, N.; Syabri, I. A heuristic method for location-inventory-routing problem in a three-echelon supply chain system. *Comput. Ind. Eng.* **2019**, *127*, 875–886. [CrossRef]
47. Fu, Y.P.; Wu, D.; Wang, H.F. Facility location and capacity planning considering policy preference and uncertain demand under the One Belt One Road Initiative. *Transp. Res. Policy Pract.* **2020**, *138*, 172–186. [CrossRef]
48. Snyder, L.V.; Daskin, M.S. Models for Reliable Supply Chain Network Design. In *Critical Infrastructure;* Springer: Berlin/Heidelberg, Germany, 2007; pp. 257–289.
49. Kleywegt, A.J.; Shapiro, A.; Homem-De-Mello, T. The sample average approximation method for stochastic discrete optimization. *SIAM J. Optim.* **2001**, *12*, 479–502. [CrossRef]
50. Karuppiah, R.; Martin, M.; Grossmann, I.E. A simple heuristic for reducing the number of scenarios in two-stage stochastic programming. *Comput. Ind. Eng.* **2010**, *34*, 1246–1255. [CrossRef]
51. Cui, X.L. Joint optimization of production planning and supplier selection incorporating customer flexibility: An improved genetic approach. *J. Intell. Manuf.* **2016**, *27*, 1017–1035. [CrossRef]

mathematics

MDPI

Article

Multi-Objective Q-Learning-Based Brain Storm Optimization for Integrated Distributed Flow Shop and Distribution Scheduling Problems

Shuo Zhang , Jianyou Xu * and Yingli Qiao

College of Information Science and Engineering, Northeastern University, Shenyang 110819, China; 1910307@stu.neu.edu.cn (S.Z.); 2370776@stu.neu.edu.cn (Y.Q.)
* Correspondence: xujianyou@mail.neu.edu.cn

Abstract: In recent years, integrated production and distribution scheduling (IPDS) has become an important subject in supply chain management. However, IPDS considering distributed manufacturing environments is rarely researched. Moreover, reinforcement learning is seldom combined with metaheuristics to deal with IPDS problems. In this work, an integrated distributed flow shop and distribution scheduling problem is studied, and a mathematical model is provided. Owing to the problem's NP-hard nature, a multi-objective Q-learning-based brain storm optimization is designed to minimize makespan and total weighted earliness and tardiness. In the presented approach, a double-string representation method is utilized, and a dynamic clustering method is developed in the clustering phase. In the generating phase, a global search strategy, a local search strategy, and a simulated annealing strategy are introduced. A Q-learning process is performed to dynamically choose the generation strategy. It consists of four actions defined as the combinations of these strategies, four states described by convergence and uniformity metrics, a reward function, and an improved ε-greedy method. In the selecting phase, a newly defined selection method is adopted. To assess the effectiveness of the proposed approach, a comparison pool consisting of four prevalent metaheuristics and a CPLEX optimizer is applied to conduct numerical experiments and statistical tests. The results suggest that the designed approach outperforms its competitors in acquiring promising solutions when handling the considered problem.

Keywords: integrated production and distribution scheduling; distributed flow shop; brain storm optimization; Q-learning

MSC: 90B50

1. Introduction

Facing the competitive market environments, an increasing number of enterprises are adjusting their production and distribution activities in an integrated manner in order to quickly deliver orders to meet customer expectations. Production and distribution are two core components which have a crucial impact in driving the business performance of the supply chain [1]. Traditionally, these two components are individually organized and managed, resulting in poor efficiency from an economic and customer satisfaction point of view [2]. Furthermore, researchers have revealed that the integrated scheduling of production and distribution can reduce total operation costs by 3% to 20% [3]. Hence, integrated production and distribution scheduling (IPDS) is necessary to achieve overall optimization. In the real world, applications involving IPDS appear in many fields, e.g., newspapers, medicine, and furniture manufacturing [4]. In the IPDS process, orders are initially manufactured on machines and, subsequently, timely transported by vehicles to customers in diverse locations. In this situation, managers must make production and distribution decisions concurrently, leading to strong competitiveness and high service quality. Thus, IPDS has attracted much attention from scholars and practitioners [5].

With the development of the globalized economy and the intensive cooperation among enterprises, an emerging distributed manufacturing mode containing multiple factories is replacing the traditional centralized manufacturing mode with a single factory [6,7]. The distributed flow shop is highly utilized as a distributed manufacturing system [8], with its versatile functionality being beneficial in enhancing productivity and lowering costs across many industries, e.g., cell manufacturing, petrochemical, and automotive engines [9]. Motivated by this, distributed flow shop scheduling problems considering various constraints, including blocking, lot streaming, no wait, no idle, and limited buffers, have been addressed in the last decade [10–14]. Moreover, as these problems are recognized as being NP-hard, a variety of metaheuristics have been put forward as a viable means of solving them [13]. Despite the extensive efforts that have been made on distributed flow shop scheduling in terms of problem investigation and method development, few researchers have addressed its integration with distribution planning. However, their integration scheduling has far-reaching applications in reality, e.g., house customization, catering, healthcare, and e-commerce businesses. Inspired by this prospect, this work presents an integrated distributed flow shop and distribution scheduling problem.

Over the past few years, metaheuristics have become commonly used methods for tackling IPDS problems, and their search efficiency has been rigorously confirmed [5]. Nevertheless, these techniques still exhibit certain limitations, such as a lack of self-learning ability and less use of historical information. Hence, to identify more effective solutions, many investigations have integrated advanced tools, e.g., reinforcement learning (RL), into the framework of metaheuristics [15]. The combination of metaheuristics and RL allows for an adaptive parameter adjustment and a dynamic search operator selection, resulting in a significant improvement in optimization performance [16]. With its powerful capability to address optimization problems in diverse application areas (e.g., control, manufacturing, and routing), the combination of metaheuristics and RL has been increasingly recognized among researchers as a suitable approach [17–19]. However, it has not been investigated in the context of IPDS problems by prior studies. Accordingly, this work combines a brain storm optimization (BSO) [20] with a RL algorithm, namely, Q-learning, to construct a solution approach. Against the previous literature, threefold contributions are summarized below:

- A multi-objective integrated distributed flow shop and distribution scheduling problem is addressed. To clearly describe it, this work formulates a mathematical model with makespan and total weighted earliness and tardiness minimization;
- A multi-objective Q-learning-based brain storm optimization (MQBSO) is designed to handle the addressed problem. In MQBSO, a double-string representation approach is used to denote a solution, and a random method is employed to initialize the population. In the clustering phase, a dynamic clustering method is adopted to create clusters. In the generating phase, a Q-learning process is performed to guide MQBSO in choosing the generation strategy, where four actions, four states, a reward function, and an improved ε-greedy method are included. In the selecting phase, a new selection method is applied to obtain a better population;
- To examine the performance of MQBSO, experiments are implemented on a group of instances in comparison with four metaheuristics and a CPLEX solver. The experimental results reveal that MQBSO exhibits excellent performance.

We organize the rest of this work as follows: in Section 2, the relative literature is reviewed; in Section 3, the problem under study is presented and formulated; in Section 4, BSO and Q-learning are described; in Section 5, the introduced method is given in detail; numerical experiments and statistical tests are provided in Section 6; and finally, Section 7 ends this work with some conclusions and points out research directions for the future.

2. Literature Review

In this section, three parts are included. First, we reviewed the relevant literature on IPDS problems with respect to production scheduling models, distribution models, objective functions, and solution methods. Second, we reviewed the studies involving the combination of metaheuristics with Q-learning in scheduling problems. Finally, the related studies about the BSO were reviewed.

2.1. Relevant Literature on IPDS

The research of IPDS problems can be traced back to the 1970s and was introduced by Potts [21]. This research addressed a scheduling problem with a single machine, job release time, and job ship time but not the loading capacity or vehicle routing. In recent years, a significant amount of work on IPDS under different environments has been reported [5,22]. Liu and Liu [4] explored an IPDS regarding perishable items, where multiple orders, multiple vehicles, multiple customers, and one machine were involved. They employed CPLEX and an improved large neighborhood search mechanism to minimize total weighted delivery time. Roberto and Marcelo [23] focused on an IPDS to reach total system makespan minimization. They adopted a set of equivalent parallel machines to process jobs and employed a single vehicle to perform multiple route tasks. To address this problem, they developed an iterated greedy algorithm. Jia et al. [24] studied an IPDS aiming at minimizing total weighted tardiness. In this problem, non-identical parallel batch machines were used to process jobs, and multiple vehicles were adopted to execute distribution tasks. They presented an ant colony optimization as a solution approach. In light of the advancements made in the economy and technology, manufacturing systems have become more complex. Yagmur and Kesen [25] put forward an integrated flow shop and distribution scheduling aimed at minimizing the sum of total traveling time and total tardiness. In this problem, jobs were processed on machines in a flow shop and delivered to customers in batches. They proposed a memetic algorithm to deal with it. Mohammadi et al. [26] investigated an integrated flexible job shop and distribution scheduling to minimize the sum of scheduling costs and the weighted sum of earliness and tardiness. To tackle it, a hybrid particle swarm optimization was given.

Unlike the above IPDS problems that dealt with one factory and a vehicle routing problem during production and distribution stages, respectively, research concerning distributed production environments and multi-depot vehicle routing problems have been reported. Gharaei and Jolai [27] addressed an IPDS with minimizing total tardiness and total delivery cost. This problem involved the fabrication of jobs across several non-identical factories, followed by transportation to customers via vehicles. They used a multi-objective evolutionary algorithm combined with a bee method to solve it. Fu et al. [28] introduced an integrated distributed flow shop and a vehicle routing problem with the aim of minimizing the makespan. To figure it out, they designed an enhanced black widow optimization. Additionally, they extended this IPDS problem with time window constraints [29]. To confront the problem, they presented an enhanced brain storm optimization. Qin et al. [30] put forward an IPDS in a distributed hybrid flow shop environment to reach a minimal sum of earliness, tardiness, and delivery cost. Given the NP-hard nature of the problem, they developed an adaptive human-learning-based genetic algorithm.

By analyzing the IPDS problems in the literature, we observed that they have the following characteristics:

- Most studies considered a single factory at the production stage, while the distributed manufacturing system was not fully considered;
- Most research concentrated on a single-objective optimization which usually involved time and cost criteria, while not enough consideration was given to multi-objective optimization;
- Metaheuristics have become the mainstream method to cope with IPDS problems, and their outstanding performance has been verified.

2.2. Q-Learning Applied to Scheduling

Recently, RL has provided an effective approach to handling optimization problems, and has attracted increasing concern from researchers and engineers [31]. Q-learning is a typical RL method, which guides agents to decide the optimum behavior through the trial-and-error method [32]. Motivated by this, many researchers have combined it with metaheuristics to tackle production scheduling problems in recent years. Li et al. [16] applied a Q-learning algorithm to an artificial bee colony algorithm for solving a flow shop scheduling. Zhao et al. [32] put forward a hyper-heuristic combining with a Q-Learning process to deal with a distributed blocking flow shop scheduling. Li et al. [15] developed a new shuffled frog-leaping algorithm with a RL algorithm named Q-learning to work out a distributed assembly hybrid flow shop scheduling. Li et al. [33] introduced a multi-objective evolutionary algorithm based on decomposition with Q-learning for a fuzzy, flexible job shop scheduling. Wang et al. [34] devised a dual Q-learning method to handle an assembly job shop scheduling. Cheng et al. [18] designed a multi-objective Q-learning-based hyper-heuristic method to figure out a mixed shop scheduling. In the aforementioned literature, the combination of metaheuristics with Q-Learning has been studied in various production scheduling problems, e.g., flow shops, job shops, and mix shops. Nevertheless, research on IPDS in a distributed flow shop environment remains scarce. To this end, this work presents a combination of BSO and Q-Learning to address an integrated distributed flow shop and distribution scheduling.

2.3. Relevant Literature on BSO

The BSO algorithm is a promising metaheuristic method, introduced by Shi in 2011 [20]. It has many advantages, such as easy implementation, high stability, and a fine search ability. In past years, BSO and its various variants have been widely developed to settle all kinds of complex and intractable optimization problems. Xu et al. [35] introduced an improved BSO to handle a real-parameter numerical optimization problem. Cheng et al. [36] proposed a modified BSO for solving a knowledge spillover problem. Hao et al. [37] designed a hybrid BSO to tackle a distributed hybrid flow shop scheduling problem. Zhao et al. [38] developed a Q-learning-based BSO to cope with an energy-efficient distributed assembly no-wait flow shop scheduling problem. Ma et al. [39] presented a BSO method with multi-objective search mechanisms to handle a home health care scheduling and routing problem. Ke [40] devised an enhanced BSO with new convergent and divergent operations to deal with a cumulative capacitated vehicle routing problem. Many existing studies have verified its powerful exploration and exploitation abilities. However, to the best of our knowledge, it has rarely been applied to IPDS problems. Thus, this work considers it as a basic optimizer.

3. Proposed Problem and Model

3.1. Problem Description

This work delves into a multi-objective IPDS with minimizing makespan and total weighted earliness and tardiness, consisting of two stages, namely the production stage and the distribution stage. The former comprises multiple identical factories, and each one is a flow shop. A specific set of jobs must be allocated across the flow shops, and each job must follow a fixed route on the machines at their respective flow shop. After processing, the jobs need to be shipped to customers located in different geographical areas via vehicles within time windows during the distribution stage. Consequently, to handle this problem, four decisions are made simultaneously, i.e., factory assignment of jobs, job processing sequence, vehicle allocation of jobs, and the job delivery sequence.

Note that a job is an order from a unique customer. Thus, the terms "job", "order", and "customer" are interchangeable as they are directly related to each other on a one-to-one basis. To clarify the problem being investigated, a visual example is shown in Figure 1 along with a mathematical model. A comprehensive listing of the related parameters and variables involved in constructing this model is provided in Table 1.

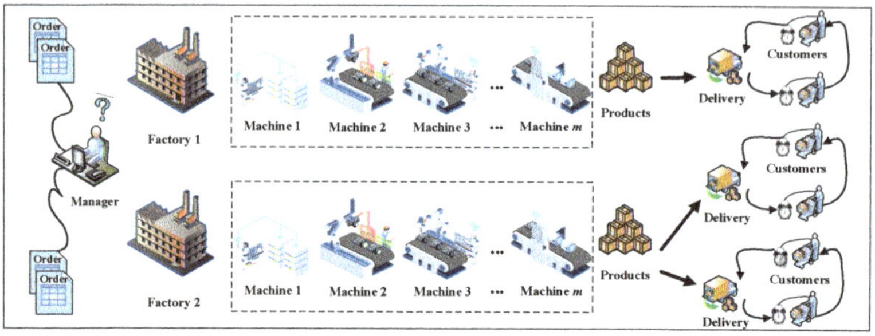

Figure 1. A visual example of the devised problem.

Table 1. The parameters and variables.

Symbol	Description
F	Set of f factories, $F = \{1, 2, \ldots, f\}$.
M	Set of m machines, $M = \{1, 2, \ldots, m\}$.
N	Set of n jobs, $N = \{0, 1, 2, \ldots, n\}$, where 0 means a virtual job.
V	Set of v vehicles at a factory, $V = \{1, 2, \ldots, v\}$.
g	The factory index, $g \in F$.
i	The machine index, $i \in M$.
k, j, l	The job index, $k, j, l \in N$.
h	The vehicle index, $h \in V$.
α_{ij}	The production time of job j on machine i.
β_{kj}	The drive time between customers k and j.
γ_{gj}	The drive time between factory g and customer j.
ψ_j	The load of job j.
φ_j	The service time at customer j.
$\left[d'_j, d''_j\right]$	The delivery time window of customer j.
E_j	The unit earliness weight of customer j.
T_j	The unit tardiness weight of customer j.
ϕ	The maximum load capacity of the vehicle.
G	An extremely positive integer.
X_{kjg}	=1, if job j is directly processed after job k at factory g, 0, otherwise.
Y_{jg}	=1, if job j is assigned to factory g, 0, otherwise.
Z_{kjh}	=1, if customer j is directly delivered after customer k by vehicle h, 0, otherwise.
C_{ij}	The completion time of job j on machine i.
S_h	The delivery start time of vehicle h.
A_j	The arrival time at customer j.
L_j	The departure time from customer j.
C_{max}	The makespan criterion.
$TWET$	The total weighted earliness and tardiness criterion.

3.2. Mathematical Model

For a solution to be considered viable, it must adhere to the following restrictions:

- At time zero, all machines must be available for use;
- Once a machine processes a job, it cannot process another one;
- At no time can a single job be worked on by multiple machines;
- Interrupting a job that has already started on a machine is not allowed;
- Each customer is visited only once;
- Vehicles must obey capacity limits.

Using the definitions provided above, we constructed the mathematical model below.

$$\text{Minimize } C_{max} \tag{1}$$

$$\text{Minimize } TWET \tag{2}$$

s.t.

$$\sum_{g\in F}\sum_{k\in N} X_{kjg} = 1, \forall j \in N, j \neq 0, k \neq j \tag{3}$$

$$\sum_{g\in F}\sum_{j\in N} X_{kjg} = 1, \forall k \in N, k \neq j \tag{4}$$

$$\sum_{g\in F} Y_{jg} = 1, \forall j \in N, j \neq 0 \tag{5}$$

$$\sum_{k\in N} X_{kjg} + \sum_{l\in N} X_{jlg} \leq 2\cdot Y_{jg}, \forall j \in N, j \neq 0, k \neq j \neq l, \forall g \in F \tag{6}$$

$$\sum_{g\in F}\left(X_{kjg} + X_{jkg}\right) \leq 1, \forall k, j \in N, k \neq j \neq 0 \tag{7}$$

$$C_{ij} \geq C_{(i-1)j} + \alpha_{ij}, \forall j \in N, j \neq 0, \forall i \in M \tag{8}$$

$$C_{ij} \geq C_{ik} + \alpha_{ij} + G\cdot(\sum_{g\in F} X_{kjg} - 1), \forall k, j \in N, j \neq 0, k \neq j, \forall i \in M \tag{9}$$

$$\sum_{h\in V}\sum_{j\in N} Z_{kjh}\cdot Y_{kg} \leq |V|, \forall g \in F, j \neq 0 \tag{10}$$

$$\sum_{h\in V}\sum_{k\in N} Z_{kjh} = 1, \forall j \in N, j \neq 0 \tag{11}$$

$$\sum_{h\in V}\sum_{j\in N} Z_{kjh} = 1, \forall k \in N, k \neq 0 \tag{12}$$

$$\sum_{k\in N} Z_{kjh} - \sum_{l\in N} Z_{jlh} = 0, \forall j \in N, \forall h \in V \tag{13}$$

$$\sum_{k\in N}\sum_{j\in N} Z_{kjh}\cdot \psi_j \leq \phi, \forall h \in V, k \neq j, j \neq 0 \tag{14}$$

$$\sum_{j\in N} Z_{0jh}\cdot Y_{jg} \leq 1, \forall h \in V, \forall g \in F,\ j \neq 0 \tag{15}$$

$$S_h \geq C_{mj} + G\cdot\left(Z_{kjh} - 1\right), \forall k, j \in N, k \neq j, \forall h \in V \tag{16}$$

$$A_j \geq S_h + \gamma_{gj} + G\cdot\left(Z_{0jh} + Y_{jg} - 2\right), \forall j \in N, j \neq 0, \forall h \in V, \forall g \in F \tag{17}$$

$$A_j \geq L_k + \beta_{kj} + G\cdot\left(Z_{kjh} - 1\right), \forall k, j \in N, k \neq j \neq 0, \forall h \in V, \forall g \in F \tag{18}$$

$$L_j = A_j + \varphi_j, \forall j \in N, j \neq 0 \tag{19}$$

$$C_{max} \geq C_{mj}, \forall j \in N, j \neq 0 \tag{20}$$

$$TWET = \sum_{j=1}^{n}\left(E_j \times max\left(d'_j - A_j, 0\right) + T_j \times max\left(L_j - d''_j, 0\right)\right) \tag{21}$$

$$C_{ij} \geq 0, \forall i \in M, \forall j \in N, j \neq 0 \tag{22}$$

$$X_{kjg} \in \{0,1\}, \forall k, j \in N, k \neq j, \forall g \in F \tag{23}$$

$$Y_{jg} \in \{0,1\}, \forall j \in N, j \neq 0, \forall g \in F \tag{24}$$

$$Z_{kjh} \in \{0,1\}, \forall k, j \in N, k \neq j, \forall h \in V \tag{25}$$

$$A_j, L_j \geq 0, \forall j \in N, j \neq 0 \tag{26}$$

The objective functions represented by Equations (1) and (2) are to minimize makespan and total weighted earliness and tardiness, respectively. The constraints laid out in Equations (3) and (4) dictate that there is precisely one preceding job and one succeeding job for each job on the machine. The constraint outlined in Equation (5) states that each job cannot be allocated to multiple factories simultaneously. Equation (6) signifies that each job owns at most one predecessor and one successor on a machine concurrently. Equation (7) mandates that there exists a strict ordering between two consecutive jobs. Equation (8) denotes that each job is worked on by only one machine at any given time. According to Equation (9), each machine must be dedicated to processing a single job at any given time. Equation (10) limits the number of vehicles. Equations (11) and (12) guarantee that no customer is visited multiple times. Equation (13) shows the constraint of maintaining continuity in vehicle routes. Equation (14) ensures that a vehicle's maximum capacity limit is strictly observed. Equation (15) stipulates that no vehicle can be employed more than once. Equation (16) demonstrates the start time for vehicle delivery. Equations (17) and (18) provide information regarding when the vehicles arrive at customers, whereas Equation (19) determines when the vehicles depart from customers. Equations (20) and (21) define the makespan and total weighted earliness and tardiness, respectively. Equations (22)–(26) show the variable's domain.

4. BSO and Q-Learning

4.1. BSO

Vitalized by the human inventive idea creation process, i.e., brainstorming process, Shi initially proposed a promising swarm-based metaheuristic: BSO [20]. The original BSO is straightforward in its design and can be easily implemented. Over the past years, BSO and its derivatives have achieved impressive results in tackling a range of complex problems, including real-parameter numerical optimization, distributed flow shops, and knowledge spillover problems [35–40]. Comprehensive experiments have verified that BSO possesses powerful performance to provide an outstanding compromise between exploration and exploitation abilities.

BSO begins with a population composed of multiple candidate individuals and each one means a solution to the optimization problem. Then, it performs three phases called the clustering phase, generating phase, and selecting phase to search solutions. The clustering phase involves using a clustering method to partition the population into several distinct clusters. For each cluster, the best individual in it is denoted as the center individual and the remaining are regarded as the normal ones. In the generating phase, new individuals are produced by employing one or two individuals from clusters. Each newly created individual is paired with an individual from the existing population. In the selecting phase, a selection method is adopted to store the better one from the paired individuals and save it for the next population. Finally, the three phases are iterated until a termination criterion is reached and the optimal solution is returned.

4.2. Q-Learning

Q-learning, as a typical model-free algorithm in RL, was originally introduced by Watkins and Dayan in 1992 [41]. Through a trial-and-error process, the method guides agents towards selecting the most beneficial behavior, and it comprises an environment, an agent, an action set, a state set, and a reward function. The main procedure of Q-learning is shown below. An agent selects an action a_t in terms of its state s_t at time t in the environment. Then, it will obtain an immediate reward r_{t+1} and its state will be transferred to a new state s_{t+1}. Meanwhile, the Q-table is updated according to Equation (27), where $Q(s_t, a_t)$ stands for the Q-value of conducting an action a_t at state s_t, θ represents the learning rate, ϑ refers to the discount rate, and $\max_a Q(s_{t+1}, a)$ means the biggest Q-value in the Q-table at state s_{t+1}.

$$Q(s_t, a_t) \leftarrow Q(s_t, a_t) + \theta \cdot \left[r_{t+1} + \vartheta \cdot \max_a Q(s_{t+1}, a) - Q(s_t, a_t) \right] \quad (27)$$

The action selection is carried out in line with the Q-table. The values in an initial Q-table are equal to 0, in which the quantity of rows and columns matches the quantity of states and actions, respectively. The ϵ-greedy approach is commonly applied, and its details are described below. If a random value $r_v \in (0,1)$ is less than ϵ, then choose an action a randomly. Otherwise, the action a with a maximum Q-value is selected.

5. Presented MQBSO Algorithm

This section introduces the framework of MQBSO as follows: Step 1, initialize the population and parameters; Step 2, implement a dynamic clustering method to construct multiple clusters; Step 3, employ a Q-learning process to determine a search strategy for generating new individuals; Step 4, apply a selection approach to create the next population; and Step 5, update the population state and Q-table.

5.1. Solution Representation and Initial Population

A double-string representation method is employed to represent solutions, that is, individuals. The solution is denoted as a job scheduling sequence string $[\pi_1, \pi_2, \ldots, \pi_n]$ and a factory assignment string $[\omega_1, \omega_2, \ldots, \omega_n]$, where π_j indicates a job index, $j \in \{1, 2, \ldots, n\}$, $\pi_j \in \{1, 2, \ldots, n\}$, ω_j means a factory index assigned to the job located at the j-th position in the job scheduling sequence string, $\omega_j \in \{1, 2, \ldots, f\}$. To better clarify this method, Figure 2 provides a visual example using a scenario where eight jobs are assigned to three factories. In it, jobs 5 and 3 are handled in factory 1, jobs 7, 4, and 2 are assigned to factory 2, and the rest belong to factory 3.

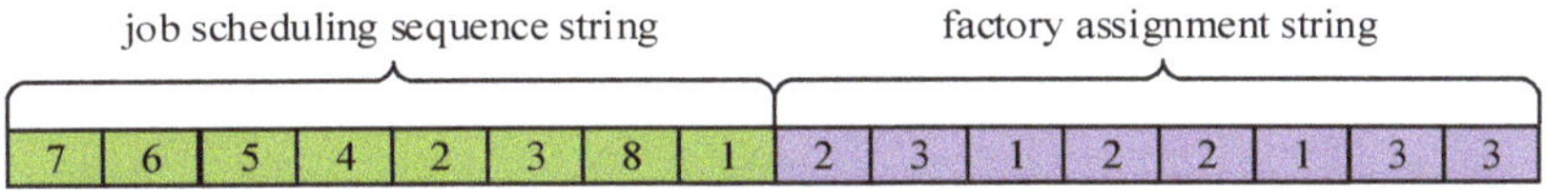

Figure 2. Illustration of the solution representation method.

Note that the aforementioned approach only focuses on assigning jobs to factories without obtaining other decisions, namely, the sequence in which jobs are processed on machines, allocation of vehicles for jobs, and delivery sequence of jobs. To convert the solution into an actionable plan, we present the following rules:

- Jobs that have been allocated to a factory are processed in a sequence that matches their assigned order on the machines;
- After the production of jobs, they are assigned in a sequential manner to a vehicle. The earlier the processing is completed, the sooner the vehicle is assigned. Meanwhile, vehicles are required not to exceed their maximum load capacity.
- Jobs are transported in the exact sequence in which they are loaded into the vehicle.

According to the above method and rules, we can successfully transform a solution into practicable decisions.

Ensuring both the stability and diversity of MQBSO, this work adopts a random method to initialize p_s feasible solutions for constructing the initial population.

5.2. Clustering

Along with the evolution of BSO, the population should be gathered into various numbers of clusters during the iteration. Thus, this work develops a dynamic clustering approach driven by a nondominated sorting method [42]. This work sorts all individuals in the population and assigns them sorted values based on their dominated relationships. The smaller the sorted value, the better the individual. Hence, this work sets the best individuals with the smallest sorted value of 1 as the center individuals, while the rest as normal individuals. For each center individual, this work constructs a cluster. To conduct such work, the normal ones are randomly assigned to these clusters. Notice that when only one individual has the sorted value of 1, this work selects the individuals with the sorted value of 2 as center individuals.

5.3. Generating

Generating is the core process of BSO, which controls the global search and local search abilities of an algorithm through applying one individual or two individuals in clusters. In this process, three vital parameters are used, i.e., r_g, r_o, r_t. Let r_g decide whether a new individual is constructed by one individual or two individuals. r_o determines whether a new individual is created by utilizing one center individual or one normal individual. r_t decides whether a new individual is produced via employing two center individuals or two normal ones. Based on them, this work introduces a global search strategy and a local search strategy. The details about them are provided as follows:

- A global search strategy is designed when utilizing two randomly chosen center or normal individuals to construct new individuals, where the sequence-based [43] and the two-point crossover [44] methods are adopted. The former is applied to update the job scheduling sequence string and the latter is utilized to update the factory assignment string. The main contents of these two methods are described below.
- Sequence-based crossover method: First, randomly have two job position indexes p_1, p_2. Then, jobs between them in the individual x_1 are copied to the same positions of a new individual x'. Finally, the missing jobs in x' are added as their appearance in the individual x_2. Hence, the job scheduling sequence string of x' is obtained. Two-point crossover method: First, two factory position indexes p_3, p_4 are generated at random. Then, extract factory assignments beyond p_3 and p_4 in x_1 and place them into the same positions of x'. Finally, the rest factory assignments in x' are filled with the elements at the same positions of x_2. Thus, the factory assignment string of x' is acquired. By employing these two methods, a new individual is successfully produced. To clearly exhibit the generation process, Figure 3 depicts an illustrative example.
- A local search strategy is developed when using one randomly selected center or normal individual to construct new individuals, where five kinds of neighborhood structures, named *NS1*, *NS2*, *NS3*, *NS4*, and *NS5* are introduced. The main idea of *NS1* is as follows: randomly produce two job positions for a chosen individual, then swap these two jobs and exchange their respective factory assignments.

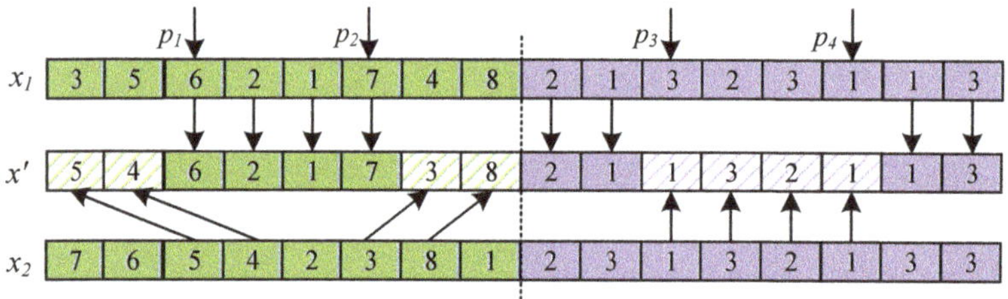

Figure 3. Illustration of a new individual generation process.

Different from *NS1*, the problem-dependent information is considered for the final four neighborhood structures. Given that one of the primary objectives of the problem investigated is to optimize the makespan criterion, it is essential to focus on improving the performance of the key factory that has a maximum completion time. To reach this, it is vital to adjust both the factory assignment and job processing sequence associated with this factory. According to the key factory theory [45] and the characteristics of the presented problem, this work designs four problem-dependent neighborhood structures. The details about them are given as follows: *NS2* randomly swaps two jobs in the key factory; *NS3* employs an insert operator, where two jobs in the key factory are randomly chosen, and one of which is inserted into the front of the other, along with corresponding changes are made to their factory assignments; *NS4* is similar to *NS2* except that the factory assignment of the two jobs is different, and one must be the key factory; and *NS5* changes the factory assignment of a job in the key factory.

It is worth mentioning that for each chosen center or normal individual, only one of five neighborhood structures is selected at random to produce a new individual. This work stores the better one between the chosen and new individuals in accordance with their dominated relationship. To intuitively understand the five neighborhood structures, Figure 4 shows five examples of these structures, and the key factory is denoted as "*".

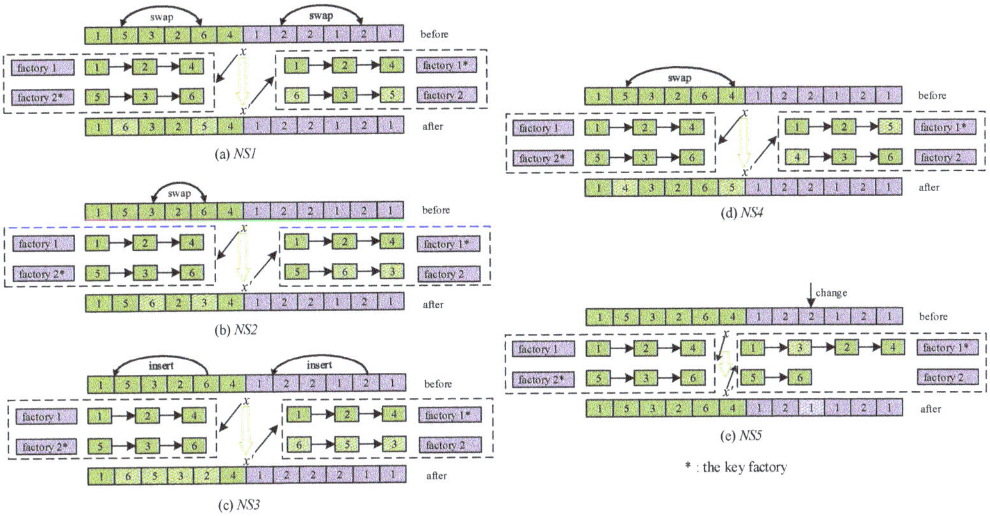

Figure 4. Examples of five types of neighborhood structures.

Furthermore, to avoid premature convergence and enhance the local search ability, we adopt a simulated annealing strategy [46]. The steps of this strategy are outlined below.

Step 1: Set an initial temperature $T_0 = 0.5\cdot\left(\sum_{i=1}^{m}\sum_{j=1}^{n}\alpha_{ij}/(10\cdot n\cdot m)\right)$, a final temperature $T_{min} = 0.5\cdot T_0$, and update the current temperature $T := T_0$.

Step 2: Select a center or normal individual x at random and set an intermediary individual $x_3 := x$.

Step 3: Randomly perform one of the five neighborhood structures on x_3 to generate a new individual x'.

Step 4: If x' dominates x_3, $x_3 := x'$; otherwise, $x_3 := x_3$.

Step 5: Adjust the temperature according to the formula: $T := T - (T\cdot 0.1)$, and repeat Steps 3–5 until $T \leq T_{min}$.

Step 6: Generate the new individual $x' := x_3$ and save it.

In the generating phase, Q-learning is implemented to assist MQBSO in choosing a generation strategy, the introduction of this process is described in Section 5.5.

5.4. Selecting

In the original BSO, the selecting phase is performed to store better individuals to enter the next population. It usually saves the better ones between new individuals and their connected individuals in the population. This method may discard some better individuals. In order to strengthen MQBSO's capability to explore promising directions, this work employs an effective selection method [44] by utilizing the nondominated sorting and crowding distance approaches. The basic idea of this method is shown as follows: First, merge the existing population with new individuals; second, sort all individuals and calculate their crowding distance values; and finally, extract the best p_s individuals as the next population based on their sorted and crowding distance values.

5.5. Q-Learning Process

In this work, Q-learning is composed of four actions, four states, a reward function, and an action selection method. Four actions are defined as the combinations of a global search strategy, a local search strategy, and a simulated annealing strategy. Four states are described by the convergence and uniformity metrics. A reward function is designed based on the states and an improved ε-greedy method is newly developed.

5.5.1. Action Set

The action set consists of four actions, and each one is a combination of a global search strategy, a local search strategy, and a simulated annealing strategy. Action $a(1)$ contains a global search strategy. Action $a(2)$ includes a local search strategy. Action $a(3)$ is composed of a global search strategy and a local search strategy. Action $a(4)$ is made up of a global search strategy and a simulated annealing strategy. According to the above designs, Figure 5 gives the framework of an action set in MQBSO, where r_n denotes a random number between $(0, 1)$.

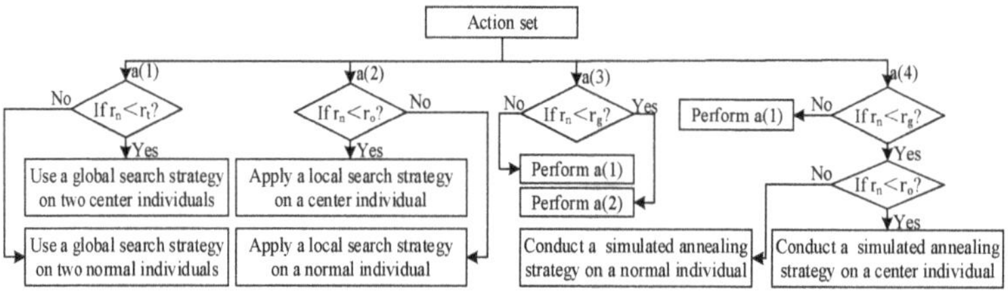

Figure 5. Framework of an action set in MQBSO.

This work uses an improved ε-greedy method [32] to conduct the selection of an action, where ε is calculated by Equation (28). In Equation (28), ρ_c denotes the current number of fitness function evaluations, and ρ_{max} represents a stopping condition equaling to $150 \cdot n \cdot m$ fitness function evaluations. Randomly generate a float number $\lambda \in (0, 1)$, if λ is bigger than $1 - \varepsilon$, one of four actions is chosen at random; otherwise, the agent selects the action with the highest Q-value as its preferred option. This method ensures that the selection probability of the two cases is about half in the beginning, along with the agent maintaining a certain ability to explore during the early stage. As the algorithm evolves, the action with the highest Q-value is favored. Thus, MQBSO can effectively intensify the exploration ability and reduce the possibility of dropping into local optima.

$$\varepsilon = 0.5 / \left(1 + e^{(10 \cdot (\rho_c - 0.6 \cdot \rho_{\max})) / \rho_{\max}}\right), \tag{28}$$

5.5.2. State Set

To clearly depict the state, a convergence index (C-metric) [47] and a uniformity index (D-metric) [33] are used, which are computed based on the formulas defined below.

$$C(U, W) = |\{w \in W | \exists u \in U : u \prec w\}| / |W| \tag{29}$$

As per Equation (29), U and W refer to the sets of non-dominated solutions acquired in the μ-th and $(\mu - 1)$-th iterations. $C(U, W)$ quantifies the percentage of solutions in set W which are dominated by solutions within set U, and $|W|$ stands for the size of W. Generally, a bigger $C(U, W)$ suggests that the performance of set U is better.

$$D = \left|\sum_{e=1}^{|E|} z_e - \bar{z}\right| / ||E| \cdot \bar{z}|, \tag{30}$$

$$\bar{z} = \sum_{e=1}^{|E|} z_e / |E|, \tag{31}$$

As per Equation (30), E is a non-dominated solution set and $|E|$ indicates its size. z_e refers to the shortest Euclidean distance from the e-th solution and any other solution in E, and $\bar{z}$ means the average distance as measured using the formula presented in Equation (31). Usually, a higher D-metric value implies a better performance of uniformity.

$$\Delta D(U,W) = D(U) - D(W) \quad (32)$$

The occurrence percentage of $C(U,W) > 0$, $C(U,W) \leq 0$, $\Delta D(U,W) > 0$, and $\Delta D(U,W) \leq 0$ in the entire search process of MQBSO on four instances are displayed in Figure 6. We see that each of the four cases appear. As a result, it is rational to consider four combinations of $C(U,W)$ and $\Delta D(U,W)$ as four states, i.e., $s(1)$: $C(U,W) > 0$ and $\Delta D(U,W) > 0$, $s(2)$:$C(U,W) > 0$ and $\Delta D(U,W) \leq 0$, $s(3)$: $C(U,W) \leq 0$ and $\Delta D(U,W) > 0$, and $s(4)$: $C(U,W) \leq 0$ and $\Delta D(U,W) \leq 0$.

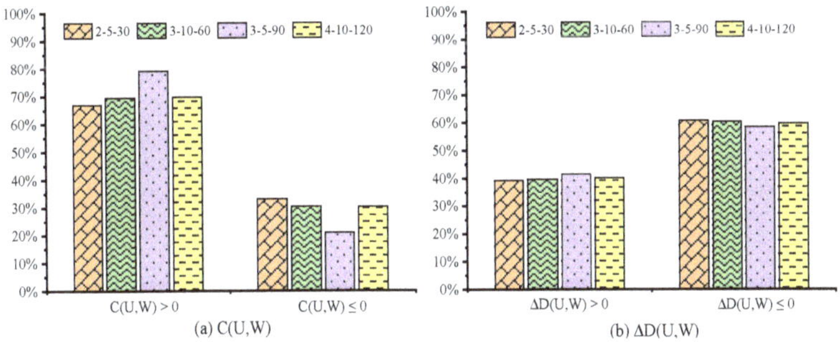

Figure 6. The occurrence percentage on each case of $C(U,W)$ and $\Delta D(U,W)$ on four instances.

5.5.3. Reward

In this work, four states are labeled as $s(1), s(2), s(3)$, and $s(4)$. The bigger the label value of the state, the worse the state. $s(1)$ means the best state while $s(4)$ is the worst one. Thus, rewards are set based on the label value of states. Four reward values r_v are 5, 3, 3, and 1 for these four states, respectively.

After a detailed discussion, Algorithm 1 provides the main procedure of MQBSO.

Algorithm 1: MQBSO

Input: Population size p_s, three generation parameters r_g, r_o, r_t, learning rate θ, discount rate ϑ, and a stopping condition ρ_{max}.
Output: A non-dominated solution set.
Initialize the population and parameters (c.f. Section 5.1)
While the stopping condition is not reached **do**
Implement a dynamic clustering method in the clustering phase (c.f. Section 5.2).
Employ a Q-learning process in the generating phase (c.f. Sections 5.3 and 5.5).
Apply a selection method in the selecting phase (c.f. Section 5.4).
Update the population state and Q-table.
End while

---

6. Experimental Evaluations

In this section, comparison experiments and statistical tests are conducted to study MQBSO's performance. MQBSO and comparison algorithms are programmed in C++ and performed on a personal computer equipped with HUAWEI Core i5-8265U CPU and 8 GB RAM in Qingdao, China. Four comparison methods are well-known metaheuristics: multi-objective whale swarm algorithm (MOWSA) [43], multi-objective brain storm optimization (MOBSO) [44], nondominated sorting genetic algorithm II (NSGA-II) [42], and multi-objective evolutionary algorithm based on decomposition (MOEA/D) [48]. In fairness, this work sets $150 \cdot n \cdot m$ fitness function evaluations as a termination criterion, and all methods independently solve each instance 20 times.

6.1. Test Instances

Since the previous work does not address the presented problem, we cannot find available benchmarks. Therefore, we produce a set of instances based on the problems' features. The benchmarks regarding flow shop scheduling and vehicle routing problems are employed to construct instances, i.e., the VFR benchmark [49] for the former, and the Gehring & Homberger benchmark [50] for the latter.

In the VFR benchmark, "VFR*a*_*b*_*c*" means the *c*-th instance of a test problem having *a* jobs and *b* machines. Four instances are adopted, including VFR30_5_1, VFR30_10_1, VFR60_5_1, and VFR60_10_1, respectively. The instances VFR90_5_1, VFR90_10_1, VFR120_5_1, and VFR120_10_1 do not exist in the VFR benchmark. Thus, this work creates them by applying the information of the first 90, 120 jobs and the first 5, 10 machines regarding the VFR100_20_1 and VFR200_20_1.

In the Gehring & Homberger benchmark, an instance named C1_2_1 is applied, where coordinates, time windows, and service times are provided. Through choosing the first 30, 60, 90, and 120 customers from it, four instances, namely, C1_2_1, C1_2_1, C1_2_1, and C1_2_1 are obtained. The chosen instances contain eight combinations of $n \times m$: $(30, 60, 90, 120) \times (5, 10)$, where n and m indicate the number of jobs and machines, respectively. This work sets the number of factories $f \in \{2, 3, 4\}$. Hence, a total of 24 test instances are successfully generated.

For convenience, Table 2 provides abbreviations for the 24 test instances. In it, the first instance called "2-5-30" consists of 2 factories, 5 machines, and 30 jobs, in which the production and distribution data are from VFR30_5_1 and C1_2_1, respectively. The remaining can be deduced by analogy. Furthermore, this work sets the load of jobs from an interval [10,40], the maximum load capacity of vehicles is 100, 125, 150, and 200 when the quantity of jobs is 30, 60, 90, and 120, respectively, and the unit earliness and tardiness weights of jobs are generated at random from $\{0.1, 0.2, 0.3, 0.4, 0.5\}$.

Table 2. Abbreviation information of 24 test instances.

Instance	*f*	Production	Distribution	Instance	*f*	Production	Distribution
2-5-30	2	VFR30_5_1	C1_2_1	2-10-30	2	VFR30_10_1	C1_2_1
2-5-60	2	VFR60_5_1	C1_2_1	2-10-60	2	VFR60_10_1	C1_2_1
2-5-90	2	VFR90_5_1	C1_2_1	2-10-90	2	VFR90_10_1	C1_2_1
2-5-120	2	VFR120_5_1	C1_2_1	2-10-120	2	VFR120_10_1	C1_2_1
3-5-30	3	VFR30_5_1	C1_2_1	3-10-30	3	VFR30_10_1	C1_2_1
3-5-60	3	VFR60_5_1	C1_2_1	3-10-60	3	VFR60_10_1	C1_2_1
3-5-90	3	VFR90_5_1	C1_2_1	3-10-90	3	VFR90_10_1	C1_2_1
3-5-120	3	VFR120_5_1	C1_2_1	3-10-120	3	VFR120_10_1	C1_2_1
4-5-30	4	VFR30_5_1	C1_2_1	4-10-30	4	VFR30_10_1	C1_2_1
4-5-60	4	VFR60_5_1	C1_2_1	4-10-60	4	VFR60_10_1	C1_2_1
4-5-90	4	VFR90_5_1	C1_2_1	4-10-90	4	VFR90_10_1	C1_2_1
4-5-120	4	VFR120_5_1	C1_2_1	4-10-120	4	VFR120_20_1	C1_2_1

6.2. Parameters Setting

An orthogonal experiment method [51] is employed in this research to implement the parameter experiment on a moderate-size instance named "3-5-60" with 3 factories, 5 machines and 60 jobs. This method is viewed as a modern technique for analyzing and optimizing parameters across various research fields. Generally, practical engineering design and optimization tasks require the consideration of three or more influential factors, leading to the application of full factorial design analysis. MQBSO considers four parameters, i.e., p_s, r_g, r_o, and r_t. Each parameter has four levels: $p_s \in \{20, 40, 60, 80\}$, $r_g \in \{0.20, 0.40, 0.60, 0.80\}$, $r_o \in \{0.20, 0.40, 0.60, 0.80\}$, $r_t \in \{0.20, 0.40, 0.60, 0.80\}$, and an array $L_{16^4_4}$ containing 16 combinations is created. To promote fairness in the comparison of different algorithms, this work sets the same number of fitness function evaluations as a stopping condition, i.e., $150 \cdot n \cdot m$, where n and m are the quantity of jobs and machines, respectively. Each combination is executed 20 times individually and the results are analyzed by applying the IGD-metric. The average IGD (AIGD) results are calculated and provided in Table 3. Through analyzing the obtained results, a hopeful parameter combination is produced, i.e., $p_s = 40$, $r_g = 0.40$, $r_o = 0.20$, $r_t = 0.80$.

Table 3. Orthogonal array and AIGD results of MQBSO.

No.	p_s	r_g	r_o	r_t	AIGD
1	20	0.20	0.20	0.20	0.1016
2	20	0.40	0.40	0.40	0.0927
3	20	0.60	0.60	0.60	0.0904
4	20	0.80	0.80	0.80	0.0861
5	40	0.20	0.40	0.60	0.1056
6	40	0.40	0.20	0.80	0.0852
7	40	0.60	0.80	0.20	0.0909
8	40	0.80	0.60	0.40	0.1232
9	60	0.20	0.60	0.80	0.1005
10	60	0.40	0.80	0.60	0.0952
11	60	0.60	0.20	0.40	0.0939
12	60	0.80	0.40	0.20	0.0984
13	80	0.20	0.80	0.40	0.0931
14	80	0.40	0.60	0.20	0.0956
15	80	0.60	0.40	0.80	0.0868
16	80	0.80	0.20	0.60	0.0867

Similarly, the parameters of four peers are achieved via using the same method, and their parameters are displayed in Table 4. In addition, the learning rate θ and discount rate ϑ are set by drawing on existing research [32], which are 0.5 and 0.8, respectively.

Table 4. Parameter settings of four compared algorithms.

Algorithm	Parameter	Levels	Value
MOWSA	population size	20, 40, 60, 80	20
	crossover probability	0.80, 0.85, 0.90, 0.95	0.85
	mutation probability	0.10, 0.15, 0.20, 0.25	0.15
MOBSO	p_s	20, 40, 60, 80	80
	r_g	0.20, 0.40, 0.60, 0.80	0.80
	r_o	0.20, 0.40, 0.60, 0.80	0.20
	r_t	0.20, 0.40, 0.60, 0.80	0.60
NSGA-II	population size	20, 40, 60, 80	80
	mutation probability	0.10, 0.15, 0.20, 0.25	0.15
MOEA/D	population size	20, 40, 60, 80	40
	neighborhood size	10, 15, 20, 25	25

6.3. Performance Metrics

Convergence and uniformity are two significant measures for examining the efficiency of multi-objective algorithms. Hence, this work utilizes three common performance metrics to carry out algorithmic measurements, i.e., C-metric [47], Inverted Generational Distance-metric (IGD-metric) [47], and Hypervolume-metric (HV-metric) [52]. The C-metric is defined in Equation (29), and the details of the IGD- and HV-metrics are offered below.

The IGD-metric is applied to reflect both convergence and uniformity of a method and its calculation formula is shown as:

$$IGD(P^*, P) = \sum\nolimits_{p \in P^*} dist(p, P)/|P^*| \quad (33)$$

where P and P^* mean an obtained solution set by an algorithm and the Pareto optimal front, respectively. In reality, the Pareto optimal front is difficult to achieve for the examined problem. Hence, this work generates P^* by merging the obtained solution sets of all employed algorithms and discarding the dominated solutions. $dist(p, P)$ represents the shortest Euclid distance from a solution p in P^* and any other solution in P, and $|P^*|$ is the quantity of solutions in P^*. In this work, all objective values are normalized within $(0, 1)$, and an algorithm with lower IGD-metric values is ideal.

The HV-metric is also used to account for the convergence and uniformity of an algorithm. It estimates the volume of the area covered by the obtained nondominated solutions of an algorithm and a known reference point H^*. It is calculated as:

$$HV = \delta\left(\cup_{o=1}^{|O|} sv_o\right) \tag{34}$$

where the Lebesgue measure δ is implemented to determine the volume of a set. $|O|$ denotes the quantity of solutions in the solution set O, and sv_o is the super volume of the area coved by the o-th solution in O and P^*. As in the IGD-metric, the obtained objective values of all algorithms are transformed into the range of $(0, 1)$, and H^* is $(1, 1)$. Generally, a larger HV-metric value shows a better performance.

6.4. Experimental Results and Analysis

This section compares MQBSO with its four rivals on the C-metric, IGD-metric, and HV-metric. The four peers are, respectively, MOWSA, MOBSO, NSGA-II, and MOEA/D, and the results are presented in Tables 5–7.

Table 5. Results of MQBSO and its peers concerning C-metric.

Instance	C(QB,WS)	C(WS,QB)	C(QB,BS)	C(BS,QB)	C(QB,GA)	C(GA,QB)	C(QB,EA)	C(EA,QB)
2-5-30	0.7951	0.0161	0.9908	0.0000	0.9889	0.0000	0.9709	0.0031
2-5-60	0.9810	0.0000	0.9729	0.0000	1.0000	0.0000	1.0000	0.0000
2-5-90	0.9735	0.0000	1.0000	0.0000	1.0000	0.0000	1.0000	0.0000
2-5-120	0.9389	0.0000	0.9739	0.0018	0.9818	0.0000	1.0000	0.0000
2-10-30	0.0000	0.6810	0.0065	0.5785	0.0439	0.2361	0.0696	0.2504
2-10-60	0.9481	0.0000	1.0000	0.0000	1.0000	0.0000	1.0000	0.0000
2-10-90	0.9297	0.0000	1.0000	0.0000	1.0000	0.0000	1.0000	0.0000
2-10-120	0.9569	0.0000	1.0000	0.0000	1.0000	0.0000	1.0000	0.0000
3-5-30	0.9782	0.0000	0.9519	0.0000	0.8082	0.1250	0.6868	0.2206
3-5-60	0.9306	0.0000	0.9731	0.0000	1.0000	0.0000	0.9750	0.0000
3-5-90	0.9816	0.0000	1.0000	0.0000	1.0000	0.0000	1.0000	0.0000
3-5-120	0.9687	0.0024	0.9964	0.0000	1.0000	0.0000	1.0000	0.0000
3-10-30	0.1077	0.5823	0.2163	0.5048	0.4705	0.2068	0.3565	0.2504
3-10-60	0.9921	0.0000	1.0000	0.0000	1.0000	0.0000	1.0000	0.0000
3-10-90	0.9658	0.0000	1.0000	0.0000	1.0000	0.0000	1.0000	0.0000
3-10-120	0.9764	0.0000	1.0000	0.0000	1.0000	0.0000	1.0000	0.0000
4-5-30	0.8991	0.0000	0.9064	0.0000	0.1531	0.7797	0.0640	0.8341
4-5-60	0.9820	0.0000	0.9753	0.0000	0.9952	0.0000	1.0000	0.0000
4-5-90	0.9792	0.0000	0.9957	0.0000	1.0000	0.0000	1.0000	0.0000
4-5-120	0.9464	0.0000	0.9918	0.0000	1.0000	0.0000	1.0000	0.0000
4-10-30	0.6849	0.0225	0.9400	0.0038	0.1859	0.4120	0.1172	0.4602
4-10-60	0.9605	0.0000	1.0000	0.0000	1.0000	0.0000	1.0000	0.0000
4-10-90	0.9796	0.0000	1.0000	0.0000	1.0000	0.0000	1.0000	0.0000
4-10-120	0.9796	0.0000	0.9981	0.0000	1.0000	0.0000	1.0000	0.0000
Average	0.8682	0.0543	0.9120	0.0454	0.8595	0.0733	0.8433	0.0841

Table 5. *Cont.*

Table 6. Results of MQBSO and its peers about IGD-metric.

Instance	MQBSO	MOWSA	MOBSO	NSGA-II	MOEA/D
2-5-30	0.1595	0.2585	0.2788	0.3784	0.3512
2-5-60	0.0668	0.4456	0.4132	0.5073	0.4948
2-5-90	0.0695	0.4587	0.4252	0.5485	0.5790
2-5-120	0.0946	0.2911	0.2813	0.4224	0.4837
2-10-30	0.4201	0.1777	0.2311	0.3187	0.3576
2-10-60	0.1246	0.3708	0.3807	0.5254	0.5820
2-10-90	0.1147	0.3676	0.4778	0.6540	0.9409
2-10-120	0.1023	0.3686	0.4377	0.6161	0.7933
3-5-30	0.1038	0.3638	0.3531	0.2781	0.2269
3-5-60	0.0963	0.4956	0.4784	0.5185	0.5287
3-5-90	0.0466	0.4270	0.4263	0.4711	0.4883
3-5-120	0.0558	0.2064	0.2535	0.3055	0.3883
3-10-30	0.1799	0.1421	0.1626	0.2380	0.2398
3-10-60	0.0561	0.4702	0.4162	0.5000	0.5307
3-10-90	0.0603	0.4344	0.4224	0.4797	0.5345
3-10-120	0.0506	0.2067	0.2748	0.3302	0.4071
4-5-30	0.2378	0.4851	0.4845	0.1161	0.1381
4-5-60	0.0616	0.5063	0.5201	0.5465	0.5696
4-5-90	0.0646	0.4412	0.4888	0.5184	0.5581
4-5-120	0.0842	0.1863	0.2955	0.3124	0.3523
4-10-30	0.1882	0.2383	0.2371	0.2016	0.2659
4-10-60	0.0511	0.4222	0.4571	0.4807	0.5007
4-10-90	0.0471	0.4030	0.4150	0.4480	0.4806
4-10-120	0.0477	0.2245	0.2720	0.3113	0.3809
Average	0.1077	0.3497	0.3714	0.4178	0.4655

Table 7. Results of MQBSO and its peers regarding HV-metric.

Instance	MQBSO	MOWSA	MOBSO	NSGA-II	MOEA/D
2-5-30	0.9106	0.7331	0.6655	0.5222	0.5543
2-5-60	0.9537	0.5126	0.4992	0.3914	0.3804
2-5-90	0.9474	0.4825	0.4625	0.3292	0.2711
2-5-120	0.8697	0.5955	0.5678	0.3848	0.3024
2-10-30	0.3208	0.8071	0.7052	0.5291	0.5064
2-10-60	0.9489	0.6054	0.5272	0.3515	0.3027
2-10-90	0.9615	0.6476	0.4196	0.2637	0.0894
2-10-120	0.9062	0.5797	0.4067	0.2397	0.1076
3-5-30	0.8422	0.5379	0.4982	0.6579	0.6860
3-5-60	0.9302	0.4018	0.3822	0.3312	0.2990
3-5-90	0.9177	0.4260	0.4011	0.3464	0.3141
3-5-120	0.8111	0.5519	0.5074	0.4383	0.3359
3-10-30	0.5548	0.7481	0.6640	0.5827	0.5695
3-10-60	0.9583	0.4643	0.4265	0.3714	0.3171
3-10-90	0.9385	0.4756	0.4193	0.3525	0.2742

Table 7. *Cont.*

Instance	MQBSO	MOWSA	MOBSO	NSGA-II	MOEA/D
3-10-120	0.7802	0.5197	0.4477	0.3680	0.2821
4-5-30	0.7839	0.4464	0.4105	0.8864	0.8946
4-5-60	0.9305	0.3777	0.3268	0.2951	0.2602
4-5-90	0.9097	0.3970	0.3596	0.3166	0.2671
4-5-120	0.8098	0.5521	0.4477	0.4121	0.3497
4-10-30	0.6532	0.5663	0.5291	0.8053	0.8131
4-10-60	0.9167	0.4544	0.3952	0.3578	0.3262
4-10-90	0.9036	0.4083	0.3459	0.3110	0.2636
4-10-120	0.7958	0.5252	0.4558	0.4019	0.3179
Average	0.8440	0.5340	0.4696	0.4269	0.3785

Table 5 exhibits the comparison results concerning C-metric, where the symbols "QB", "WS", "BS", "GA", and "EA" indicate the nondominated solution sets obtained by MQBSO, MOWSA, MOBSO, NSGA-II, and MOEA/D, respectively. A higher value of $C(QB, R)$ suggests a superior performance of MQBSO, $R \in \{WS, BS, GA, EA\}$. As shown in Table 5, the values of $C(QB, WS)$ and $C(QB, BS)$ are bigger than those of $C(WS, QB)$ and $C(BS, QB)$ in 22 instances, along with the values of $C(QB, GA)$ and $C(QB, EA)$ which are larger than those of $C(GA, QB)$ and $C(EA, QB)$ in 21 instances. Thus, MQBSO is significantly better than its peer methods. Furthermore, we find that MQBSO obtains better average results than MOWSA, MOBSO, NSGA-II, and MOEA/D. In light of the comparative analysis results, it is evident that MQBSO is a valid method.

Table 6 reports the comparison results with respect to the IGD-metric. Usually, a lower IGD-metric value means a better performance of an algorithm. As displayed in Table 6, MQBSO produces the best results in 22 out of 24 test instances compared with MOWSA, MOBSO, NSGA-II, and MOEA/D. Furthermore, the average values of all instances are shown at the bottom of Table 6. The average values of MQBSO, MOWSA, MOBSO, NSGA-II, and MOEA/D are 0.1077, 0.3497, 0.3714, 0.4178, and 0.4655, respectively. Clearly, MQBSO achieves a minimum average result. Thereby, we verify that MQBSO can obtain more promising solutions than its competitors in settling the studied problem.

Table 7 provides the comparison results regarding the HV-metric, where an algorithm with higher HV-metric values exhibits better than those with lower values. The results demonstrated in Table 7 ensure that the solutions obtained by MQBSO can cover a large volume on most test instances, meaning that MQBSO is superior. MQBSO is better than MOWSA and MOBSO in 22 instances, and it performs better than NSGA-II and MOEA/D in 20 out of 24 test instances. Thereby, we verify that MQBSO is competent at generating better solutions. In addition, by analyzing the average values acquired by MQBSO, MOWSA, MOBSO, NSGA-II, and MOEA/D, we draw a similar conclusion, the average values are, respectively, 0.8440, 0.5340, 0.4696, 0.4269, and 0.3785. Based on the ongoing study, we declare that MQBSO is an outstanding solver.

To clearly illustrate the experimental findings of MQBSO and other four rivals, boxplots are drawn to visualize the performance of all algorithms across nine instances with varying sizes. Figures 7 and 8, respectively, display the boxplots of MQBSO and its competitors with respect to IGD- and HV-metric. According to Figure 7, we find that MQBSO achieves a significantly lower median value than its rivals across all selected instances concerning IGD-metric. Similarly, as can be observed from Figure 8, MQBSO owns a greater median value than its rivals in all the chosen instances in terms of the HV-metric. Therefore, the collected experimental results and subsequent analysis state that MQBSO has an obvious advantage over its rivals in handling the problem under study.

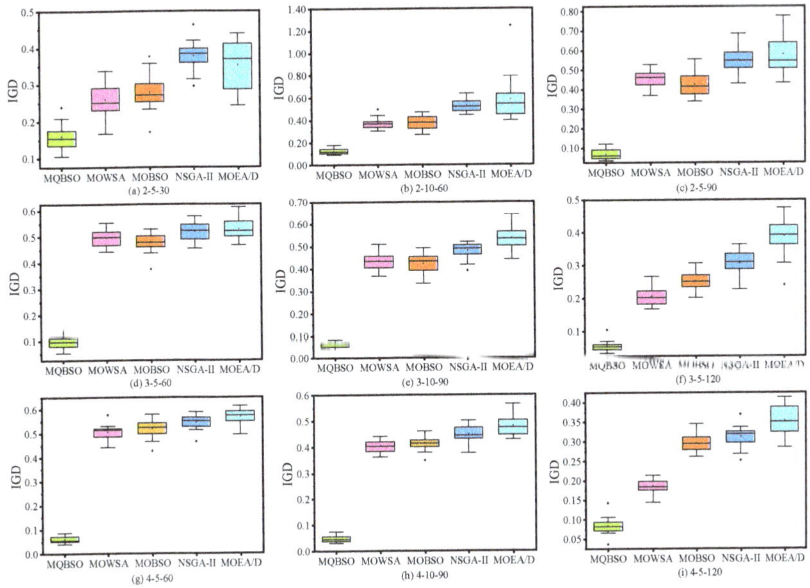

Figure 7. Boxplots for the results of nine test instances regarding the IGD-metric.

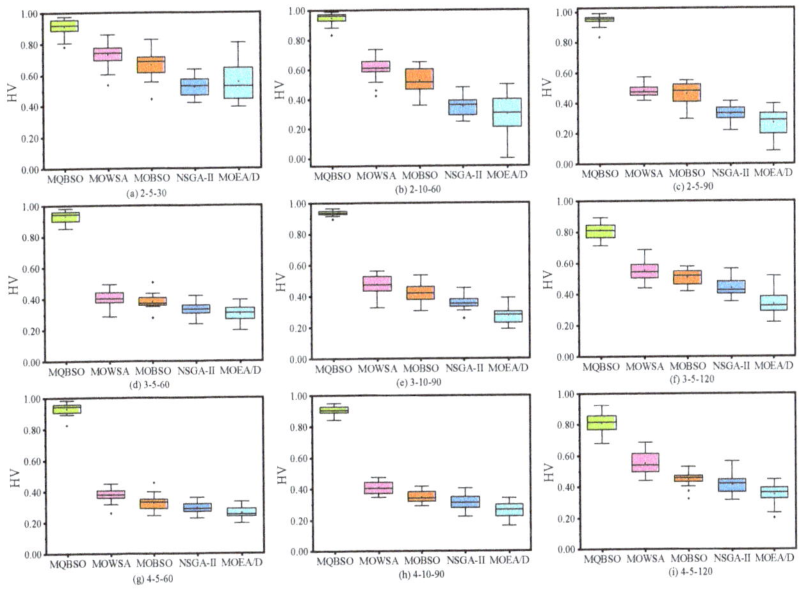

Figure 8. Boxplots for the results of nine test instances regarding the HV-metric.

For a further comparison, Figure 9 shows the distribution graphs of the nondominated solutions achieved by MQBSO and its peers in settling six instances with different sizes. From Figure 9, it is apparent that the nondominated solutions obtained by MQBSO are consistently much better than its rivals on the chosen test instances. Specifically, we see that MQBSO produces uniformly distributed and better approximated solutions. Hence, MQBSO can be taken as an outstanding optimizer.

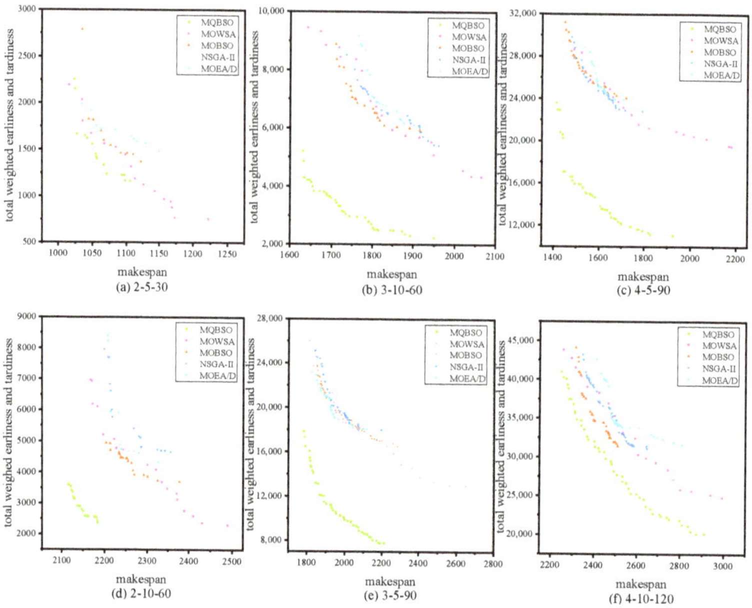

Figure 9. Nondominated solutions obtained by MQBSO and its peers.

Moreover, this work applies statistical tests to verify whether the performance difference between MQBSO and its peers is significantly different. The Friedman and Wilcoxon signed rank tests [53–55] are carried out on each instance of the IGD- and HV-metrics at $\alpha = 0.05$ level of significance. The average rank values of MQBSO, MOWSA, MOBSO, NSGA-II, and MOEA/D with respect to the IGD-metric are 1.3333, 2.5417, 2.7083, 3.7917, and 4.6250, respectively, and those of the five algorithms regarding the HV-metric are 1.5000, 2.1667, 3.1667, 3.7500, and 4.4167, respectively. Obviously, MQBSO obtains a minimum average rank value on the two metrics. Furthermore, the test statistic indices T_F regarding the IGD- and HV-metrics are calculated, i.e., 39.8483 and 8.0714. These values surpass the critical value of 2.53. Accordingly, the performance difference among all algorithms is statistically significant. The statistical results of the Wilcoxon signed rank test are displayed in Table 8, with respect to the IGD- and HV-metrics. The acquired R^+ values are greater than the R^- values, and the obtained p-values are lower than 0.05. As a consequence, we state that MQBSO significantly outperforms its peers.

Table 8. Results of the Wilcoxon signed rank test.

MQBSO vs.	Metric	R^+	R^-	z	p
MOWSA	IGD	290	10	4.00	0.0000
	HV	279	21	3.69	0.0001
MOBSO	IGD	294	6	4.11	0.0000
	HV	288	12	3.94	0.0000
NSGA-II	IGD	293	7	4.09	0.0000
	HV	289	11	3.97	0.0000
MOEA/D	IGD	294	6	4.11	0.0000
	HV	288	12	3.94	0.0000

6.5. Effectiveness of the Q-Learning Process in MQBSO

To demonstrate the effect of the Q-learning process in MQBSO, a variant without using it (named MBSO) is constructed. In MBSO, the generation strategy is selected at random to produce new individuals. Table 9 displays the comparison results of MQBSO and MBSO regarding the C-, IGD-, and HV-metrics. MQBSO acquires better results than MBSO on 21 instances of the C- and HV-metrics and performs better than MBSO in 20 instances with respect to the IGD-metric. In addition, MQBSO has an advantage over MBSO in terms of the average value for three metrics. Thus, the Q-learning process is effective in MQBSO when solving the investigated problem.

Table 9. Results of MQBSO and MBSO in the C-, IGD-, and HV-metrics.

Instance	C		IGD		HV	
	C(MQBSO,MBSO)	C(MBSO,MQBSO)	MQBSO	MBSO	MQBSO	MBSO
2-5-30	0.6230	0.1384	0.1716	0.2167	0.8012	0.6947
2-5-60	0.9721	0.0000	0.1210	0.3698	0.9096	0.4643
2-5-90	0.9746	0.0000	0.0997	0.3849	0.8930	0.4789
2-5-120	0.7014	0.1848	0.1085	0.1525	0.7541	0.6730
2-10-30	0.0000	0.8176	0.5289	0.1392	0.2769	0.8436
2-10-60	0.7192	0.0295	0.1888	0.1792	0.8035	0.5949
2-10-90	0.6700	0.1205	0.1949	0.2577	0.8191	0.6260
2-10-120	0.6206	0.2857	0.1464	0.1888	0.7612	0.6732
3-5-30	0.9776	0.0000	0.1142	0.3174	0.9177	0.5385
3-5-60	0.9564	0.0000	0.0905	0.4709	0.9189	0.3773
3-5-90	0.9871	0.0000	0.0564	0.3688	0.8724	0.4316
3-5-120	0.7571	0.1462	0.0621	0.0911	0.7148	0.6578
3-10-30	0.0450	0.6833	0.3210	0.1640	0.4751	0.7644
3-10-60	0.9878	0.0000	0.0696	0.3819	z	0.5006
3-10-90	0.9939	0.0000	0.0651	0.3697	0.9119	0.5338
3-10-120	0.7203	0.1812	0.0519	0.0906	0.7115	0.6547
4-5-30	0.9608	0.0000	0.0637	0.4683	0.9180	0.3940
4-5-60	0.9786	0.0000	0.0637	0.5151	0.8905	0.3329
4-5-90	0.9882	0.0000	0.0708	0.4126	0.8715	0.3920
4-5-120	0.5761	0.2595	0.0787	0.0961	0.7174	0.6761
4-10-30	0.3218	0.3746	0.1525	0.1183	0.6851	0.7460
4-10-60	0.9904	0.0000	0.0632	0.3645	0.8812	0.4630
4-10-90	0.9934	0.0000	0.0487	0.3538	0.8665	0.4476
4-10-120	0.7838	0.1182	0.0540	0.0966	0.7224	0.6465
Average	0.7625	0.1391	0.1244	0.2737	0.7928	0.5669

6.6. Comparison of Five Algorithms in CPU Time

To examine the computation efficiency of MQBSO, this work records the CPU time of MQBSO and its competitors in handling all the employed test instances. The instances are organized into groups based on their job quantity, and the average CPU time is computed for each group, as provided in Table 10. The average CPU time of MOWSA and MOBSO is longer than that of MQBSO in all groups. Thus, MQBSO has better abilities to tackle the considered problem by utilizing less time. The average CPU time of NSGA-II and MOEA/D exhibits a slight advantage over MQBSO in all groups. However, the difference between MQBSO and NSGA-II, along with MQBSO and MOEA/D is not very large. Thus, MQBSO is still regarded as an outstanding solver.

Table 10. Average CPU time of all the used algorithms in different groups.

n	Average CPU Time (s)				
	MQBSO	MOWSA	MOBSO	NSGA-II	MOEA/D
30	48.338	44.144	48.624	21.072	33.675
60	143.127	152.184	170.268	67.990	106.256
90	275.020	358.952	347.227	142.793	250.765
120	470.585	638.195	582.547	249.867	474.062
Average	234.268	298.369	287.166	120.430	216.189

6.7. Comparison of MQBSO and CPLEX

To verify MQBSO's performance for seeking optimal solutions, CPLEX is used for comparisons. The experiments are conducted as follows: this work develops three instances based on the first 8 jobs, the first 10 jobs, and all jobs of a test problem with 12 jobs, respectively. Tables 11 and 12 provide the information of the used test problem.

Table 11. Information for the test problem.

Job	Processing Time		Time Window		Load	Unit Earliness and Tardiness Weight	
	α_{1j}	α_{2j}	$d_j^{'}$	$d_j^{''}$	ψ_j	el_j	td_j
J_1	36	45	105	130	20	0.2	0.4
J_2	79	82	193	253	20	0.3	0.2
J_3	21	19	162	192	30	0.2	0.3
J_4	16	82	190	294	10	0.4	0.3
J_5	23	57	141	160	20	0.2	0.3
J_6	31	73	157	192	10	0.3	0.2
J_7	29	90	234	300	10	0.2	0.3
J_8	95	3	311	345	40	0.1	0.2
J_9	45	30	308	353	20	0.3	0.2
J_{10}	50	93	278	364	20	0.2	0.4
J_{11}	54	86	332	378	20	0.3	0.5
J_{12}	54	20	371	400	10	0.4	0.5

Table 12. The drive time for the numerical example.

	F_1	F_2	J_1	J_2	J_3	J_4	J_5	J_6	J_1	J_8	J_9	J_{10}	J_{11}	J_{12}
F_1	0	999	52	70	55	76	94	54	23	45	44	12	94	113
F_2	999	0	43	47	53	70	86	60	35	53	18	44	37	46
J_1	52	43	0	89	94	113	129	24	33	75	22	48	76	70
J_2	70	47	89	0	35	37	46	107	37	45	22	67	53	75
J_3	55	53	94	35	0	21	39	105	12	18	16	29	53	70
J_4	76	70	113	37	21	0	18	125	43	27	36	93	33	37
J_5	94	86	129	46	39	18	0	143	28	39	47	56	35	53
J_6	54	60	24	107	105	125	143	0	25	36	48	69	23	35
J_7	23	35	33	37	12	43	28	25	0	12	33	44	53	75
J_8	45	53	75	45	18	27	39	36	12	0	23	34	107	37
J_9	44	18	22	22	16	36	47	48	33	23	0	84	18	22
J_{10}	12	44	48	67	29	93	56	69	44	34	84	0	24	107
J_{11}	94	37	76	53	53	33	35	23	53	107	18	24	0	17
J_{12}	113	46	70	75	70	37	53	35	75	37	22	107	17	0

Considering that CPLEX cannot cope with a multi-objective optimization problem, we employ the weighted sum method to develop a variant of the problem under study. For each instance, three weight vectors are used, i.e., (1.0, 0.0), (0.5, 0.5), and (0.0, 1.0), to construct three sub-problems. There are two factories, and each factory contains two machines and two vehicles. The maximum load capacity of vehicles is 60, 80, and 100 when the number of jobs is 8, 10, and 12, respectively. The service time of customers is 90. This work sets the maximum running time of CPLEX as 3600 s. In scenarios where CPLEX fails to identify the global optimal solution in the allowed time, it outputs an approximate optimal value (AOV) instead. Table 13 shows the comparison results.

From Table 13, we can see that CPLEX achieves an optimal solution on two sub-problems and obtains the same value as MQBSO on one sub-problem when solving the instance with 8 jobs. On the contrary, MQBSO shows better than CPLEX on two sub-problems for solving the instances with 10 and 12 jobs, and it acquires the same value as CPLEX on one sub-problem. Moreover, the running time of MQBSO is significantly shorter than CPLEX. Thus, we can infer that MQBSO exhibits clear advantages over CPLEX in handling the proposed problem if the problem scale is larger.

Table 13. Comparison results of MQBSO and CPLEX.

n	Weight	CPLEX		MQBSO	
		Output	Time (s)	Output	Time (s)
8	(1.0, 0.0)	246.000	25.140	246.000	2.828
	(0.5, 0.5)	292.050	2242	300.500	2.213
	(0.0, 1.0)	322.700	245	324.000	2.203
10	(1.0, 0.0)	307.000(AOV)	3600	307.000	3.383
	(0.5, 0.5)	428.800(AOV)	3600	419.500	2.474
	(0.0, 1.0)	499.300(AOV)	3600	498.000	2.894
12	(1.0, 0.0)	360.000(AOV)	3600	360.000	2.187
	(0.5, 0.5)	583.650(AOV)	3600	571.500	3.347
	(0.0, 1.0)	767.800(AOV)	3600	723.000	4.079

Through analyzing the achieved experimental and statistical results in the previous sections, we verify that MQBSO has a powerful ability to gain better results in handling the problem under consideration. In MQBSO, a dynamic clustering method is designed in the clustering phase. A global search strategy, a local search strategy, and a simulated annealing strategy are used in the generating phase. A Q-learning process is conducted to dynamically choose the generation strategy. It includes four actions defined as the combinations of these strategies, four states described by convergence and uniformity metrics, a reward function, and an improved ε-greedy method. A selection method is employed in the selecting phase. By employing these methods iteratively, MQBSO has a superior trade-off between its abilities to explore and exploit the solution space, thus rendering it an outstanding solver for the problem being examined.

7. Conclusions

This work, for the first time, addresses a multi-objective integrated distributed flow shop and distribution scheduling to minimize makespan and total weighted earliness and tardiness. A mathematical model is given to define it and an MQBSO is developed to cope with it. In MQBSO, a double-string representation method is applied, and a dynamic clustering method is designed. Q-learning is applied to choose the generation strategy, where four actions, four states, a reward function, and an improved ε-greedy approach are designed. To assess the performance of MQBSO, numerical experiments are implemented on test instances by comparing with MOWSA, MOBSO, NSGA-II, MOEA/D, and CPLEX. The results suggest that MQBSO is superior.

The future directions are pointed out, which are encouraged to expand our study in several aspects, e.g., inventory, multiple time windows, stochastic models, flexible distributed scheduling, and energy-related objectives [56,57]. In addition, we will focus on RL to design effective solution methods.

Author Contributions: Conceptualization, J.X. and S.Z.; methodology, S.Z.; software, S.Z. and Y.Q.; validation, S.Z. and Y.Q.; formal analysis, S.Z. and Y.Q.; investigation, S.Z.; resources, J.X.; data curation, Y.Q.; writing—original draft preparation, S.Z. and Y.Q.; writing—review and editing, S.Z., J.X. and Y.Q.; visualization, S.Z.; supervision, J.X.; project administration, J.X.; funding acquisition, J.X. All authors have read and agreed to the published version of the manuscript.

Funding: This research was supported in part, by the National Natural Science Foundation of China: grant number 72271048.

Data Availability Statement: The data presented in this study are available on request from the corresponding author. The data are not publicly available due to privacy restrictions.

Conflicts of Interest: The authors declare no conflict of interest.

References

1. Rafiei, H.; Safaei, F.; Rabbani, M. Integrated production-distribution planning problem in a competition-based four-echelon supply chain. *Comput. Ind. Eng.* **2018**, *119*, 85–99. [CrossRef]
2. Ganji, M.; Kazemipoor, H.; Molana, S.M.H.; Sajadi, S.M. A green multi-objective integrated scheduling of production and distribution with heterogeneous fleet vehicle routing and time windows. *J. Clean. Prod.* **2020**, *259*, 120824. [CrossRef]
3. Chandra, P.; Fisher, M.L. Coordination of production and distribution planning. *Eur. J. Oper. Res.* **1994**, *72*, 503–517. [CrossRef]
4. Liu, L.; Liu, S. Integrated production and distribution problem of perishable products with a minimum total order weighted delivery time. *Mathematics* **2020**, *8*, 146. [CrossRef]
5. Moons, S.; Ramaekers, K.; Caris, A.; Arda, Y. Integrating production scheduling and vehicle routing decisions at the operational decision level: A review and discussion. *Comput. Ind. Eng.* **2017**, *104*, 224–245. [CrossRef]
6. Wang, J.J.; Wang, L. A bi-population cooperative memetic algorithm for distributed hybrid flow-shop scheduling. *IEEE Trans. Emerg. Top. Comput. Intell.* **2020**, *5*, 947–961. [CrossRef]
7. Shao, W.S.; Shao, Z.S.; Pi, D.C. Modeling and multi-neighborhood iterated greedy algorithm for distributed hybrid flow shop scheduling problem. *Knowl.-Based Syst.* **2020**, *194*, 105527. [CrossRef]
8. Wang, J.J.; Wang, L. A knowledge-based cooperative algorithm for energy-efficient scheduling of distributed flow-shop. *IEEE Trans. Syst. Man Cybern. Syst.* **2020**, *50*, 1805–1819. [CrossRef]
9. Lu, C.; Gao, L.; Gong, W.Y.; Hu, C.Y.; Yan, X.S.; Li, X.Y. Sustainable scheduling of distributed permutation flow-shop with non-identical factory using a knowledge-based multi-objective memetic optimization algorithm. *Swarm Evol. Comput.* **2021**, *60*, 100803. [CrossRef]
10. Shao, W.S.; Pi, D.C.; Shao, Z.S. Optimization of makespan for the distributed no-wait flow shop scheduling problem with iterated greedy algorithms. *Knowl.-Based Syst.* **2017**, *137*, 163–181. [CrossRef]
11. Gong, D.W.; Han, Y.Y.; Sun, J.Y. A novel hybrid multi-objective artificial bee colony algorithm for blocking lot-streaming flow shop scheduling problems. *Knowl.-Based Syst.* **2018**, *148*, 115–130. [CrossRef]
12. Zheng, J.; Wang, L.; Wang, J.J. A cooperative coevolution algorithm for multi-objective fuzzy distributed hybrid flow shop. *Knowl.-Based Syst.* **2020**, *194*, 105536. [CrossRef]
13. Fu, Y.P.; Hou, Y.S.; Wang, Z.F.; Wu, X.W.; Gao, K.Z.; Wang, L. A review of distributed scheduling problems in intelligent manufacturing systems. *Tsinghua Sci. Technol.* **2021**, *26*, 625–645. [CrossRef]
14. Zhao, F.Q.; Shao, D.Q.; Wang, L.; Xu, T.P.; Zhu, N.N.; Jonrinal, D. An effective water wave optimization algorithm with problem-specific knowledge for the distributed assembly blocking flow-shop scheduling problem. *Knowl.-Based Syst.* **2022**, *243*, 108471. [CrossRef]
15. Li, H.X.; Gao, K.Z.; Duan, P.Y.; Li, J.Q.; Zhang, L. A novel shuffled frog-leaping algorithm with reinforcement learning for distributed assembly hybrid flow shop scheduling. *Int. J. Prod. Res.* **2022**, *61*, 1233–1251. [CrossRef]
16. Li, H.X.; Gao, K.Z.; Duan, P.Y.; Li, J.Q.; Zhang, L. An improved artificial bee colony algorithm with Q-learning for solving permutation flow-shop scheduling problems. *IEEE Trans. Syst. Man Cybern. Syst.* **2022**, *53*, 2684–2693. [CrossRef]
17. Luo, B.; Liu, D.; Huang, T.; Wang, D. Model-free optimal tracking control via critic-only Q-learning. *IEEE Trans. Neural Netw. Learn. Syst.* **2016**, *27*, 2734–2744. [CrossRef] [PubMed]
18. Cheng, L.X.; Tang, L.X.; Zhang, L.P.; Zhang, Z.K. Multi-objective Q-learning-based hyper-heuristic with Bi-criteria selection for energy-aware mixed shop scheduling. *Swarm Evol. Comput.* **2022**, *69*, 100985. [CrossRef]
19. Bdeir, A.; Boeder, S.; Dernedde, T.; Tkachuk, K.; Falkner, J.K.; Schmidt-Thieme, L. RP-DQN: An application of Q-learning to vehicle routing problems. *Adv. Artif. Intell.* **2021**, *12873*, 3–16. [CrossRef]
20. Shi, Y.H. Brain storm optimization algorithm. In *International Conference in Swarm Intelligence*; Springer: Berlin/Heidelberg, Germany, 2011; pp. 303–309.
21. Potts, C.N. Analysis of a heuristic for one machine sequencing with release dates and delivery times. *Oper. Res.* **1980**, *28*, 1436–1441. [CrossRef]
22. Chen, Z.L. Integrated production and outbound distribution scheduling: Review and extensions. *Oper. Res.* **2010**, *58*, 120–148. [CrossRef]
23. Roberto, F.T.N.; Marcelo, S.N. An iterated greedy approach to integrate production by multiple parallel machines and distribution by a single capacitated vehicle. *Swarm Evol. Comput.* **2019**, *44*, 612–621. [CrossRef]
24. Jia, Z.H.; Cui, Y.F.; Li, K. An ant colony-based algorithm for integrated scheduling on batch machines with non-identical capacities. *Appl. Intell.* **2022**, *52*, 1752–1769. [CrossRef]
25. Yagmur, E.; Kesen, S.E. A memetic algorithm for joint production and distribution scheduling with due dates. *Comput. Ind. Eng.* **2020**, *142*, 106342. [CrossRef]
26. Mohammadi, S.; Al-e-Hashem, S.M.; Rekik, Y. An integrated production scheduling and delivery route planning with multi-purpose machines: A case study from a furniture manufacturing company. *Int. J. Prod. Econ.* **2020**, *219*, 347–359. [CrossRef]
27. Gharaei, A.; Jolai, F. A multi-agent approach to the integrated production scheduling and distribution problem in multi-factory supply chain. *Appl. Soft Comput.* **2018**, *65*, 577–589. [CrossRef]

28. Fu, Y.P.; Hou, Y.S.; Chen, Z.H.; Pu, X.J.; Gao, K.Z.; Sadollah, A. Modelling and scheduling integration of distributed production and distribution problems via black widow optimization. *Swarm Evol. Comput.* **2021**, *68*, 101015. [CrossRef]
29. Hou, Y.S.; Fu, Y.P.; Gao, K.Z.; Zhang, H.; Sadollah, A. Modelling and optimization of integrated distributed flow shop scheduling and distribution problems with time windows. *Expert Syst. Appl.* **2021**, *187*. [CrossRef]
30. Qin, H.; Li, T.; Teng, Y.; Wang, K. Integrated production and distribution scheduling in distributed hybrid flow shops. *Memetic Comput.* **2021**, *13*, 185–202. [CrossRef]
31. Wang, L.; Pan, Z.X.; Wang, J.J. A review of reinforcement learning based intelligent optimization for manufacturing scheduling. *Complex Syst. Model. Simul.* **2021**, *1*, 257–270. [CrossRef]
32. Zhao, F.; Di, S.; Wang, L. A hyperheuristic with Q-learning for the multiobjective energy-efficient distributed blocking flow shop scheduling problem. *IEEE Trans. Cybern.* **2022**, *53*, 3337–3350. [CrossRef] [PubMed]
33. Li, R.; Gong, W.Y.; Lu, C. A reinforcement learning based RMOEA/D for bi-objective fuzzy flexible job shop scheduling. *Expert Syst. Appl.* **2022**, *203*, 117380. [CrossRef]
34. Wang, H.X.; Sarker, B.R.; Li, J.; Li, J. Adaptive scheduling for assembly job shop with uncertain assembly times based on dual Q-learning. *Int. J. Prod. Res.* **2020**, *59*, 5867–5883. [CrossRef]
35. Xu, P.; Luo, W.; Lin, X. BSO20: Efficient brain storm optimization for real-parameter numerical optimization. *Complex Intell. Syst.* **2021**, *7*, 2415–2436. [CrossRef]
36. Cheng, S.; Zhang, M.; Ma, L.; Lu, H.; Wang, R.; Shi, Y.H. Brain storm optimization algorithm for solving knowledge spillover problems. *Neural Comput. Appl.* **2021**, *35*, 12247–12260. [CrossRef]
37. Hao, J.H.; Li, J.Q.; Du, Y.; Song, M.X.; Duan, P.; Zhang, Y.Y. Solving distributed hybrid flowshop scheduling problems by a hybrid brain storm optimization algorithm. *IEEE Access* **2019**, *7*, 66879–66894. [CrossRef]
38. Zhao, F.Q.; Hu, X.T.; Wang, L.; Xu, T.P.; Zhu, N.N.; Jonrinaldi. A reinforcement learning-driven brain storm optimisation algorithm for multi-objective energy-efficient distributed assembly no-wait flow shop scheduling problem. *Int. J. Prod. Res.* **2023**, *61*, 2854–2872. [CrossRef]
39. Ma, X.M.; Fu, Y.P.; Gao, K.Z.; Zhu, L.H.; Sadollah, A. A multi-objective scheduling and routing problem for home health care services via brain storm optimization. *Complex Syst. Model. Simul.* **2023**, *3*, 32–46. [CrossRef]
40. Ke, L. A brain storm optimization approach for the cumulative capacitated vehicle routing problem. *Memetic Comput.* **2018**, *10*, 411–421. [CrossRef]
41. Watkins, C.J.C.H.; Dayan, P. Technical note: Q-learning. *Mach. Learn.* **1992**, *8*, 279–292. [CrossRef]
42. Deb, K.; Pratap, A.; Agarwal, S. A fast and elitist multiobjective genetic algorithm: NSGA-II. *IEEE Trans. Evol. Comput.* **2002**, *6*, 182–197. [CrossRef]
43. Wang, G.C.; Gao, L.; Li, X.Y.; Li, P.G.; Tasgetiren, M.F. Energy-efficient distributed permutation flow shop scheduling problem using a multi-objective whale swarm algorithm. *Swarm Evol. Comput.* **2020**, *57*, 100716. [CrossRef]
44. Fu, Y.P.; Tian, G.D.; Fard, A.M.H.; Ahmadi, A.; Zhang, C.Y. Stochastic multi-objective modelling and optimization of an energy-conscious distributed permutation flow shop scheduling problem with the total tardiness constraint. *J. Clean. Prod.* **2019**, *226*, 515–525. [CrossRef]
45. Lu, C.; Gao, L.; Yi, J.; Li, X. Energy-efficient scheduling of distributed flow shop with heterogeneous factories: A real-world case from automobile industry in China. *IEEE Trans. Ind. Inform.* **2020**, *17*, 6687–6696. [CrossRef]
46. Kuidi, M. A memetic algorithm with novel semi-constructive evolution operators for permutation flowshop scheduling problem. *Appl. Soft Comput.* **2020**, *94*, 106458. [CrossRef]
47. Zitzler, E.; Deb, K.; Thiele, L. Comparison of multiobjective evolutionary algorithms: Empirical results. *Evol. Comput.* **2000**, *8*, 173–195. [CrossRef]
48. Zhang, Q.F.; Li, H. A multiobjective evolutionary algorithm based on decomposition. *IEEE Trans. Evol. Comput.* **2007**, *11*, 712–731. [CrossRef]
49. Vallada, E.; Ruiz, R.; Framinan, J.M. New hard benchmark for flowshop scheduling problems minimising makespan. *Eur. J. Oper. Res.* **2015**, *240*, 666–677. [CrossRef]
50. Gehring, H.; Homberger, J. A parallel hybrid evolutionary metaheuristic for the vehicle routing problem with time windows. In *Proceedings of EUROGEN99*; Springer: Berlin/Heidelberg, Germany, 1999; Volume 2, pp. 57–64.
51. Karna, S.K.; Sahai, R. An overview on Taguchi method. *Int. J. End. Math. Sci.* **2012**, *1*, 1–7.
52. Zitzler, E.; Thiele, L. Multiobjective evolutionary algorithms: A comparative case study and the strength Pareto approach. *IEEE Trans. Evol. Comput.* **1999**, *3*, 257–271. [CrossRef]
53. Friedman, M. The use of ranks to avoid the assumption of normality implicit in the analysis of variance. *J. Am. Stat. Assoc.* **1937**, *32*, 675–701. [CrossRef]
54. Wilcoxon, F.; Katti, S.K.; Wilcox, R.A. Critical values and probability levels for the Wilcoxon rank sum test and the Wilcoxon signed rank test. *Sel. Tables Math. Stat.* **1970**, *1*, 171–259.
55. Hou, Y.S.; Wang, H.F.; Fu, Y.P.; Gao, K.Z.; Zhang, H. Multi-objective brain storm optimization for integrated scheduling of distributed flow shop and distribution with maximal processing quality and minimal total weighted earliness and tardiness. *Comput. Ind. Eng.* **2023**, *179*, 109217. [CrossRef]

56. Li, F.; Chen, Z.L.; Tang, L. Integrated production, inventory and delivery problems: Complexity and algorithms. *INFORMS J. Comput.* **2017**, *29*, 232–250. [CrossRef]
57. Wang, J.; Song, G.; Liang, Z.; Demeulemeester, E.; Hu, X.; Liu, J. Unrelated parallel machine scheduling with multiple time windows: An application to earth observation satellite scheduling. *Comput. Oper. Res.* **2023**, *149*, 106010. [CrossRef]

mathematics

MDPI

Article

Demand Prediction of Shared Bicycles Based on Graph Convolutional Network-Gated Recurrent Unit-Attention Mechanism

Jian-You Xu [1,*], Yan Qian [1], Shuo Zhang [1] and Chin-Chia Wu [2]

[1] College of Information Science and Engineering, Northeastern University, Shenyang 110819, China; 2170764@stu.neu.edu.cn (Y.Q.); 1910307@stu.neu.edu.cn (S.Z.)

[2] Department of Statistics, Feng Chia University, Taichung 40724, Taiwan; cchwu@fcu.edu.tw

* Correspondence: xujianyou@mail.neu.edu.cn

Abstract: Shared bicycles provide a green, environmentally friendly, and healthy mode of transportation that effectively addresses the "final mile" problem in urban travel. However, the uneven distribution of bicycles and the imbalance of user demand can significantly impact user experience and bicycle usage efficiency, which makes it necessary to predict bicycle demand. In this paper, we propose a novel shared-bicycle demand prediction method based on station clustering. First, to address the challenge of capturing patterns in station-level bicycle demand, which exhibits significant fluctuations, we employ a clustering method that combines graph information from the bicycle transfer graph and potential energy. This method aggregates closely related stations into corresponding prediction regions. Second, we use the GCN-CRU-AM (Graph Convolutional Network-Gated Recurrent Unit-Attention Mechanism) model to predict bicycle demand in each region. This model extracts the spatial information and correlation between regions, integrates time feature data and local weather data, and assigns weights to the input features. Finally, experimental results based on the data from Citi Bike System in New York City demonstrate that the proposed model achieves a more accurate demand prediction.

Keywords: shared bicycles; station clustering; demand prediction; graph convolutional network

MSC: 68T07; 90B20

1. Introduction

With the accelerated process of urbanization and the escalating problem of traffic congestion, shared bicycles have experienced rapid growth as a green, low-carbon, and convenient mode of transportation. According to statistical data, as of 2021, the global market size of shared bicycles has exceeded 15 billion USD and is expected to reach 30 billion USD by 2025 [1]. However, in many cities, there are significant spatial and temporal variations in the distribution and demand for shared bicycles [2]. Without predicting the occurrence of bicycle shortages and surpluses in advance, these variations can result in underutilized shared-bicycle resources and inadequate supply in certain areas. Therefore, predicting the user demand in shared-bicycle systems plays a crucial role in promoting the intelligent and sustainable development of urban transportation.

Shared-bicycle demand prediction refers to the process of forecasting the demand for shared bicycles during a specific future time period through the analysis and modeling of historical data. Currently, shared-bicycle demand prediction methods can be broadly categorized into two types.

The first type is station-level methods, in which each individual shared-bicycle station is considered as the basic prediction unit, and the demand for bicycles within each station is predicted separately. Huang et al. [3] proposed a Bimodal Gaussian Inhomogeneous Poisson (BGIP) algorithm for predicting the number of bicycles at each station. Chen et al. [4] developed a model based on recurrent neural networks (RNN) to predict the real-time rental and return demand at each bicycle station, which can be used to formulate load-balancing strategies between stations. Zi et al. [5] introduced the TAGCN (Temporal Attention Graph Convolution Network) model, which combines graph convolutional neural networks with attention mechanisms to address the problem of the bike check-out/in number prediction of each station.

The other method category is based on cluster-level analysis. Due to the fact that the usage patterns of bicycles at each station are susceptible to factors such as time and weather, it is challenging to predict the demand for shared bicycles at individual stations. Algorithms of this type group similar stations into the same cluster and predict the demand for bicycles within each cluster.

Feng et al. [6] proposed a hierarchical traffic prediction model that utilizes iterative spectral clustering to cluster stations and employs a gradient boosting regression tree to predict the rental count for the entire shared-bicycle system. Jia et al. [7] proposed a two-stage Gaussian mixture model (GMM) clustering algorithm for shared bicycle stations, which considers bicycle migration trends and geographic location information between stations. Hua et al. [8] divided the virtual stations of dockless bike-sharing through K-means clustering and used random forest to predict the demand. Chen et al. [9] introduced a cluster-based dynamic prediction algorithm that constructed a weighted relationship network based on the current environment to simulate the relationships between bicycle stations. Stations with similar usage patterns are dynamically grouped into clusters.

Table 1 summarizes the differences between these two types of methods for predicting shared-bicycles demand and demonstrates whether the features are considered in each study.

Table 1. Two types of shared-bicycle demand prediction methods considering different features.

Type	Authors	Prediction Method	Spatial Features	Time Feature	Weather Feature
Station-level	Huang et al. [3]	BGIP (a Bimodal Gaussian Inhomogeneous Poisson)	✔	✔	×
	Chen et al. [4]	RNN (Recurrent Neural Networks)	✔	✔	✔
	Zi et al. [5]	TAGCN (a graph convolutional network model with temporal attention)	✔	×	✔
Clustering-level	Feng et al. [6]	Iterative spectral clustering; Gradient boosting regression tree	✔	×	✔
	Jia et al. [7]	TL-GMM (A two-level Gaussian Mixture Model); Gradient boosting regression tree	✔	×	✔
	Hua et al. [8]	K-means clustering; Random forest	✔	✔	×

Through the analysis of Table 1 and the current research status, its limitations are as follows:

1. Most studies do not consider the connection between shared-bicycle stations. Simply studying the demand of a single station is not enough to improve the service quality of the entire city's shared bicycle system.
2. Previous studies primarily utilized the bipartite clustering model (BC) [10], the unified geographic grid clustering (GC) algorithm, and K-means [9] to cluster bike stations. These methods have disadvantages such as not considering the migration trend of shared bikes between stations and relying heavily on randomly initialized parameters [11].

3. Some existing demand prediction models use traditional machine learning methods, such as random forest [9,12], support vector machine [13], linear regression [14], gradient boosting regression tree [6,8], etc. These models have shortcomings such as difficulty in handing complex relationships, limitations in feature interactions, and limited ability to model time series in the prediction of shared-bicycle demand. Additionally, some deep learning methods [5,15] used for demand prediction have limitations in terms of incomplete consideration and insufficient prediction. Specifically, these methods only take into account two aspects of spatial, temporal, or weather features, neglecting the holistic nature of the problem.

In order to overcome the deficiencies of existing bicycle demand prediction methods, this paper provides a novel shared-bicycle demand prediction method based on GIPE (Graph Information and Potential Energy) clustering and the GCN–GRU–AM (Graph Convolutional Network–Gated Recurrent Unit–Attention Mechanism) deep neural network. Its main contributions include the following:

1. We construct a bicycle transfer graph that considers the migration trend of shared bicycles between stations and extract graph information by calculating the importance degree of each station. Making full use of the graph information can effectively improve the clustering accuracy of shared-bicycle stations.
2. We apply the idea of potential energy to the correlation between stations, so that stations with more similar bicycle usage patterns and more frequent circulation can be reasonably clustered into the same regions.
3. In addition to historical bicycle demand features, we also consider the impact of weather features and time features on shared-bicycle demand prediction and evaluate different features through experiments.
4. Based on the deep neural network, we construct a GCN–GRU–AM model to predict the demand for shared bicycles, which can capture the spatial correlation between regions and the long-term and short-term dependencies in time series data and assign weights to different features. The experimental results show that the model's prediction accuracy is better than that of other models.

The rest of the paper is organized as follows: In Section 2, we provide a comprehensive description of our station clustering method and the shared-bicycle demand prediction model, offering detailed insights into their methodologies and techniques. In Section 3, we present the experimental process, including a comparative analysis of our approach with other models, as well as an exploration of the different feature inputs and various clustering methods. In Section 4, we outline the findings and conclusions of this study, providing a comprehensive summary and highlighting the implications of our research.

2. Materials and Methods

In this section, we present the methods proposed in this paper, which contain the station clustering method and the demand prediction model.

2.1. Station Clustering Method

The usage of bicycles in a shared-bicycle system is influenced by multiple factors such as the bicycle's time of use, weather conditions, and the unique relationships between stations [16]. This implies that the demand for bicycles varies significantly depending on these conditions, which makes it difficult to capture its regularity and predictability. By aggregating stations with similar characteristics, the accuracy of demand prediction can be improved, especially when compared to analyzing individual stations. Additionally, the users' riding habits are not limited to one station, so when users cannot find bicycles at their current station, they will go to nearby stations to search for bicycles. When users want to return their bicycles but find that the parking spots are full, they may also go to nearby stations to park their bicycles. Therefore, the proximity between stations has some correlation from the users' perspective [6].

In this section, we propose a clustering method based on graph information and potential energy to solve the problem of inter-station correlations.

2.1.1. Graph Information

1. Bicycle Transfer Graph; The bicycle transfer between shared-bicycle stations is essentially similar to the strong and weak associations between nodes in a graph. The correlation between different bicycle stations can also be represented by a graph. We define a bicycle transfer graph as a weighted directed network $G = (S,\ F)$, in which the nodes represent the set of single stations $S = \{\Sigma s_i | \ i = 1,\ 2,\ \ldots,\ n\}$, the lines with arrows represent the set of edges $F = \{\Sigma f_{ij} | i,\ j = 1,\ 2,\ \ldots,\ n\}$, and the f_{ij} means represents the transfer quantity from station s_i to station s_j. The bicycle transfer relationship between nodes is shown in Figure 1, which is a schematic diagram.

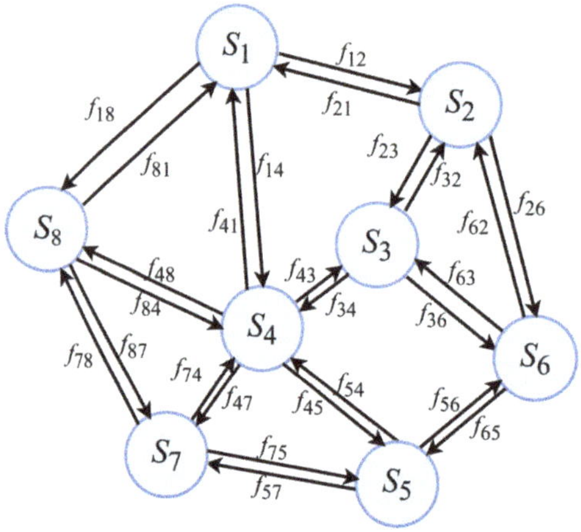

Figure 1. Bicycle transfer graph.

2. Station Importance Degree Matrix; The initial importance degree matrix P for each station is defined as the proportion of bicycle usage at each station to the bicycle usage at all stations in a certain time period. Assuming there are n nodes in the bicycle transfer graph and that the total bicycle usage in this period is sum, the bicycle usage of station s_i is p_i; the calculation formula for the initial importance matrix P is shown as follows:

$$P = \begin{bmatrix} p_1 & \cdots & 0 \\ \vdots & \ddots & \vdots \\ 0 & \cdots & p_n \end{bmatrix} / sum \tag{1}$$

3. Adjacency Matrix; The adjacency matrix S represents the bicycle flow between each station. We calculate the number of bicycles that can be transferred from one station to another and the total number of bicycles that can be reached from other stations to the current station to construct the bicycle transfer matrix O and the station bicycle arrival volume matrix A. The calculation method for the adjacency matrix S is as follows:

$$S = \frac{O}{A} = \begin{bmatrix} o_{11} & \cdots & o_{1n} \\ \vdots & \ddots & \vdots \\ o_{n1} & \cdots & o_{nn} \end{bmatrix} * \left(1 / \begin{bmatrix} a_1 & \cdots & a_1 \\ \vdots & \ddots & \vdots \\ a_n & \cdots & a_n \end{bmatrix} \right) \tag{2}$$

o_{ij} represents the number of bicycle transfer from station s_i to station s_j in a certain period, and a_i represents the total number of bicycles arriving at station s_i within a certain period.

The importance degree of each station is calculated from the above adjacency matrix and the initial station importance degree matrix P. The specific calculation process is as follows:

$$P = \lambda P + (1 - \lambda) S * P \tag{3}$$

$$P = \begin{bmatrix} p_{11} & \cdots & p_{1n} \\ \vdots & \ddots & \vdots \\ p_{n1} & \cdots & p_{nn} \end{bmatrix} \tag{4}$$

In the above equations, λ is a parameter between 0 and 1 that determines the relative importance of the station's borrowing behavior and the bicycle flow behavior between stations. In the final station importance degree matrix, p_{ii} represents the station importance degree obtained by the user's bicycle usage behavior at station s_i, and p_{ii} represents the circulation importance degree feedback from station s_j's user bicycle usage importance degree to site s_i due to the bicycle flow between station s_i and station s_j. Similar to graph nodes, the importance degree of each node in the graph is not only related to itself but also affected by the nodes with which it is connected.

By extracting the graph information from the bicycle transfer graph through the above calculation process, the final station importance degree $V = [c_1, c_2, \ldots, c_n]^T$ is obtained from the node importance degree matrix, in which $c_i = \sum_{1 \le j \le n} p_{ij}$, indicating the importance degree of station i in the bicycle transfer graph.

2.1.2. Potential Energy between Stations

The correlation between bicycle stations is determined by the distance between stations and the overall importance of each station in the bicycle network. The mutual influence between stations can be compared to the attraction between different planets, where stations with higher importance have a larger range and capability of influence. Comparing the complex bicycle network to a large galaxy, the clustering process is equivalent to distinguishing small galaxies with strong correlations, such as the solar system in which the Earth is located. Referring to the universal gravitational formula between planets, the potential energy E_{ij} between station s_i and station s_j is calculated as follows:

$$E_{ij} = c_i * c_j * e^{-\left(\frac{\|d_i - d_j\|}{\varepsilon}\right)^2} \tag{5}$$

c_i and c_j represent the importance of stations s_i and s_j, $\|d_i - d_j\|$ represents the distance between two stations, and ε represents the corresponding distance influence factor, which is a customizable parameter used to adjust the degree of influence caused by distance between stations.

2.1.3. Station Clustering Method

The main idea of the clustering method in this paper is based on the importance degree and correlation between the stations in the bicycle station network. The goal of the clustering method is to select the most important and closely related stations from the bicycle transfer graph and then classify them into clusters based on their distance from the cluster center. In addition, each cluster only contains stations that have a maximum potential energy with the current cluster center.

The main process of the clustering method is as follows:

1. Extract station information from the bicycle order data and construct the bicycle transfer graph;
2. Extract graph information by calculating the importance degree and nearest-neighbor distance with high-importance degrees for all stations by using the bicycle transfer graph;
3. Construct a decision diagram based on station importance degrees and nearest neighbor distance with high-importance degrees. Based on this diagram, nodes with

higher importance degrees and high-importance degree nearest-neighbor distances are selected as cluster centers; and

4. Classify the remaining nodes according to their potential energy with the cluster center based on the principle of maximizing potential energy.

Figure 2 illustrates the clustering process of the proposed method.

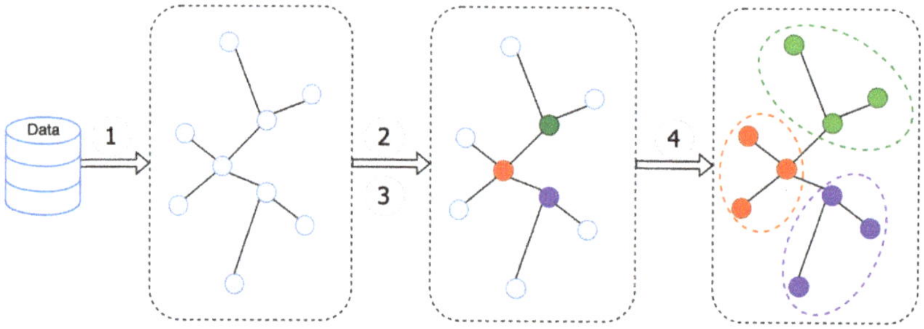

Figure 2. Process of the GIPE clustering method.

The core steps of the GIPE clustering method include calculating the importance of stations in the bicycle transfer graph and allocating the remaining stations based on their potential energy. The specific allocation process of the remaining stations after selecting the cluster centers is shown in Figure 3.

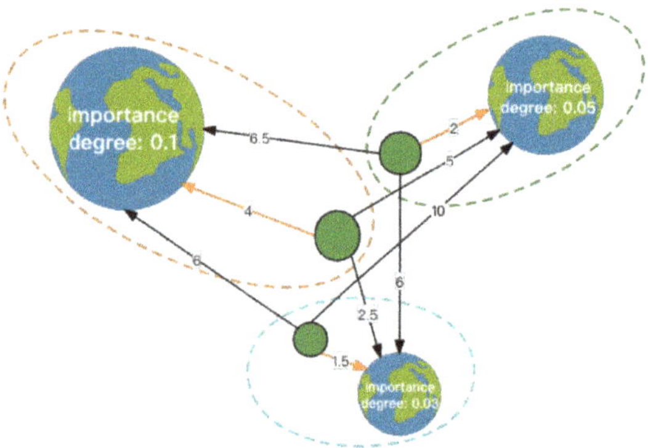

Figure 3. Station allocation of the GIPE clustering method.

In the station allocation diagram, there are three cluster centers with importance degrees of 0.1, 0.05, and 0.03, respectively. These three green circles represent the stations to be allocated. The values on the arrows represent the potential energy between the current station to be allocated and the cluster center, and the orange line indicates the final allocation result of the station. Through the station allocation process, it can be seen that the degree of association between stations not only depends on their importance but also relates to the distance between different stations. The cluster centers with higher importance and closer distance to the current station are more attractive, and the mutual circulation of bicycles between them is also more frequent.

2.2. Demand Prediction Model

This paper proposes a deep learning model for bicycle demand prediction. The input features include historical bicycle demand data in various regions, time-related feature data, and corresponding weather feature data at the same time. Firstly, the GCN is employed to capture spatial correlations, and then a multi-layer GRU is designed to learn the associations between time series. Additionally, an attention mechanism is adopted to extract historical time step data information and inter-regional features with different weights, enabling the final model to have a good ability to predict demand. Finally, the dense layer outputs the bicycle demand in each time period for the 26 clustered regions. The model includes the input layer, the GCN layer, the GRU layer, the attention layer, and the output layer, as shown in Figure 4 [17].

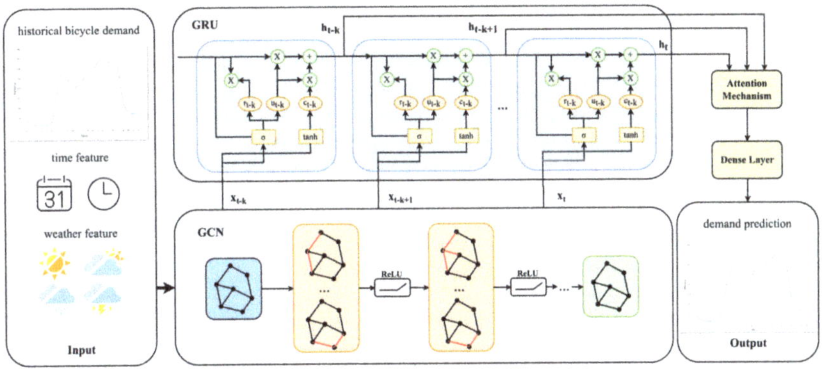

Figure 4. The structure of the GCN–CRU–AM model.

1. Input Layer:
This layer is used to receive bicycle demand, time features, and weather features. The data form can be expressed as $X = [x_1, x_2, \ldots, x_{t-1}, x_t]^T$, in which $X \in R^{t \times d}$, t represents the time length of the input sequence, d represents the feature dimension of the input data, and x_i represents the feature vector at time i. In this paper, the value of d is 32, including bicycle demand in 26 areas, three-dimensional time features and three-dimensional weather features.
2. GCN Layer [18]:
This layer used to capture the spatial correlation between regions. First, we construct a region adjacency matrix A to represent the connection relationship between regions. Assuming that there are n bicycle station regions, the amount of bicycle transfers from region i to region j in a certain period is f_{ij}, and the total number of bicycles arriving in region j during this period is t_j, then the adjacency matrix A between regions can be expressed as follows:

$$A = \begin{bmatrix} A_{11} & \cdots & A_{1n} \\ \vdots & \ddots & \vdots \\ A_{n1} & \cdots & A_{nn} \end{bmatrix} \quad (6)$$

The adjacency matrix is a 26×26 matrix, where A_{ij} represents the connection strength between region i to region j, which can be expressed as $A_{ij} = f_{ij}/t_j$. The original adjacency matrix is normalized to obtain the matrix $\widetilde{A}$:

$$\widetilde{A} = \begin{bmatrix} a_{11}+1 & \cdots & a_{1n} \\ \vdots & \ddots & \vdots \\ a_{n1} & \cdots & a_{nn}+1 \end{bmatrix} \quad (7)$$

The basic operation of the GCN can be expressed as:

$$H^{(l+1)} = \sigma\left(\widetilde{A}H^{(l)}W^{(l)}\right) \quad (8)$$

Here, $\widetilde{A}$ is the normalized adjacency matrix, $H^{(l)}$ is the feature representation of the l-th layer, $W^{(l)}$ is the weight matrix of the l-th layer, and σ is the activation function (such as ReLU). We applied multiple GCN layers to extract spatial features. The GCN operation of each layer will update the node features in order to capture the higher-order spatial correlations [19].

3. GRU Layer [20]:
This layer is used to capture long -short-term dependencies in time series data. This module receives feature sequences from the GCN module and processes them in sequence over time, capturing temporal features in the input sequence, such as trends and periodicity. The GRU utilizes gate structures to control the generation and forgetting of information. Meanwhile, it also uses the state of the previous moment to calculate the state of the current moment, thereby achieving the modeling of sequence historical data and long-term memory [21]. We used a fully connected layer to fuse the spatial features extracted by the GCN layer with other input features (weather features and time features). Next, we employed multiple GRU units to model the fused features, with each GRU layer containing 128 hidden neurons and using sigmoid activation functions to learn the time series relationships between data. The hidden layer output $\{h_1, h_2, \ldots, h_t\}$ serves as the input for the subsequent attention mechanism layer. The gated structure of the GRU can effectively handle dependencies at different time scales, thereby capturing the temporal dynamics of bicycle demand. In Figure 4, X_{t-k} represents the output of the GCN layer when the input data at time $t-k$ is provided to it, and h_{t-k} denotes the hidden layer output of the GRU layer after memorizing and forgetting the current input X_{t-k} and the historical information. Ultimately, these are passed to the attention mechanism layer to assign weights from different inputs.

4. Attention Layer:
This layer is used to address the issues of information loss and the vanishing gradient encountered by the GRU layer when handling long sequences. This mechanism computes the feature weights for the hidden layer in the GRU, which can preserve important features and reduce the impact of interference information. In this paper, we adopt the additive attention mechanism and the specific calculation process is as follows:

$$e_{ij} = a(h_i, h_j) = LeakyReLU(W_a[h_i \parallel h_j] + b_a) \tag{9}$$

$$\alpha_{ij} = \frac{exp(e_{ij})}{\sum_{k=1}^{26} exp(e_{ik})} \tag{10}$$

$$Attention(h_i) = \sum_{j=1}^{26} \alpha_{ij} h_j \tag{11}$$

$a(h_i, h_j)$ is used to calculate the similarity score between h_i and h_j, where $\parallel$ represents vector splicing and $LeakyReLU$ is an activation function. Additionally α_{ij} is the normalized attention weight.

5. Output Layer
This fully connected layer is used to map the attention-weighted GRU output to the predicted bicycle demand, that is, the future bicycle demand in 26 regions. Assuming that the output is y_i, the calculation process of the output layer is:

$$y_i = \sigma(W_o Attention(h_i) + b_o) \tag{12}$$

W_o and b_o are the weight matrix and bias of the output layer, respectively.

3. Results and Discussion

3.1. Experimental Datasets

3.1.1. Shared Bicycle Data

This study utilizes a publicly available dataset from Citi Bike in New York City for research purposes [22]. The dataset consists of 6.14 million bicycle ride order records from July to August 2021, obtained from the official Citi Bike website. Table 2 presents a partial overview of the raw data fields collected for Citi Bike orders in this study.

Table 2. Citi Bike order data.

Rideable_Type	Started_At	Ended_At	Start_Lat	Start_Lng	User_Type
electric_bike	02/07/2021 16:57	02/07/2021 17:09	40.790179	−73.97288	casual
electric_bike	10/07/2021 07:40	10/07/2021 07:58	40.749156	−73.9916	casual
electric_bike	09/07/2021 13:25	09/07/2021 13:30	40.842842	−73.94212	member
classic_bike	09/07/2021 12:45	09/07/2021 12:59	40.717571	−74.00554	member
classic_bike	29/07/2021 19:28	29/07/2021 19:52	40.710762	−73.99400	casual

3.1.2. Weather Data

This study collected hourly weather report data for New York City from July to August 2021 to complement the analyzed Citi Bike dataset [23,24]. The weather report data from Weather Underground includes hourly reports for various weather parameters in New York City during this period. The report format consists of timestamps, wet bulb temperatures, dry bulb temperatures, humidity, pressure, and wind speeds. It should be noted that the original data may contain missing values for wind speed and humidity. To ensure the continuity of the meteorological data, this study employs a method for filling in the missing values using the previous hour's weather report data.

3.2. Result of Clustering

From the original bicycle order data, this study extracted 1451 station records. To ensure the reasonability of the research, a rectangular division approach was adopted. Stations within the longitude range of 40.68° N to 40.77° N and the latitude range of −74.02° W to −73.95° W were selected. A total of 487 stations were filtered for subsequent experimental research. For extracting station graph information and calculating inter-station potential energy, data from five consecutive working days were selected. Figure 5 illustrates the selected research stations and the clustering results of the stations using the graph information and potential energy clustering method.

The clustering results from Figure 5 reveal that the centers of each clustered region are reasonably spaced, with no closely located cluster centers. Furthermore, the number and distribution of stations within each cluster region are relatively even. These observations indicate that the clustering algorithm effectively selected appropriate cluster centers and achieved a satisfactory division of stations. The clustering results align well with the actual distribution of the stations.

From the comparison of the clustering results in Figure 6, it is evident that the K-means algorithm [25] can relatively evenly aggregate stations in different regions. However, it tends to overlook the influence of actual geographical factors and local residents' travel habits. The clustering results do not align with the actual distribution of user demand, which may result in the aggregation of unrelated stations. As a result, the demand for station clusters fluctuates significantly, impacting the model's ability to predict the demand for different cluster groups.

DBSCAN [26], on the other hand, performs station clustering by setting the minimum number of points in each cluster and the corresponding search radius. However, the stations in this study were extracted from the bicycle order data, and the actual stations are fixed stations with their locations determined by the bike-sharing operator. The station distribution is relatively uniform, and density clustering does not effectively capture the actual correlations between stations. Additionally, determining the number of clusters is challenging, and the sizes of the clusters vary significantly, deviating from the actual rules for dividing stations into regions.

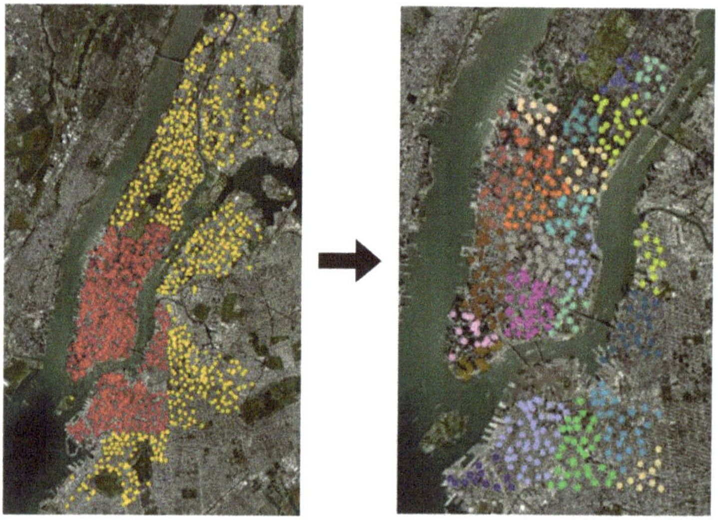

(**a**) (**b**)

Figure 5. Regional site screening and clustering results: (**a**) station filter, and (**b**) clustering results.

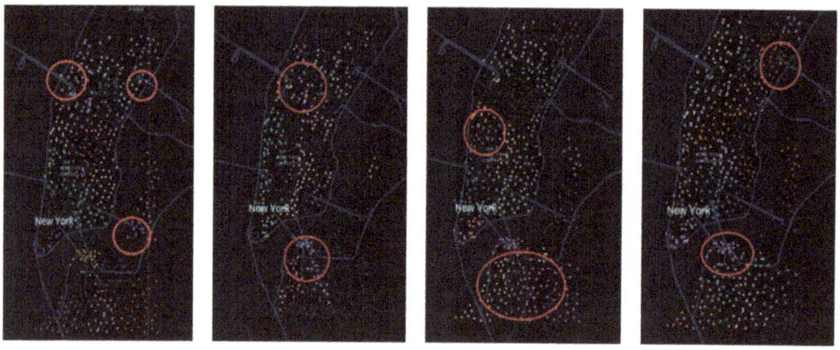

(**a**) (**b**) (**c**) (**d**)

Figure 6. Comparison of the results of the four clustering methods: (**a**) K-means, (**b**) DBSCAN, (**c**) DPC, and (**d**) GIPE.

DPC clustering [27], as a density peak-based algorithm, has similar reference metrics to DBSCAN but has different rules for assigning the remaining points. DPC clustering is better able to specify the number of cluster regions, select high-density stations as cluster centers, and divide the remaining stations based on density and distance correlations. However, similar to DBSCAN, DPC clustering also exhibits significant differences in cluster sizes. Some clusters become excessively large, which hinders accurate bicycle predictions between regions.

The GIPE clustering method proposed in this study, which combines graph information and potential energy, not only evaluates the importance degree of each station in the bicycle transfer graph from the perspective of actual demand but also selects distant stations with high-importance degrees as cluster centers. Additionally, it utilizes potential theory to calculate the attractiveness of each cluster center to the remaining stations, representing the degree of correlation between stations. This approach enables the final clustering of stations. The clustering results align well with reality, and the distribution of the stations within each cluster is relatively even, meeting the basic requirements of regional prediction and bicycle scheduling research.

3.3. Result of Demand Prediction

3.3.1. Baseline Method

The problem of demand prediction in the different regions and time periods of shared bicycles, can essentially be formulated as a time series forecasting task. Various deep models are commonly used to address such problems. In this study, the GCN–GRU–AM model is employed, and its performance is evaluated by comparing it with several benchmark methods from existing research or state-of-the-art approaches.

- CNN [28]: The convolutional neural network (CNN) model is a typical model for extracting spatial information from data. It can also be applied to bicycle demand prediction tasks by extracting useful information from the raw bicycle demand data and weather data, enabling effective prediction of future bicycle demand.
- LSTM [29]: As a variant of the recurrent neural network (RNN), the long short-term memory (LSTM) is one of the most commonly used deep models for handling time series forecasting problems and has been widely applied in various research studies.
- GRU [21]: GRU is similar to LSTM but has a simpler internal structure. It discards the complex cell state and uses only the memory gate and the forget gate to achieve a similar functionality to LSTM. GRU has fewer parameters and is simpler to train.
- XGBoost [30]: XGBoost is a model that employs decision trees for prediction or classification tasks. Compared to traditional random forest models, XGBoost demonstrates superior performance, wider applicability, and a significantly improved training speed.
- GCN [31]: The GCN combines graph theory with CNN by constructing a reasonable graph relationship (adjacency matrix) for node-type data. It effectively captures spatial information between nodes and achieves significant performance improvement by integrating with the CNN module.
- GRU-AM [32]: GRU–AM is a hybrid model, in which the GRU structure is first used to preserve historical information, and then the temporal attention mechanism (AM) is used to give different weights to the features.
- CNN-GRU [33]: The CNN–GRU model is a fusion deep-learning approach that combines a convolution neural network (CNN) and gated recurrent units (GRUs).
- CNN–GRU–AM [34]: The CNN–GRU–AM model is a combination of three different techniques. First, CNN is used to extract local features from the data. Second, GRU is employed to capture the time-series relationships of the output data of CNN. Finally, the AM is introduced to mine the potential relationships of the series features.
- T-GCN [19]: The temporal graph convolutional network (T–GCN) model is combined with the GCN and GRU to capture the spatial and temporal dependences simultaneously.

3.3.2. Evaluation Indicators

- Mean Absolute Error (MAE):

$$MAE = \frac{\sum_{i=1}^{n}|y_i - \hat{y}_i|}{n} \tag{13}$$

- Root Mean Square Error (RMSE):

$$RMSE = \sqrt{\frac{1}{n}\sum_{i=1}^{n}(y_i - \hat{y}_i)^2} \tag{14}$$

- Root Mean Squared Logarithmic Error (RMSLE) is a metric commonly used to evaluate the performances of different models on the same research problem across different datasets. It measures the relative error and is defined as follows:

$$RMSE = \sqrt{\frac{1}{n}\sum_{i=1}^{n}(\log(\hat{y}_i + 1) - \log(\hat{y}_i + 1))^2} \tag{15}$$

In this equation, y_i represents the actual value, and $\hat{y}_i$ represents the model predicted value.

MAE and RMSE are used to evaluate the deviation between model prediction results and actual demand, that is, the absolute error, while RMSLE is used to evaluate the deviation between model prediction results and actual demand, reflecting the model's ability to predict the overall change trend.

3.3.3. Experimental Setup

When considering the demand prediction problem, it is necessary to identify the data characteristics of the main objective and subjective factors related to bicycle demand and assess the importance of different features. In this study, demand-related features, time features, peak-hour features, and weather features, which are closely related to bicycle demand prediction, were selected. XGBoost was used to evaluate the different features.

According to the feature analysis results in Figure 7, it is evident that the original demand sequence is crucial for model training. Hourly information, morning and evening peak indicators (represented by 1 and 2, respectively), and the weekday attribute (ranging from 1 to 7) also exhibit significant effects. On the other hand, weather features have a relatively smaller impact as compared to other features. However, they still contribute to improving the model's demand prediction performance. In this study, selected weather features include temperature, humidity, and wind speed.

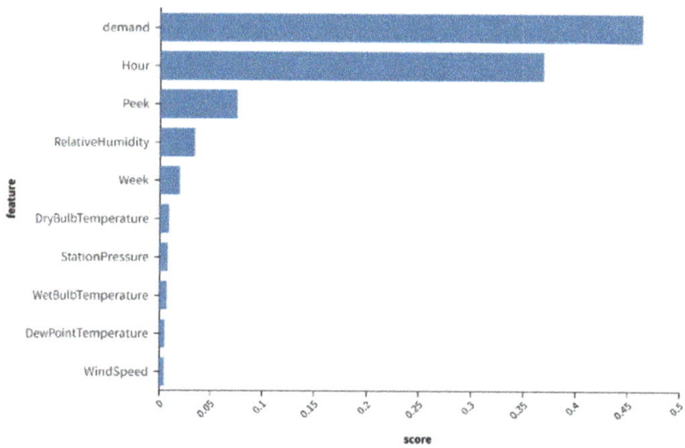

Figure 7. Feature importance degree analysis.

The impact of the time step on the prediction performance of the basic GRU model was investigated. The most appropriate time step was selected and used as the "time_step" parameter for all of the deep models. The input features for the GRU model consist of the combination of bicycle demand, time features, and weather features. Experimental results for the different regions' bicycle demand predictions using the GRU model under different time steps are presented in Table 3.

Table 3. Performance of the GRU model at different time steps.

Time_Step	RMSE	RMSLE	MAE
1	19.162	0.398	12.359
2	18.001	0.379	11.992
3	17.659	0.376	11.834
4	17.516	0.372	11.708
5	18.257	0.378	12.396
6	18.758	0.381	12.325
8	19.018	0.388	11.957
16	19.831	0.407	12.974
32	19.976	0.412	13.335

From the experiment results in Table 3, it can be observed that the demand prediction performance of the GRU model shows an overall trend of first increasing and then weakening with the time steps. Normally, considering that the station status in the previous time period affects the station status in the current time period, the accuracy of the prediction is higher with the larger time step. However, when the time step reaches a certain value, due to the addition of noise features that are irrelevant to time series prediction, the prediction performance does not increase but rather decreases, and the training time is increased. Therefore, the time step is selected to be four through the experiments. At this time, the RMSE, MAE, and RMSLE of the GRU model are all minimum values.

3.3.4. Performance Analysis

1. Performance Analysis of the GCN–CRU–AM model

Based on the station-clustering results, we compared the performance of different deep learning models in predicting the actual bicycle demand under the same input data features. The input features include historical demand, time, and weather characteristics. We used the data of 34 consecutive working days as the training and validation set, and the subsequent nine working days as the test set. Each model is trained for 100 epochs, and the demand prediction results are calculated by subtracting the actual demand. The multiple error values are obtained and statistically analyzed, as shown in Table 4.

Table 4. Comparison of the demand prediction performances of different deep learning models.

Model	Check-Out Demand			Check-In Demand		
	RMSE	RMSLE	MAE	RMSE	RMSLE	MAE
LSTM	18.320	0.377	12.003	18.706	0.386	11.978
GRU	17.516	0.372	11.708	17.396	0.378	11.657
XGBoost	16.879	0.369	11.441	16.951	0.368	11.472
GRU-AM	16.582	0.361	11.561	16.566	0.368	11.383
CNN-GRU	17.182	0.363	11.431	17.378	0.367	11.816
CNN-GRU-AM	16.238	0.355	11.226	16.476	0.358	11.277
GCN	17.390	0.375	12.281	17.479	0.376	12.032
T-GCN	15.935	0.347	10.687	16.052	0.346	10.804
GCN-GRU-AM	15.291	0.335	10.325	14.905	0.331	10.133

From the experimental data presented in Table 4, it can be observed that among the various deep learning models, the GCN–GRU–AM model adopted in this study exhibits a good demand prediction performance. The RMSLE of predicting check-out demand in various regions reaches 0.335, and the RMSE is 15.291. For check-in demand, the RMSLE and RMSE are 0.331 and 14.905, respectively. These figures are significantly lower than those of other models, indicating that the GCN–GRU–AM model has a strong capability for predicting the future demands for shared bicycles in each region.

Among the remaining models, the basic LSTM performs worst, and the GRU shows a certain degree of performance improvement over LSTM. Compared to the LSTM and

GRU models, XGBoost has smaller demand prediction error values, indicating that its basic performance is superior to the LSTM and GRU in the context of this study. After incorporating the Attention Mechanism into the GRU model, its RMSE, MAE, and RMSLE errors decrease, suggesting that the combination of the attention mechanism and the GRU module enhances the model's predicting performance.

The performance of the original GCN model is better than that of LSTM and GRU models but is somewhat inferior to XGBoost. Although the GCN extracts information from different regional demand and other features, it lacks a time-series learning module, which may cause the temporal information to be overlooked and hinder the learning of associativity between time series. By incorporating the GRU module to effectively extract input information, the model performance improves significantly, with the RMSLE, RMSE, and MAE slightly better than those of the CNN–GRU–AM model, which exhibits the best performance among the remaining models.

To intuitively demonstrate the effectiveness of the GRU module and the attention mechanism module in the GCN model, the check-out demand prediction results of the 2nd clustering region from the GCN, GCN–GRU, and GCN–GRU–AM models are compared with the actual check-out demand. This comparison aims to investigate the influence of the different modules on the final model performance.

By comparing the demand prediction results of the GCN, GCN–GRU, and GCN–GRU–AM models with the actual demand prediction results in Figure 8, it can be observed that the prediction results of the GCN model have the lowest fitting degree with the actual demand. The demand prediction results during the morning and evening rush hours are relatively accurate, while the prediction deviation of bicycle demand during lunchtime is relatively large. With the addition of the GRU model, the prediction performance of bicycle demand during the day improves. On this basis, the GCN–GRU–AM model, which incorporates the attention mechanism, enhances the prediction accuracy during the morning and evening rush hours and lunchtime, thereby improving the overall performance of the model.

In order to present the demand prediction performance of different models more intuitively, Figure 9 shows the check-in demand prediction results of the different models compared with the actual demand data in Region 22 for four consecutive working days, from 22 to 25 August 2021. We compared the GCN–GRU–AM model with the XGBoost model, which preforms better in the basic models, and the CNN–GRU–AM model, which has a better performance among the hybrid models.

It can be seen from Figure 9 that each model has a certain deviation from the original demand when making actual predictions of working-day demand. Among them, the model with a larger error index has a larger performance deviation in actual prediction. The GCN–GRU–AM model used in this article hac the best performance and has a high degree of fit with the original demand curve.

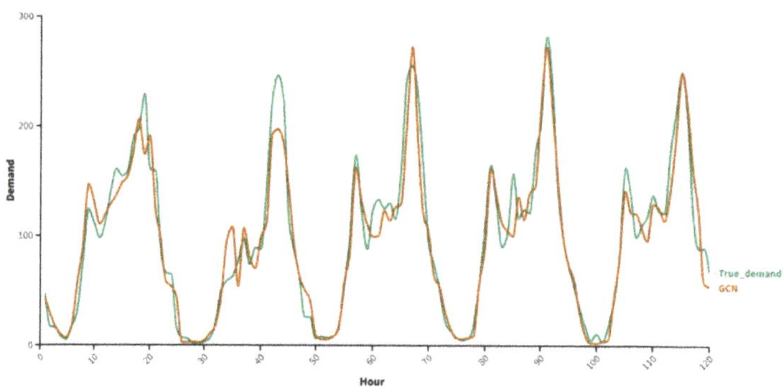

(a)

Figure 8. *Cont.*

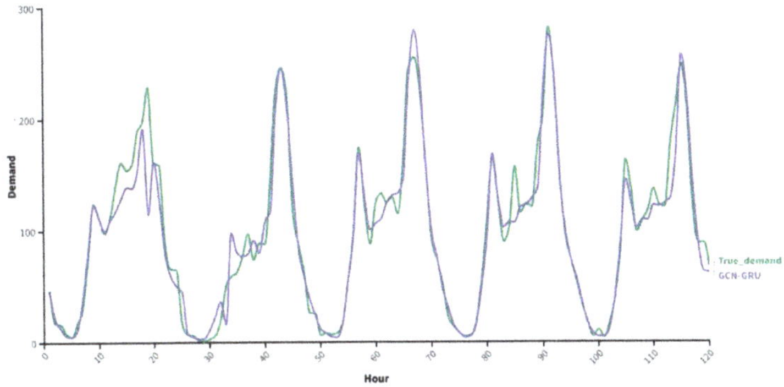

(**b**)

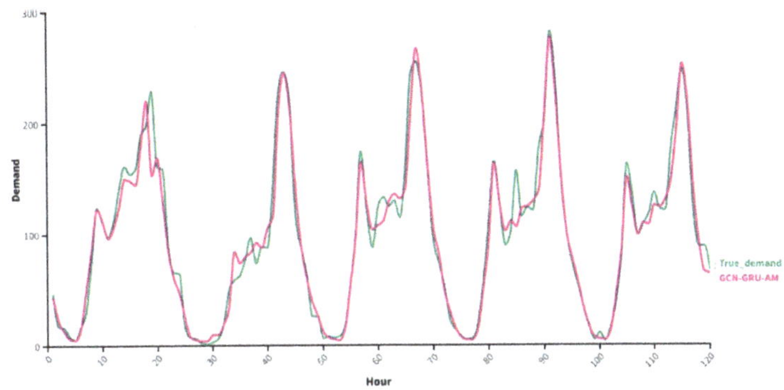

(**c**)

Figure 8. Comparison of the prediction result with the actual demand in Region 2. (**a**) Comparison of the GCN prediction results with the actual demand in Region 2, (**b**) Comparison of the GCN–GRU prediction result with actual demand in Region 2, and (**c**) Comparison of the GCNGRU–AM prediction result with actual demand in Region 2.

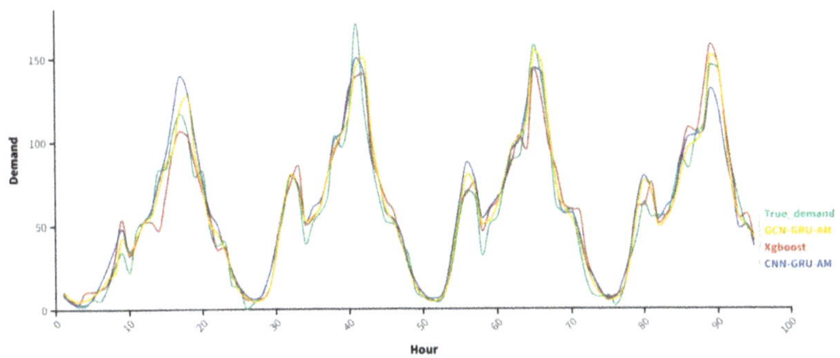

Figure 9. Prediction results of the different models over multiple working days.

2. The Impact of Input Features on Model Performance

For deep learning models, their performance not only depends on their structure but also on the quality of the input data and the feature dimension, which greatly affect the final performance of the model. Using the GCN–GRU–AM model, we conducted experiments by combining the different input data features to test the impact of the various features on the model's demand prediction performance. The specific experimental data is presented in Table 5.

Table 5. Analysis of model demand prediction performances with different feature combinations.

Feature Combination	Check-Out Demand			Check-In Demand		
	RMSE	RMSLE	MAE	RMSE	RMSLE	MAE
Demand	16.219	0.367	10.961	16.213	0.361	10.715
Demand + Time	15.604	0.343	10.557	15.784	0.341	10.405
Demand + Weather	16.102	0.362	10.844	16.049	0.358	10.672
Demand + Time + Weather	15.291	0.335	10.325	14.905	0.331	10.133

In the comparison of model performance under different features, the GCN–GRU–AM model trained with the input data of the demand in different regions and time periods performs worst. By adding time-based and weather features for model training, the demand prediction performance improves. Among them, the model trained with time-based features performed better than the model trained with weather features, indicating that time-based feature data contributes more to the improvement of the model performance than the weather features. This is consistent with the results of the analysis using the XGBoost model to assess the different features in Section 3.3.3. By combining time-based and weather features, the demand prediction error rate of the model further decreases. The input feature data used in the final demand forecasting model of this paper includes the combination of demand data, time-based feature data, and weather feature data.

3. Effectiveness Analysis of Clustering Method

To validate the effectiveness of the proposed GIPE clustering method, we perform clustering on the initial 577 stations using other clustering methods. Combining the clustering results with the calculated demand for each clustering region and time period, we obtained the demand data under different clustering methods. Then, we trained the GCN–CRU–AM model using the demand data estimated by the different clustering methods and predicted the future demand in each region. This enabled us to assess the model's performance under various clustering methods. In addition, K-means and DPC clustering methods generate 26 clusters, the same as the GIPE clustering method. Because the DBSCAN clustering algorithm has an uncertain number of clusters, it is not included in the comparison among the different clustering methods.

After re-constructing the adjacent matrix and re-statistically calculating the historical demand for each region, the GCN–GRU–AM model is trained for the future demand prediction of each region based on the clustering results from different clustering methods. Table 6 summarizes the experimental performance data of the GCN–GRU–AM model trained using the clustering results of different clustering methods.

Table 6. Performance analysis of demand forecasting models with different clustering methods.

Clustering Method	Check-Out Demand			Check-In Demand		
	RMSE	RMSLE	MAE	RMSE	RMSLE	MAE
K-means	16.637	0.356	10.924	16.432	0.354	10.831
DPC	17.427	0.371	11.518	17.641	0.375	11.665
GIPE	15.291	0.335	10.325	14.905	0.331	10.133

Compared with the K-means clustering method that only considers node distance and the DPC clustering method that only considers node density and distance, the clustering method in this paper considers the actual bicycle usage and distance factors. In this case, the bicycle demand forecast error value is smaller thanks to the use of the same GCN-GRU-AM model for training.

4. Conclusions

Shared bicycle systems are an important part of urban public transportation, and demand prediction can improve resource allocation, optimize bicycles management, and enhance user experience. Furthermore, our research on this subject can support policymakers in making informed decisions and formulating effective strategies, such as optimizing the distribution of shared bicycles across different regions, planning for infrastructure development, and designing targeted promotional campaigns to encourage bicycle usage.

In this paper, we propose a novel shared-bicycle demand prediction model based on station clustering. Taking into consideration the user's riding habits and the correlation between the different stations in the actual shared-bicycle system, we constructed a bicycle transfer graph based on bicycle trip data and cluster stations by calculating each station's importance degree and the inter-station potential energy. In the demand prediction problem, we consider time features and weather features that affect the demand for shared bicycles and incorporate them as key features into the GCN-GRU-AM model constructed in this paper for analyzing the shared-bicycle demand within clusters during different time periods. The experimental results demonstrate that the proposed demand prediction model has a high degree of alignment with the actual bicycle demand data and can effectively predict the bicycle demand in different regions and time periods, thereby outperforming other models in terms of performance.

In future works, we will utilize annual data for research and incorporate seasonal features into the deep-model training to enhance the model's versatility. Moreover, because the current method to solve the imbalance of bicycle demand within stations is manual dispatch, future research will seek optimal inter-station paths in order to reduce the cost of manual dispatch.

Author Contributions: Conceptualization, J.-Y.X. and Y.Q.; methodology, Y.Q. and C.-C.W.; software, Y.Q. and S.Z.; validation, J.-Y.X. and Y.Q.; formal analysis, C.-C.W. and J.-Y.X.; investigation, Y.Q.; resources, J.-Y.X.; data curation, Y.Q. and J.-Y.X.; writing—original draft preparation, S.Z. and Y.Q.; writing—review and editing, J.-Y.X., C.-C.W. and Y.Q.; visualization, S.Z.; supervision, J.-Y.X.; project administration, J.-Y.X.; funding acquisition, J.-Y.X. All authors have read and agreed to the published version of the manuscript.

Funding: This work was supported in part by the National Natural Science Foundation of China grant number 72271048, and by the National Science and Technology Council of Taiwan, NSTC 112-2221-E-035-060-MY2.

Data Availability Statement: The corresponding author will provide the relative datasets upon request.

Conflicts of Interest: The authors declare no conflict of interest.

References

1. Zheng, L.; Li, Y. The Development, Characteristics and Impact of Bike Sharing Systems. *Int. Rev. Spat. Plan. Sustain. Dev.* **2020**, *8*, 37–52. [CrossRef] [PubMed]
2. Li, Y.; Zheng, Y. Citywide Bike Usage Prediction in a Bike-Sharing System. *IEEE Trans. Knowl. Data Eng.* **2020**, *32*, 1079–1091. [CrossRef]
3. Huang, F.; Qiao, S.; Peng, J.; Guo, B. A Bimodal Gaussian Inhomogeneous Poisson Algorithm for Bike Number Prediction in a Bike-Sharing System. *IEEE Trans. Intell. Transp. Syst.* **2019**, *20*, 2848–2857. [CrossRef]
4. Chen, P.-C.; Hsieh, H.-Y.; Sigalingging, X.K.; Chen, Y.-R.; Leu, J.-S. Prediction of Station Level Demand in a Bike Sharing System Using Recurrent Neural Networks. In Proceedings of the 2017 IEEE 85th Vehicular Technology Conference (VTC Spring), Sydney, NSW, Australia, 4–7 June 2017; pp. 1–4. [CrossRef]
5. Zi, W.; Xiong, W.; Chen, H.; Chen, L. TAGCN: Station-Level Demand Prediction for Bike-Sharing System via a Temporal Attention Graph Convolution Network. *Inf. Sci.* **2021**, *561*, 274–285. [CrossRef]
6. Feng, S.; Chen, H.; Du, C.; Li, J.; Jing, N. A Hierarchical Demand Prediction Method with Station Clustering for Bike Sharing System. In Proceedings of the 2018 IEEE Third International Conference on Data Science in Cyberspace (DSC), Guangzhou, China, 18–21 June 2018; pp. 829–836. [CrossRef]
7. Jia, W.; Tan, Y.; Liu, L.; Li, J.; Zhang, H.; Zhao, K. Hierarchical Prediction Based on Two-Level Gaussian Mixture Model Clustering for Bike-Sharing System. *Knowl.-Based Syst.* **2019**, *178*, 84–97. [CrossRef]

8. Hua, M.; Chen, J.; Chen, X.; Gan, Z.; Wang, P.; Zhao, D. Forecasting Usage and Bike Distribution of Dockless Bike-Sharing Using Journey Data. *IET Intell. Transp. Syst.* **2020**, *14*, 1647–1656. [CrossRef]
9. Chen, L.; Zhang, D.; Wang, L.; Yang, D.; Ma, X.; Li, S.; Wu, Z.; Pan, G.; Nguyen, T.-M.-T.; Jakubowicz, J. Dynamic Cluster-Based over-Demand Prediction in Bike Sharing Systems. In Proceedings of the 2016 ACM International Joint Conference on Pervasive and Ubiquitous Computing, Heidelberg, Germany, 12–16 September 2016; pp. 841–852. [CrossRef]
10. Li, Y.; Zheng, Y.; Zhang, H.; Chen, L. Traffic Prediction in a Bike-Sharing System. In Proceedings of the 23rd SIGSPATIAL International Conference on Advances in Geographic Information Systems, Seattle, WA, USA, 3–6 November 2015. [CrossRef]
11. Frey, B.J.; Dueck, D. Clustering by Passing Messages Between Data Points. *Science* **2007**, *315*, 972–976. [CrossRef]
12. Xu, H.; Duan, F.; Pu, P. Dynamic Bicycle Scheduling Problem Based on Short-Term Demand Prediction. *Appl. Intell.* **2019**, *49*, 1968–1981. [CrossRef]
13. Sathishkumar, V.E.; Park, J.; Cho, Y. Using Data Mining Techniques for Bike Sharing Demand Prediction in Metropolitan City. *Comput. Commun.* **2020**, *153*, 353–366. [CrossRef]
14. Almannaa, M.H.; Elhenawy, M.; Rakha, H.A. Dynamic Linear Models to Predict Bike Availability in a Bike Sharing System. *Int. J. Sustain. Transp.* **2020**, *14*, 232–242. [CrossRef]
15. Li, X.; Xu, Y.; Chen, Q.; Wang, L.; Zhang, X.; Shi, W. Short-Term Forecast of Bicycle Usage in Bike Sharing Systems: A Spatial-Temporal Memory Network. *IEEE Trans. Intell. Transp. Syst.* **2022**, *23*, 10923–10934. [CrossRef]
16. Kim, K. Investigation on the Effects of Weather and Calendar Events on Bike-Sharing According to the Trip Patterns of Bike Rentals of Stations. *J. Transp. Geogr.* **2018**, *66*, 309–320. [CrossRef]
17. Zhu, J.; Han, X.; Deng, H.; Tao, C.; Zhao, L.; Tao, L.; Li, H. KST-GCN: A Knowledge-Driven Spatial-Temporal Graph Convolutional Network for Traffic Forecasting. *IEEE Trans. Intell. Transp. Syst.* **2020**, *23*, 15055–15065. [CrossRef]
18. Kipf, T.; Welling, M. Semi-Supervised Classification with Graph Convolutional Networks. *arXiv* **2016**. [CrossRef]
19. Zhao, L.; Song, Y.; Zhang, C.; Liu, Y.; Wang, P.; Lin, T.; Deng, M.; Li, H. T-GCN: A Temporal Graph Convolutional Network for Traffic Prediction. *IEEE Trans. Intell. Transp. Syst.* **2020**, *21*, 3848–3858. [CrossRef]
20. Chung, J.; Gulcehre, C.; Cho, K.; Bengio, Y. Empirical Evaluation of Gated Recurrent Neural Networks on Sequence Modeling. *arXiv* **2014**. [CrossRef]
21. Fu, R.; Zhang, Z.; Li, L. Using LSTM and GRU Neural Network Methods for Traffic Flow Prediction. In Proceedings of the 2016 31st Youth Academic Annual Conference of Chinese Association of Automation (YAC), Wuhan, China, 11–13 November 2016; pp. 324–328. [CrossRef]
22. Data. Available online: https://www.citibikenyc.com/system-data (accessed on 18 September 2023).
23. Data. Available online: https://www.wunderground.com/history/monthly/us/ny/new-york-city/KLGA/date/2021-7 (accessed on 18 September 2023).
24. Data. Available online: https://www.wunderground.com/history/monthly/us/ny/new-york-city/KLGA/date/2021-8 (accessed on 18 September 2023).
25. Ahmed, M.; Seraj, R.; Islam, S.M.S. The K-Means Algorithm: A Comprehensive Survey and Performance Evaluation. *Electronics* **2020**, *9*, 1295. [CrossRef]
26. Ester, M.; Kriegel, H.-P.; Sander, J.; Xu, X. A Density-Based Algorithm for Discovering Clusters in Large Spatial Databases with Noise. In Proceedings of the Second International Conference on Knowledge Discovery and Data Mining (KDD-96), Portland, OR, USA, 2–4 August 1996; pp. 226–231.
27. Rodriguez, A.; Laio, A. Clustering by Fast Search and Find of Density Peaks. *Science* **2014**, *334*, 1492–1496. [CrossRef]
28. Yang, H.; Xie, K.; Ozbay, K.; Ma, Y.; Wang, Z. Use of Deep Learning to Predict Daily Usage of Bike Sharing Systems. *Transp. Res. Rec.* **2018**, *2672*, 92–102. [CrossRef]
29. Yu, Y.; Si, X.; Hu, C.; Zhang, J. A Review of Recurrent Neural Networks: LSTM Cells and Network Architectures. *Neural Comput.* **2019**, *31*, 1235–1270. [CrossRef]
30. Zheng, H.; Yuan, J.; Chen, L. Short-Term Load Forecasting Using EMD-LSTM Neural Networks with a Xgboost Algorithm for Feature Importance Evaluation. *Energies* **2017**, *10*, 1168. [CrossRef]
31. Kim, T.S.; Lee, W.K.; Sohn, S.Y. Graph Convolutional Network Approach Applied to Predict Hourly Bike-Sharing Demands Considering Spatial, Temporal, and Global Effects. *PLoS ONE* **2019**, *14*, e0220782. [CrossRef] [PubMed]
32. Zhang, L.; Zhang, J.; Niu, J.; Wu, Q.M.J.; Li, G. Track Prediction for HF Radar Vessels Submerged in Strong Clutter Based on MSCNN Fusion with GRU-AM and AR Model. *Remote Sens.* **2021**, *13*, 2164. [CrossRef]
33. Wu, Y.-W.; Hsu, T.-P. Mid-term prediction of at-fault crash driver frequency using fusion deep learning with city-level traffic violation data[J/OL]. *Accid. Anal. Prev.* **2021**, *150*, 105910. [CrossRef]
34. Peng, Y.; Liang, T.; Hao, X.; Chen, Y.; Li, S.; Yi, Y. CNN-GRU-AM for Shared Bicycles Demand Forecasting. *Comput. Intell. Neuroscience* **2021**, *2021*, 5486328. [CrossRef]

mathematics

MDPI

Article

Multiple Control Policy in Unreliable Two-Phase Bulk Queueing System with Active Bernoulli Feedback and Vacation

S. P. Niranjan [1], S. Devi Latha [1], Miroslav Mahdal [2] and Krishnasamy Karthik [3,*]

1 Department of Mathematics, Vel Tech Rangarajan Dr. Sagunthala R&D Institute of Science and Technology, Chennai 600062, India; niran.jayan092@gmail.com (S.P.N.); devilathamphil7485@gmail.com (S.D.L.)
2 Department of Control Systems and Instrumentation, Faculty of Mechanical Engineering, VSB-Technical University of Ostrava, 17, Listopadu 2172/15, 70800 Ostrava, Czech Republic; miroslav.mahdal@vsb.cz
3 Department of Mechanical Engineering, Vel Tech Rangarajan Dr. Sagunthala R&D Institute of Science and Technology, Chennai 600062, India
* Correspondence: karthikk@veltech.edu.in

Abstract: In this paper, a bulk arrival and two-phase bulk service with active Bernoulli feedback, vacation, and breakdown is considered. The server provides service in two phases as mandatory according to the general bulk service rule, with minimum bulk size $'a'$ and maximum bulk size $'b'$. In the first essential service (FES) completion epoch, if the server fails, with probability $'\delta'$, then the renewal of the service station is considered. On the other hand, if there is no server failure, with a probability $'1-\delta'$, then the server switches to a second essential service (SES) in succession. A customer who requires further service as feedback is given priority, and they join the head of the queue with probability β. On the contrary, a customer who does not require feedback leaves the system with a probability $'1-\beta'$. If the queue length is less than $'a'$ after SES, the server may leave for a single vacation with probability $'1-\beta'$. When the server finds an inadequate number of customers in the queue after vacation completion, the server becomes dormant. After vacation completion, the server requires some time to start service, which is attained by including setup time. The setup time is initiated only when the queue length is at least $'a'$. Even after setup time completion, the service process begins only with a queue length 'N' ($N > b$). The novelty of this paper is that it introduces an essential two-phase bulk service, immediate Bernoulli feedback for customers, and renewal service time of the first essential service for the bulk arrival and bulk service queueing model. We aim to develop a model that investigates the probability-generating function of the queue size at any time. Additionally, we analyzed various performance characteristics using numerical examples to demonstrate the model's effectiveness. An optimum cost analysis was also carried out to minimize the total average cost with appropriate practical applications in existing data transmission and data processing in LTE-A networks using the DRX mechanism.

Keywords: multiple control policy; renewal time; breakdown; Bernoulli feedback

MSC: 60K25; 68M20; 90B22

1. Introduction

Several academicians have tested queue systems with vacations and their numerous combos. Some of those studies are queue structures with vacation queue fashions via Tian and Zhang [1]. In many actual applications, there can be a couple of arrivals into the machine. These types of systems are labeled as bulk arrival queue structures. For bulk carrier queue structures with multiple vacations, Arumuganathan and Jeyakumar obtained consistent national conditions for numerous performance measures and value optimization [2]. Jeyakumar and Senthilnathan recently obtained the steady-state queue size distribution for the $M^X/G\ (a, b)/1$ queue system with multiple vacations [3]. In all queue models with vacations that have been studied in this context, the server remains on vacation, even whilst the queue period is excessive enough to initiate the primary provider. The modeling of actual-time systems can benefit from those vacation methods. Baba examined the M/PH/1 line with working vacations and interruptions [4]. The $M^X/G\ (a, b)/1$ queue model with vacation interruption was also researched by Haridass and Arumuganathan [5]. Through real-time applications, they deduced diverse queue device functions. Gao and Liu investigated the M/G/1 queue under a Bernoulli agenda with a single working vacation and vacation interruption [6]. Customers arrive at a queue served by a single server, and their arrivals follow a Poisson process. The duration of the service provided by the server conforms to an exponential distribution. However, the server takes periodic vacations which are scheduled based on a Bernoulli process. During the vacations, the server can be interrupted and resume service if a customer arrives, preventing the vacation from being completed, as studied by Tao et al. [7]. A countless-buffer bulk arrival queue with a bulk-size-dependent provider was tested by Pradhan and Gupta [8]. Madan et al. studied the consistent state of two $M^X/M\ (a, b)/1$ queue models with random breakdowns. In 2003, they took into account the reality that the repair time is deterministic for one version and exponential for every other. It has been cited in the literature on queue fashions with server breakdown that, excluding Madan et al., each creator who discusses server breakdown in the context of a bulk provider queue version deals with a server that can only serve one customer at a time. The server may also interrupt right away if trouble arises. Yet, in the majority of instances, it is impossible to disturb the server before it has completed providing its bulk services [9]. Jeyakumar and Senthilnathan also studied breakdown without carrier disruption in a bulk carrier queue model and a bulk arrival queue model. They developed a model using closedown time and constructed probability-generating functions for the completion epochs of services, vacations, and renewals [10]. Wu et al. investigated an M/G/1 queue system with an N-policy, a solitary vacation, an unreliable service station, and a replaceable repair facility [11,12].

Hanumantha Rao Sama et al. introduced an unstable server and delayed repair for a bulk arrival Markovian queueing system with state-dependent arrival and an N-policy [13]. Ankamma Rao et al. examined a two-phase queueing model, denoted M/M/1, incorporating server startup, time-out, and breakdowns [14]. Samuel U. Enogwe et al. investigated a non-Markovian queueing system that incorporates two distinct types of service mechanisms: balking and Bernoulli server vacation. The model is referred to as a bivariate Markov process and includes the elapsed service time and vacation time as supplementary variables [15]. GnanaSekar and Indhira Kandaiyan delved into the dynamics of a retrial queueing system with distinctive features, including delayed repair, a feedback mechanism, and the incorporation of a working vacation policy, as outlined in their article. If the essential and sufficient requirements are viable, the system can be stabilized [16]. Server breakdown based on service modes was introduced by Niranjan. In this paper, the author used supplementary variable techniques to derive important performance measures [17]. Blondia analyzed energy harvesting in the queueing model for a wireless sensor node [18]. C.K. Deena Merit and Haridass worked on a simulation analysis of the bulk queueing system with a working breakdown [19]. An application of a queueing system in 4G/5G networks was presented by V. Deepa et al. [20]. Niranjan et al. introduced two types of breakdown with two phases of service in bulk queueing systems [21]. In this study, we examine an $M^X/G\ (a, b)/1$ queuing system with an optional additional service and numerous vacations, and setup time is examined by Ayyappan and Deepa [22]. Niranjan et al. analyzed a non-Markovian bulk queueing system with renewal and startup/shutdown times [23]. Nithya and Haridass conducted a maximum entropy analysis of a queueing system that controls both arrival and bulk service, incorporating breakdowns and multiple vacation periods [24]. In their article, Enogwe and Obiora-Ilouno explored the impacts of three pivotal factors—reneging, server breakdown, and server vacation—on various stages of a queueing system with bulk arrivals and a single server [25]. Khan IE and Paramasivam R analyzed the quality control policy for the Markovian model with feedback, balking, and maintaining reneged clients using an iterative method for the nth customer in the system [26]. Ammar, Rajadurai P analyzed an innovative type of retry queueing system with functional breakdown services presented in this inquiry. Priority and regular clients are two different categories that are taken into consideration [27]. Gabi Hanukov and Shraga Shoval introduce a compelling vacation queue model that accounts for dynamic server service rates affected by factors like human fatigue and machinery wear. The analysis employed multidimensional methods to explore the impact of different vacation policies on system efficiency. The findings underscore the significant positive effect of strategic vacation scheduling on mean customer waiting time, suggesting potential benefits even when switching to a temporary server during times of higher main-server service rates [28]. Xing et al. investigated traffic accident patterns in undersea tunnels, offering valuable insights into the evolution of vehicle congestion queuing. The authors present precise queue-length estimation models based on shockwave theory and real-time data input, demonstrating optimal accuracy with a 30 s time interval. The results highlight the effectiveness of the model, with an accuracy of 92.34% for the maximum queue-length estimation model and 83.50% for the real-time whole-process queue-length estimation model. The proposed approach outperforms the input–output model, indicating its potential for supporting timely and effective control measures in undersea tunnel traffic management [29]. Mohan Chaudhry et al. addresses a finite-space, single-server queueing system with a unique (a, b)-bulk service rule and finite-buffer capacity 'N'. It introduces a novel approach utilizing embedded Markov chains, Markov renewal theory, and semi-Markov processes to derive probability distributions for queue lengths at post-departure and random epochs. This investigation establishes a functional relationship between the probability-generating function representing the queue-length distribution and the Laplace–Stieltjes transform (LST) of the queueing-time distribution. This connection facilitates the derivation of waiting-time distributions for individual random customers. The use of LSTs facilitates a comprehensive discussion of the probability density function of waiting times, emphasizing numerical implementations for practical applications [30]. Laurentiu Rece et al. introduce a novel approach using queueing theory models to optimize production department size, production costs, and provisioning. This method employs queuing mathematical models to form the basis for an experimental algorithm and a numerical approach. This research effectively employed these models in designing a practical industrial engineering unit, aligning with technological flow and equipment schemes. The focus on minimizing costs in terms of server count is addressed using the Monte Carlo method, showcasing the practicality of iterative methods like Jacobi and Gauss–Seidel in solving the associated linear system for Jackson queueing networks [31]. Mustafa Demircioglu et al. investigated the influence of disasters on a discrete-time single-server queueing system featuring general independent arrivals and service times. Disasters, modeled as a Bernoulli process, lead to the simultaneous removal of all customers. This study employs a two-dimensional Markovian state description, providing expressions for probability-generating functions, and average values, variances, and tail probabilities for both system content and customer sojourn time are analyzed under a first-come-first-served policy. The derivation of customer loss probability due to disaster occurrences is also addressed, with numerical illustrations enhancing the understanding of the proposed models [32]. In all the above queueing models, essential two-phase bulk service is not considered. It is mandatory to analyze many real-time systems such as communication systems, the manufacturing industry, production systems, network systems, etc. Multiple control policies and renewal of service stations in first-phase customer feedback are the technical terms introduced in this paper which will be useful the studying the performance analysis of DRX mechanisms in network systems.

2. Motivation

Long term evolution-advanced (LTE-A) networks are characterized by two critical elements: power saving and quality of service (QoS). 'Discontinuous reception' (DRX) is a widely utilized mechanism in mobile communication networks to improve power efficiency. By employing DRX, mobile devices can conserve battery life effectively while maintaining seamless connectivity. This method is crucial in enhancing the overall performance and longevity of mobile devices. The first essential service starts using power saving and LTE. The data signals are passed, the data transfer is authenticated, and the minimum value is 1024 mbps and the maximum 4096 mbps. In LTE-A networks, data transfer between the mobile device and the network is orchestrated through a series of negotiated phases for the user equipment (UE). During the data transfer, sometimes the system may be affected by a virus. The service will not be abruptly interrupted; instead, it will be sustained for the ongoing bulk of data, attached or else transferred by carrying out some technical arrangements. After the service is completed, the antivirus is activated and detects the problems in the system. If there are no issues, the process is continued. In this paper, we propose the development of a novel appliance that adapts its functionality based on the type of traffic being processed by the user equipment (UE).

The second essential service is proposed to switch the DRX mechanism combined with the quality of service, and it helps to check the quantity and quality of data that are going to be transferred. The minimum value is 1000 mbps and maximum 4000 mbps as it transfers data at a speed of 1 GB to 4 GB; as of today, the 4th generation. For example, during the wireless connection, it asks for a passcode for the essential verification of data and confirms whether the data are strong enough for communication and transfer of information. If the transfer of data is not successful, as the data are delayed or the customer is not satisfied after the data are sent, they go for feedback, and the system is checked and verified on the server side and rectified for further huge data transfers using DRX. Following data transmission, in the absence of accessible data for processing, the server will be allocated to secondary tasks such as system updates and clearing temporary files. During the data transfer check, the setup time indicates the progress of the necessary service. The data are thoroughly examined and verified before being allowed to proceed. Once the setup time has elapsed, the data meet the threshold value, prompting the server to resume the service. The above scenario may be represented as a 'multiple control policy in an unreliable two-phase bulk queueing system with active Bernoulli feedback and vacation'.

3. System Analysis

3.1. Arrival Process

The arrival process refers to the specific way in which entities enter the system. Customers are added to the system in large quantities according to a Poisson process with a defined arrival rate λ_1, as described in our work. The inter-arrival time adheres to a certain pattern. The distribution of group size follows a geometric distribution, while the distribution of the exponential follows an exponential distribution.

3.2. Service Process

The service process indicates how the server provides service for the customers. In this model, the server provides service in batches according to the general bulk service rule. The service process is split into two phases called FES and SES. The service process will be completed only if each customer undergoes both phases of service. Service time follows the general distribution.

3.3. Bernoulli Feedback

Customer feedback is an important phenomenon in network systems. In this model, after the completion of each service, customers have the option to obtain additional service as feedback. Upon completion of SES, the customer who requires feedback can be taken immediately for service with a specified probability.

3.4. Renewal Time

Due to proactive technical measures that have been set in place, the service process will seamlessly continue in the event of a server failure while serving customers in the ongoing batch. The server will undergo repairs upon the completion of the ongoing service. The duration needed to restore the server is referred to as the renewal time. If a server failure occurs after the completion of the current batch of customer FES, the renewal process for the service station comes into play. Throughout the renewal time, maintenance or repair activities may be conducted on the server.

3.5. Vacation

Upon completing SES, the server embarks on a vacation if the queue length falls below 'a'. Following the vacation period, if the queue length remains below 'a', the server remains idle until the queue length reaches the threshold 'a'. To optimize this idle interval, the server is allocated a secondary task (vacation) that has the potential to enhance the quality of subsequent service.

3.6. Setup Time

Upon the completion of the vacation period, the server may need a certain duration known as setup time before commencing the next service.

3.7. Model Description

With active Bernoulli feedback, server failure, and vacation as factors, this study examines various control approaches for a two-phase bulk arrival and bulk service queueing model. The system experiences a large influx of customers, with several customers entering at once, following the Poisson process at a rate of λ_1. The bulk size distribution of the arrival is geometric. The bulk service process is split into two phases called FES and SES with minimum server capacity $'a'$ and maximum server capacity $'b'$ by Neuts introduction of the general rule for bulk service [33]. The server will be turned on only if the queue length reaches the value 'a'. In the event of a server failure during the FES epoch, the service process persists without interruption for the ongoing group of customers, facilitated by technical precautions. The server is designed to deliver a pivotal two-phase service. In the initial FES phase, if the server experiences failure with a probability of 'δ', the renewal of the service station is triggered. Conversely, if there is no server failure with a probability of '$1-\delta$', the server transitions to a successive phase called SES. Customers who require further service as feedback will be given priority and join at the head of the queue with probability β. On the contrary, the customer who does not require feedback may leave the system with a probability $'1-\beta'$. If the queue length is less than $'a'$ after SES, the server may leave for a single vacation with probability $'1-\beta'$. When the server finds an inadequate number of customers in the queue after vacation completion, the server becomes dormant. After vacation completion, the server requires some time to start service which is the setup time. The setup time will be initiated only when the queue length is at least $'a'$. Even after setup time completion, the service process will be started only with the queue length 'N' ($N > b$).

4. Notations

Let Y be the group size random variable of the arrival, $Y(z)$ be the probability generating function of Y, λ_1 be the Poisson arrival rate, g_k be the probability that 'k' customers arrive in a bulk.

$N_q(t)$—The count of customers waiting for service at a given time 't';
$N_s(t)$—The count of customers under service at a given time 't';
β—Feedback probability;
δ—Probability of server failure.
The detailed set of notations for different state are given in Table 1.

Table 1. Notations.

	Cumulative Distribution Function	Probability Distribution Function	Laplace–Stieltjes Transform	Remaining Service Time
First essential service	$S(y)$	$s(y)$	$\tilde{S}(\theta)$	$S^0(y)$
Second essential service	$S_2(y)$	$s_2(y)$	$\tilde{S}_2(\theta)$	$S_2{}^0(y)$
Vacation	$V(y)$	$v(y)$	$\tilde{V}(\theta)$	$V^0(y)$
Renewal time	$R(y)$	$r(y)$	$\tilde{R}(\theta)$	$R^0(y)$
Preparatory work	$A(y)$	$a(y)$	$\tilde{A}(\theta)$	$A^0(y)$

$B(t) = 0$—when theserver is busy with FES, 1—when the server is busy with SES, 2—when the server is on vacation, 3—when the server is in repair, 4—when the server is in a dormant period, 5—when the server is in setup time. The state probabilities are defined as follows:

$$P_{ij}(y,t)dt = P\Big\{N_s(t) = i, N_q(t) = j,\ y \le S^0(t) \le y + dt,\ B(t) = 0\Big\}\ a \le i \le b;\ j \ge 1 \quad (1)$$

$$W_{ij}(y,t)dt = P\Big\{N_s(t) = i,\ N_q(t) = j, y \le S_2{}^0(t) \le y + dt, B(t) = 1\Big\} \quad (2)$$

$$Q_n(y,t)dt = P\Big\{N_q(t) = n,\ y \le V^0(t) \le y + dt, B(t) = 2\Big\}\ 0 \le n \le a-1 \quad (3)$$

$$R_n(y,t)dt = P\Big\{N_q(t) = n,\ y \le R^0(t) \le y + dt,\ B(t) = 3\Big\} \quad (4)$$

$$D_n(t) = P\{N_q(t) = n,\ B(t) = 4\}\ 0 \le n \le a-1 \quad (5)$$

$$A_n(y,t)dt = P\Big\{N_q(t) = n,\ y \le A^0(t) \le y + dt, B(t) = 5\Big\}\ n \ge a \quad (6)$$

5. Steady-State Queue Size Distribution

The following equations are derived by using the 'supplementary variable technique' [34].

$$-P_{i0}{}'(y) = -\lambda_1 P_{i0}(y) + (1-\beta)\Big(\sum_{m=a}^{b} W_{mi}(0)s(y)\Big) + \beta(W_{i0}(0)s(y))\ a \le i \le b \quad (7)$$

Equation (7) indicates what the different probabilities for the server in FES for 'i' customers in service and '0' customers in the queue in the remaining service time $x - \Delta t$ at time $t + \Delta t$ are. In RHS, the first term indicates there is no arrival at that time and the second term indicates that, when SES is completed, if 'i' customers are in the queue then 'i' customers go for FES and zero customers are waiting in the queue with probability $(1-\beta)$ since there is no feedback. The next term indicates that, when SES is completed, if the customer needs feedback then the 'i' customers again go for FES with the probability β. Similarly, we give the following equations for SES, vacation, repair time, dormant period, and set-up time in Equations (8)–(20).

$$-P_{ij}{}'(y) = -\lambda_1 P_{ij}(y) + \sum_{k=1}^{j} P_{i,j-k}(y)\lambda_1 g_k + \beta(W_{ij}(0)s(y))\ a \le i \le b-1\ j \ge 1 \quad (8)$$

$$-P_{bj}{}'(y) = -\lambda_1 P_{bj}(y) + (1-\beta)\left(\sum_{m=a}^{b} W_{m,b+j}(0)s(y)\right) + \beta\Big(W_{bj}(0)s(y)\Big) + \sum_{k=1}^{j} P_{b,j-k}(y)\lambda_1 g_k\ 1 \le j \le N-b-1 \quad (9)$$

$$-P_{bj}{}'(y) = -\lambda_1 P_{bj}(y) + (1-\beta)\Big(\textstyle\sum_{m=a}^{b} W_{m,b+j}(0)s(y)\Big) + \beta\Big(W_{bj}(0)s(y)\Big) + \sum_{k=1}^{j} P_{b,j-k}(y)\lambda_1 g_k + A_{b+j}(0)s(x)\ j \ge N-b \quad (10)$$

$$-W_{i0}{}'(y) = -\lambda_1 W_{i0}(y) + (1-\delta)\sum_{m=a}^{b} P_{mi}(0)s_2(y) + R_0(0)s_2(y) \quad (11)$$

$$-W_{ij}{}'(y) = -\lambda_1 W_{ij}(y) + \sum_{k=1}^{j} W_{i,j-k}(y)\lambda_1 g_k + (1-\delta)W_{ij}(0)s_2(y)\ a \le i \le b-1\ j \ge 1 \quad (12)$$

$$-W_{bj}{}'(y) = -\lambda_1 W_{ij}(y) + R_j(0)s_2(y) + (1-\delta)\Big(P_{bj}(0)s_2(y)\Big)\ j \ge 1 \quad (13)$$

$$-Q_0{}'(y) = -\lambda_1 Q_0(y) + (1-\beta)(\sum_{m=a}^{b} W_{m0}(0)v(y)) \quad (14)$$

$$-Q_n{}'(y) = -\lambda_1 Q_n(y) + (1-\beta)(\sum_{m=a}^{b} W_{mn}(0)v(y)) + \sum_{k=1}^{n} Q_{n-k}(y)\lambda_1 g_k\ 1 \le n \le a-1 \quad (15)$$

$$-A_n{}'(y) = -\lambda_1 A_n(y) + Q_n(0)a(y) + \sum_{k=1}^{n} A_{n-k}(y)\lambda_1 g_k + \sum_{m=0}^{a-1} T_m \lambda_1 g_{i-m} a(y)\ n \ge a \quad (16)$$

$$-R_0{}'(y) = -\lambda_1 R_0(y) + \delta \sum_{m=a}^{b} P_{m0}(0)r(y) \quad (17)$$

$$-R_n{}'(y) = -\lambda_1 R_n(y) + \delta \sum_{m=a}^{b} P_{mn}(0)r(y) + \sum_{k=1}^{n} R_{n-k}(y)\lambda_1 g_k\ n \ge 1 \quad (18)$$

$$0 = -\lambda_1 T_0 + Q_0(0) \quad (19)$$

$$0 = -\lambda_1 T_n + Q_n(0) + \sum_{k=1}^{n} T_{n-k}(0)\lambda_1 g_k\ 0 \le n \le a-1 \quad (20)$$

The Laplace–Stieltjes transforms of $P_{in}(y)$, $Q_n(y>)$, $W_{in}(y)$, R_n (y), and $A_n(y)$ are defined as

$$\widetilde{P}_{in}(\theta) = \int_0^\infty e^{-\theta y}\, P_{in}(y)dy \quad (21)$$

$$\widetilde{W}_{in}(\theta) = \int_0^\infty e^{-\theta x} W_{in}(x)dy \quad (22)$$

$$\widetilde{Q}_n(\theta) = \int_0^\infty e^{-\theta y} Q_n(y)dy \quad (23)$$

$$\widetilde{R}_n(\theta) = \int_0^\infty e^{-\theta y} R_n(y)dy \quad (24)$$

$$\widetilde{A}_n(\theta) = \int_0^\infty e^{-\theta y} A_n(y)dy \quad (25)$$

By applying the Laplace–Stieltjes transform to both sides of Equations (7)–(20), we obtain

$$\theta\widetilde{P}_{i0}(\theta) - P_{i0}(0) = \lambda_1 \widetilde{P}_{i0}(\theta) - \beta\Big(W_{i0}(0)\widetilde{S}(\theta)\Big) - (1-\beta)\left(\sum_{m=a}^{b} W_{mi}(0)\widetilde{S}(\theta)\right)\ a \le i \le b \quad (26)$$

$$\theta\widetilde{P}_{ij}(\theta) - P_{ij}(0) = \lambda_1 \widetilde{P}_{ij}(\theta) - \sum_{k=1}^{j} \widetilde{P}_{i,j-k}(\theta)\lambda_1 g_k - \beta\Big(W_{ij}(0)\widetilde{S}(\theta)\Big)\ a \le i \le b-1\ j \ge 1 \quad (27)$$

$$\begin{aligned}\theta\widetilde{P}_{bj}(\theta) - P_{bj}(0) = {} & \lambda_1 \widetilde{P}_{bj}(\theta) - \beta\Big(W_{bj}(0)\widetilde{S}(\theta)\Big) - (1-\beta)\Big(\sum_{m=a}^{b} W_{m,b+j}(0)\widetilde{S}(\theta)\Big) \\ & -\textstyle\sum_{k=1}^{j} \widetilde{P}_{b,j-k}(\theta)\lambda_1 g_k\ 1 \le j \le N-b-1\end{aligned} \quad (28)$$

$$\begin{aligned}\theta\widetilde{P}_{bj}(\theta) - P_{bj}(0) = {} & \lambda_1 \widetilde{P}_{bj}(\theta) - \beta\Big(W_{bj}(0)\widetilde{S}(\theta)\Big) - (1-\beta)\Big(\textstyle\sum_{m=a}^{b} W_{m,b+j}(0)\widetilde{S}(\theta)\Big) \\ & -\textstyle\sum_{k=1}^{j} \widetilde{P}_{b,j-k}(\theta)\lambda_1 g_k - A_{b+j}(0)\widetilde{S}(\theta)\ j \ge N-b\end{aligned} \quad (29)$$

$$\theta\widetilde{W}_{i0}(\theta) - W_{i0}(0) = \lambda_1 \widetilde{W}_{i0}(\theta) - R_0(0)\widetilde{S}_2(\theta) - (1-\delta)\sum_{m=a}^{b} P_{mi}(0)\widetilde{S}_2(\theta) \quad (30)$$

$$\theta\widetilde{W}_{ij}(\theta) - W_{ij}(0) = \lambda_1\widetilde{W}_{ij}(\theta) - (1-\delta)W_{ij}(0)\widetilde{S}_2(\theta)\ a \le i \le b-1 \quad (31)$$

$$\theta\widetilde{W}_{bj}(\theta) - W_{bj}(0) = \lambda_1\widetilde{W}_{bj}(\theta) - (1-\delta)\left(P_{bj}(0)\widetilde{S}_2(\theta)\right) - R_j(0)\widetilde{S}_2(\theta)\ j \ge 1 \quad (32)$$

$$\theta\widetilde{Q}_0(\theta) - Q_0(0) = \lambda_1\widetilde{Q}_0(\theta) - (1-\beta)\left(\sum_{m=a}^{b} W_{m0}(0)\widetilde{V}(\theta)\right) \quad (33)$$

$$\theta\widetilde{Q}_n(\theta) - Q_n(0) = \lambda_1\widetilde{Q}_n(\theta) - \textstyle\sum_{k=1}^{n}\widetilde{Q}_{,n-k}(\theta)\lambda_1 g_k - (1-\beta)\left(\sum_{m=a}^{b} W_{mn}(0)\widetilde{V}(\theta)\right)\quad 1 \le n \le a-1 \quad (34)$$

$$\theta\widetilde{A}_n(\theta) - A_n(0) = \lambda_1\widetilde{A}_n(\theta) - Q_n(0)\widetilde{A}(\theta) - \sum_{k=1}^{n}\widetilde{A}_{n-k}(\theta)\lambda_1 g_k - \sum_{m=0}^{a-1} T_m\lambda_1 g_{i-m}\widetilde{A}(\theta)\ n \ge a \quad (35)$$

$$\theta R_0(\theta) - R_0(0) = \lambda_1\widetilde{R}_0(\theta) - \delta\sum_{m=a}^{b} P_{m0}(0)\widetilde{R}(\theta) \quad (36)$$

$$\theta R_n(\theta) - R_n(0) = \lambda_1\widetilde{R}_n(\theta) - \delta\sum_{m=a}^{b} P_{mn}(0)\widetilde{R}(\theta) - \sum_{k=1}^{n}\widetilde{R}_{n-k}(\theta)\lambda_1 g_k\ n \ge 1 \quad (37)$$

To derive the probability-generating function (PGF) for the queue size at any given time, the following PGFs are defined:

$$\begin{aligned}
\widetilde{P}_i(z,\theta) &= \sum_{j=0}^{\infty}\widetilde{P}_{i,j}(\theta)z^j \quad P_i(z,0) = \sum_{j=0}^{\infty} P_{ij}(0)z^j \\
\widetilde{A}(z,\theta) &= \sum_{n=a}^{\infty}\widetilde{A}_n(\theta)z^n \quad A(z,0) = \sum_{n=a}^{\infty} A_n(0)z^n \\
\widetilde{W}_i(z,\theta) &= \sum_{j=0}^{\infty}\widetilde{W}_{i,j}(\theta)z^j \quad W_i(z,0) = \sum_{j=0}^{\infty} W_{ij}(0)z^j \\
\widetilde{Q}(z,\theta) &= \sum_{n=0}^{a-1}\widetilde{Q}_n(\theta)z^n \quad a \le i \le b \\
Q(z,0) &= \sum_{n=0}^{a-1} Q_n(0)z^n \quad T(z) = \sum_{n=0}^{a-1} T_n z^n \\
\widetilde{R}(z,\theta) &= \sum_{n=0}^{\infty}\widetilde{R}_n(\theta)z^n \quad R(z,0) = \sum_{n=0}^{\infty} R_n(0)z^n
\end{aligned} \quad (38)$$

By multiplying Equations (26)–(37) with suitable powers of z^n and summing over n, then by using (38), we obtain

$$(\theta - \lambda_1 + \lambda_1 y(z))\widetilde{P}_i(z,\theta) = P_i(z,0) - \beta W_i(z,0)\widetilde{S}(\theta) - (1-\beta)\left(\sum_{m=a}^{b} W_{mi}(0)\widetilde{S}(\theta)\right)\ a \le i \le b-1 \quad (39)$$

$$(\theta - \lambda_1 + \lambda_1 y(z))\widetilde{P}_b(z,\theta) = P_b(z,0)z^b - \left(\beta z^b - (1-\beta)\right)\widetilde{S}(\theta)W_b(z,0)$$
$$-\widetilde{S}(\theta)\begin{pmatrix} (1-\beta)\left(\sum_{m=a}^{b-1} W_m(z,0) - \sum_{j=0}^{b-1} W_{mj}(0)z^j\right) \\ +\left(R(z,0) - \sum_{j=0}^{b-1} R_j(0)z^j\right) \\ +\left(A(z,0) - \sum_{j=0}^{b-1} A_j(0)z^j\right)\end{pmatrix} \quad (40)$$

$$(\theta - \lambda_1 + \lambda_1 y(z))\widetilde{W}_i(z,\theta) = W_i(z,0) - \widetilde{S}_2(\theta)\left((1-\delta)\sum_{m=a}^{b} P_{mi}(0) + R(0)\right)\ a \le i \le b-1 \quad (41)$$

$$(\theta-\lambda_1+\lambda_1 y(z))\widetilde{W}_b(z,\,\theta)=W_b(z,\,0)-(1-\delta)\left(P_b(z,\,0)\widetilde{S}_2(\theta)\right)+R(z,0)\widetilde{S}_2(\theta)\ \ j\geq 1 \tag{42}$$

$$(\theta-\lambda_1+\lambda_1 y(z))\widetilde{Q}(z,\,\theta)=Q(z,\,0)-\widetilde{V}(\theta)(1-\beta)\left(\sum_{m=a}^{b}\sum_{n=0}^{a-1}W_{mn}(0)z^n\right) \tag{43}$$

$$(\theta-\lambda_1+\lambda_1 y(z))\widetilde{R}(z,\,\theta)=R(z,\,0)-\delta\widetilde{R}(\theta)\sum_{m=a}^{b}P_m(z,0) \tag{44}$$

$$(\theta-\lambda_1+\lambda_1 y(z))\widetilde{A}(z,\,\theta)=A(z,\,0)-\widetilde{A}(\theta)\left(\begin{array}{c}\left(Q(z,0)-\sum_{n=0}^{a-1}Q_n(0)z^n\right)\\+\sum_{m=0}^{a-1}T_m\lambda_1 g_{i-m}\end{array}\right) \tag{45}$$

6. Probability-Generating Function of the Queue Size at Any Time

Let $P(z)$ be the probability-generating function

$$P(z)=\sum_{m=a}^{b-1}\widetilde{P}_m(z,0)+\widetilde{P}_b(z,0)++\widetilde{Q}(z,0)+T(z)+\widetilde{R}(z,0)+\sum_{m=a}^{b-1}\widetilde{W}_m(z,0)+\widetilde{W}_b(z,0) \tag{46}$$

Substituting $\theta=\lambda_1-\lambda_1\,Y\,(z)$ in Equations (39)–(45), following algebraic manipulations, the PGF of the queue size is expressed and simplified as defined in Equation (46).

$$P(z)=\frac{M_1\left(\begin{array}{c}\left(\widetilde{S}(\lambda_1-\lambda_1 Y(z))-1\right)K_1\\+\left(\widetilde{A}(\lambda_1-\lambda_1 Y(z))-1\right)K_2\\+\left(\widetilde{V}(\lambda_1-\lambda_1 Y(z))-1\right)(1-\beta)\sum_{n=0}^{a-1}w_n z^n\\K_1\delta\left(\widetilde{R}(\lambda_1-\lambda_1 Y(z))\left(\widetilde{S}_2(\lambda_1-\lambda_1 Y(z))-1\right)+M_2\right)\end{array}\right)+K_3\left(\begin{array}{c}(\delta M_2+\delta\widetilde{R}(\lambda_1-\lambda_1 Y(z))\widetilde{S}(\lambda_1-\lambda_1 Y(z)))\\+\left(\widetilde{S}(\lambda_1-\lambda_1 Y(z))-1\right)\\+\left(\widetilde{S}_2(\lambda_1-\lambda_1 Y(z))-1\right)(1-\delta)\widetilde{S}(\lambda_1-\lambda_1 Y(z))\end{array}\right)}{M_1(-\lambda_1+\lambda_1 Y(z))} \tag{47}$$

where

$$M_1=z^b-\beta z^b-(1-\beta)\widetilde{S}(\lambda_1-\lambda_1 Y(z))\times\left(\widetilde{S}_2(\lambda_1-\lambda_1 Y(z))(1-\delta)+\delta\widetilde{R}(\lambda_1-\lambda_1 Y(z))\right)$$

$$M_2=\left(\widetilde{R}(\lambda_1-\lambda_1 Y(z))-1\right)\widetilde{S}(\lambda_1-\lambda_1 Y(z))+\widetilde{R}(\lambda_1-\lambda_1 Y(z))\widetilde{S}(\lambda_1-\lambda_1 Y(z))\widetilde{S}_2(\lambda_1-\lambda_1 Y(z))$$

$$K_1=\beta\widetilde{S}_2(\lambda_1-\lambda_1 Y(z))\left(\sum_{i=a}^{b-1}d_i+r_0\right)-(1-\beta)\sum_{i=a}^{b-1}w_i\quad d_n=\sum_{n=0}^{b-1}(A_n+p_n+R_n)$$

$$K_2=\widetilde{V}(\lambda_1-\lambda_1 Y(z))\left((1-\beta)\sum_{i=0}^{a-1}w_i z^i\right)-\sum_{i=0}^{a-1}\left(q_i+\sum_{m=0}^{a-1}T_m\lambda_1 g_{i-m}\right)$$

$$K_3=\widetilde{A}(\lambda_1-\lambda_1 Y(z))K_2+\left(\begin{array}{c}\delta\widetilde{R}(\lambda_1-\lambda_1 Y(z))\\+(1-\beta)\end{array}\right)\times\widetilde{S}_2(\lambda_1-\lambda_1 Y(z))\left(\sum_{i=a}^{b-1}d_i\right)-\sum_{n=0}^{b-1}(d_n)z^n$$

6.1. Steady-State Condition

The steady-state condition for the proposed queueing model is derived as

$$\rho = \frac{\lambda_1 E(Y)(1-\beta)\begin{pmatrix} S1 + (1-\delta)(W1) \\ +\delta(R1) \end{pmatrix}}{b(1-\beta)} \tag{48}$$

where $E(Y)$ = mean bulk size, $S1$ = expected FES time, $W1$ = expected SES time, $R1$ = expected renewal time.

6.2. Result

If we let $\Pi_n = \sum_{i=0}^{a-1}\left[\sum_{j=0}^{(a-1)-i} \alpha_{n-i-j}(\beta_j + k_j)\right]p_i$, then $q_n = \frac{\Pi_n + \sum_{i=1}^{n-a} \alpha_i q_{n-i}}{1-\alpha_0}$, where

$$n = a+1, a+2, a+3, \ldots, N-1$$

The unknown constants T_n involved in $P(z)$ are expressed in terms d_n in the following theorem.

Theorem 1. *Let B_j be the collection of a set of positive integers (not necessarily distinct) A, such that the sum of elements in A is j, then,* $T_n = \frac{1}{\lambda}\sum_{j=0}^{n} q_{n-j}\sum_{j=1}^{n(B_j)} \prod_{l\in A} g_l$.

Proof . From Equations (19) and (20), we have

$$\begin{aligned} \lambda_1 T_0 &= Q_0(0) = q_0 \\ \lambda_1 T_n &= Q_n(0) + \lambda_1 \textstyle\sum_{k=1}^{n} T_{n-k} g_k \qquad 1 \le n \le a-1 \end{aligned}$$

When n = 1,

$$\begin{aligned} \lambda_1 T_1 &= Q_1(0) + \lambda_1 T_0 g_1 \\ &= q_1 + q_0 g_1 \end{aligned}$$

When n = 2,

$$\begin{aligned} \lambda_1 T_2 &= Q_2(0) + \lambda_1 \textstyle\sum_{k=1}^{2} T_{2-k} g_k; \\ &= Q_2(0) + \lambda_1 T_1 g_1 + \lambda_1 T_0 g_2 \\ &= q_2 + q_1 g_1 + q_0({g_1}^2 + g_2) \end{aligned}$$

When n = 3,

$$\begin{aligned} \lambda_1 T_3 &= Q_3(0) + \lambda_1 \textstyle\sum_{k=1}^{3} T_{3-k} g_k \\ &= Q_3(0) + \lambda_1 T_2 g_1 + \lambda_1 T_1 g_2 + \lambda_1 T_0 g_3 \\ &= q_3 + q_2 g_1 + q_1({g_1}^2 + g_2) + q_0({g_1}^3 + 2g_1 g_2 + g_3) \\ T_3 &= \frac{1}{\lambda_1}\left(\textstyle\sum_{j=0}^{3} q_{3-j} \sum_{j=1}^{n(B_j)} \prod_{l\in A} g_l\right) \end{aligned}$$

where

$$B_1 = \{\{1\}\}, B_2 = \{\{1,1\},\{2\}\}, \text{and } B_3 = \{\{3\},\{1,1,1\}\{1,2\},\{2,1\}\}$$

By induction, we obtain

$$T(z) = \sum_{n=0}^{a-1} T_n z^n = \frac{1}{\lambda_1}\left(\sum_{n=0}^{a-1}\left(\sum_{j=0}^{n} q_{n-j} \sum_{j=1}^{n(B_j)} \prod_{l\in A} g_l\right) z^n\right)$$

Therefore,

$$T_n = \frac{1}{\lambda_1}\left(\sum_{j=0}^{n} q_{n-j} \sum_{j=1}^{n(B_j)} \prod_{l\in A} g_l\right)$$

Hence the proof. □

7. Performance Measures

7.1. Expected Number of Customers in the Queue

The average number of customers in the queue at an arbitrary time can be obtained from the given expression below:

$$E(Q) = \lim_{Z \to 1} P'(z)$$

$$E(Q) = \frac{2(H\ (\lambda_1)) - 2(G\ (\lambda_1)) - 3(H\ (\lambda_1))}{24\left(N_9''\right)^2} \quad (49)$$

where

$S1 = \lambda_1 E(S)E(Y)$ $W1 = \lambda_1 E(S_2)E(Y)$ $S2 = {\lambda_1}^2 E(S^2)(E(Y))^2$ $W2 = {\lambda_1}^2 E({S_2}^2)(E(Y))^2$
$S3 = E(S)\lambda_1 Y''(1)$ $W3 = E(S_2)\lambda_1 Y''(1)$ $S4 = {\lambda_1}^3 E(S^3)(E(Y))^3$ $W4 = {\lambda_1}^3 E({S_2}^3)(E(Y))^3$
$S5 = E(S)\lambda_1 Y'''(1)$ $S5 = E(S_2)\lambda_1 Y'''(1)\lambda_1 Y'''(1)$ $V1 = \lambda_1\ E(V)E(Y)$ $R1 = \lambda_1 E(R)E(Y)$
$V2 = {\lambda_1}^2 E(V^2)(E(Y))^2$ $R2 = {\lambda_1}^2 E(R^2)(E(Y))^2$ $V3 = E(V)\lambda_1 Y''(1)$ $R(3) = E(R)\lambda_1 Y''(1)$
$V4 = {\lambda_1}^3 E(V^3)(E(Y))^3$ $R4 = {\lambda_1}^3 E(R^3)(E(Y))^3$ $V5 = E(V)\lambda_1 Y'''(1)$ $R5 = E(R)\lambda_1 Y'''(1)$
$A1 = \lambda_1 E(A)E(Y)$ $D1 = \lambda_1 E(S^2)E(Y)\ Y''(1)$ $A2 = {\lambda_1}^2 E(A^2)(E(Y))^2$ $D2 = {\lambda_1}^2 E({S_2}^2)E(Y)\ Y''(1)$
$A3 = E(A)\lambda_1 Y''(1)$ $D3 = {\lambda_1}^2 E(V^2)E(Y)\ Y''(1)$ $A4 = {\lambda_1}^3 E(A^3)(E(Y))^3$ $D4 = {\lambda_1}^2 E(R^2)E(Y)\ Y''(1)$
$A5 = E(A)\lambda_1 Y'''(1)$ $D5 = {\lambda_1}^2 E(A^2)E(Y)\ Y''(1)$
$F(\lambda_1) = (N_5' + N_6' + N_7' + N_8')\ N_9''$ $G(\lambda_1) = (N_5'' + N_6'' + N_7'' + N_8'')\ N_9'''$
$H(\lambda_1) = (N_5''' + N_6''' + N_7''' + N_8''')\ N_9''$ $N_1'' = 2M_1'(S1)(k_1);$ $N_2'' = 2M_1'(A1)k_2$
$N_1''' = 6M_1'k_1'(S1) + 3M_1'k_1(S3 + S2) + 3M_1''k_1(S1)$
$N_2''' = 5M_1'(A1)k_2' + 2M_1'k_2(A2 + A3) + 2M_1''k_2(A1)$
$N_3'' = 2(V1)(1-\beta)M_1'f_1$ $N_3''' = nf_1\{5(V1)(1-\beta)M_1'\} + f_1\{3(V1)(1-\beta)M_1'' + 3(V2 + V3)(1-\beta)M_1'\}$
$N_4'' = 2\delta M_1'(k_1)W2;$ $N_5' = \delta M_1'(k_1)M_2$

$$N_4''' = \delta\left\{\begin{array}{c} 3M_1'(S2 + S3) \\ +3M_1'(k_1)(R1)(W2 + W1) \\ +4M_1'k_1'(W2) + M_1''k_1(W2 + W1) \\ +2M_1'k_1'((R1) + 1)(W1) \end{array}\right\}$$

$$N_5'' = \delta\begin{pmatrix} M_1(k_1 M_2'' + 2M_2'k_1' + k_1''M_2) \\ M_1'(k_1 M_2'' + 2k_1'M_2) + M_1''k_1 M_2 \end{pmatrix}$$

$$N_5''' = \delta\begin{pmatrix} M_1'(3k_1 M_2'' + 6k_1'M_2' + k_1''M_2) \\ M_1''(3k_1 M_2' + k_1'M_2) + M_1'''k_1 M_2 \end{pmatrix}$$

$N_6' = \delta(k_3(M_2' + S1 + R1) + k_3'(1 + M_2))$
$N_6'' = \delta(k_3(M_2'' + S2 + S3 + 2(S1)R1 + R2 + R3) + 2k_3'(M_2' + S1 + R1) + k_3''(M_2 + 1))$

$$N_6''' = \delta\left[\begin{array}{c} k_3\begin{pmatrix} R5 + M_2''' - \lambda_1 Y'''(1) + (S1)\lambda_1 Y''(1) \\ +2D1 + S4 + 3(S1)(R2 + R3) + D4 \\ +3(R1)(S2 + S3)\left({\lambda_1}^2 E(Y))^2 + 1\right) \end{pmatrix} \\ 2k_3'(M_2'' + (S2 + S3) + 2(R1)S1 \\ +R2 + R3) + 3k_3''(S1 + R1 + M_2') \end{array}\right] \quad N_7' = k_3 S(1);\ N_7'' =$$

$k_3(S2 + S3) + 2k_3'(S1)$
$N''' = k_3(S4 + S5 + D1) + 3k_3''(S1) + 2k_3'(S2 + S3)$ $N_8' = (1-\delta)(k_3)W1$

$$N_8'' = (1-\delta)\left[\begin{array}{c} k_3(W1(S1 + 2(S2) + 2(S3)) \\ +2k_3'(W1) \end{array}\right]$$

$$N_8''' = (1-\delta)\begin{pmatrix} k_3\begin{pmatrix} 2W1(S2 + S3) \\ +2(W2 + W3)S1 \\ +3(D2) + W4 + S5 \end{pmatrix} \\ 3k_3'(W2 + W3 + S1(W1)) \\ k_3'(S1)W1 \end{pmatrix}$$

$N_9{}'' = 2M_1{}'(\lambda_1 E(Y))$ $N_9{}''' = 3M_1{}'\lambda_1 Y'''(1) + 3M_1{}''(\lambda_1 E(Y))$ $N_9{}'^{v} = \lambda_1(4M_1{}'Y'''(1) + 6M_1{}''Y''(1) + 4M_1{}'''(E(Y))$
$r_2 = W1(1-\delta) + \delta R1$ $k_1 = (1-\beta)f_1 - c_2$ $K_1{}' = (E1)c_1$ $M_1{}' = (1-\beta)(b - S1 - r_2)$ $f_1 = \sum_{i=0}^{a-1} w_i$
$K_1{}'' = (W2+W3)\,c_1$ $K_1{}''' = (W5+W4+3D2)\,c_1$ $r_3 = (1-\delta)(W2+W3)+\delta(R2+R3)$

$$M_1{}'' = (1-\beta)\begin{pmatrix} b(b-1)-(S2+S3) \\ -2S1r_2 - r_3 \end{pmatrix} \quad M_2{}' = 2R1 + (S1+W1)$$

$$M_1{}''' = (1-\beta)\begin{pmatrix} b(b-1)(b-2) \\ -3(S2+S3)r_2 \\ -(S4+S5+3D1) - 3(S1)r_3 \\ -(1-\delta)(W5+W4+D2) \\ -\delta(R4+R5+D4) \end{pmatrix} \quad c_1 = \sum_{i=a}^{b-1} d_i + r_0$$

$$c_2 = \sum_{i=0}^{a-1}\left(q_i + \sum_{m=0}^{a-1} D_m \lambda_1 g_{i-m}\right)$$

$$M_2{}'' = 2R1S1 + 2(R2+R3) + R1\begin{pmatrix} W2+W3 \\ W1+S1 \end{pmatrix} + W3 + w2 + 2(S1)W1 + S2 + S3$$

$M_2{}''' = 3R1(S2+S3) + (R2 + R3(W2+W3)) + (3R2 + 3R3 + R5 + R4 + D4)S1 + R1(S5 + D1 + S4) + W5 + 3D2 + (S1)W2 + W4 + 2(S2+S3)W1 + 2S1(W2+W3)$
$K_2{}' = ((V1+i)(1-\beta)f_1) - c_2 + i(i-1)) - c_2$ $K_2{}'' = (1-\beta)f_1(V2 + V3 + 2i(V1)$ $f_2 = \sum_{n=0}^{a-1}(d_n + R_n)$
$K_2{}''' = (1-\beta)f_1[V5 + V4 + 3(D3) + 3(V2+V3)i + 3(V1)i(i-1) + i(i-1)(i-2)] - c_2$
$K_3{}' = K_2{}' + A1(f_1(1-\beta) - c_2) + (\delta R1 + (1-\beta)W1)c_1 - nf_2$
$K_3{}'' = 2A1K_2{}' + (A2 + A3)k_2 + \delta(R2+R3) + (1-\beta)(W2+W3)(c_1) - n(n-1)f_2$
$K_3{}''' = 2(A2+A3)K_2{}' + 2A1K_2{}'' + K_2{}''' + (A4 + A5 + 3(D5))k_2 + \delta(R5 + R4 + 3(D4)) + (1-\beta)(W5 + W4 + 3(D2))(c_1) - f_2 n(n-1)(n-2))$

7.2. Expected Waiting Time of a Customer in the Queue

By using Little's formula we have obtained the result

$$E\,(W) = \frac{E(Q)}{\lambda_1 E(Y)} \tag{50}$$

7.3. Expected Duration of the Dormant Period

When one observes the epochs marking the beginning of both the busy and vacation phases, they are said to have passed through an idle period. I will stand in for the 'idle period' random variable. The likelihood that the system state visits '*j*' during an idle time is denoted as $\alpha(j)$, $j = 0, 1, 2, \ldots, a-1$.

Let

$$I_{j=}\begin{cases} 1, \; if\ the\ state\ 'j'\ during\ an\ idle\ period. \\ \qquad 0,\ otherwise \end{cases} \tag{51}$$

Conditioning on the queue size in the service completion epoch, we have $\alpha_0 = \pi_0$.

$$\alpha_j = P(I_j = 1) = \pi_j + \sum_{k=0}^{c-1} \pi_k\, P\left(I_{j-k}{}^1 = 1\right);$$

Thus, the expected duration of the dormant period is obtained from

$$E(I) = \frac{1}{\lambda_1}\sum_{j=0}^{c-1}\alpha_j, \tag{52}$$

where $\frac{1}{\lambda_1}$ is the expected staying time in the state '*j*' during a dormant period.

7.4. Duration of the Server's Expected Busy Period

The active period random parameter is denoted by B. The time when the server is either serving users or being repaired is denoted by T. After that,

$$E(T) = E(S) + E\ (W) + \delta E(R) \tag{53}$$

$E(S)$ = expected FES time, $E(W)$ = expected SES time, $E(R)$ = expected renewal time.
We define a random variable J as

$J = 0$, if there is feedback after the service completion;
$J = 1$, if there is a departure after the service completion and there are fewer than 'a' customers after the first service;
$J = 2$, if there is a departure after the service completion and there are at least 'a' consumers following the conclusion of the service.

Then,

$$E(B) = \frac{E\ (T)}{(1-\beta)\sum_{i=0}^{a-1} d_i} \tag{54}$$

8. Cost Model

The suggested queueing model's overall average cost can be minimized by making the following assumptions.

γ_{h} : holding cost per customer

γ_0 : operating cost per unit of time

γ_{s} : startup cost per cycle

γ_{r} : reward cost per cycle due to vacation

Since the length of the cycle is the sum of the idle period and busy period,

$$E(T_c) = E(length\ of\ Idle\ period) + E(length\ of\ the\ Busy\ Period) \tag{55}$$

$$E(T_c) = \frac{1}{\lambda_1}\sum_{j=0}^{c-1} \alpha_j, + \frac{E\ (T)}{(1-\beta)\sum_{i=0}^{a-1} d_i} \tag{56}$$

$$\text{Total Average Cost} = [\gamma_s - \gamma_r E(I)]\frac{1}{E(T_c)} + \gamma_h E(Q) + \gamma_0 \rho \tag{57}$$

where $\rho = \frac{\lambda_1 E(Y)[E(B)+\delta E(R)]}{}$
It is quite difficult to derive an analytical method for finding the optimal value a^* (minimum bulk size in bulk arrival and bulk service queueing model) to minimize the total average cost (*TAC*). The simple direct search method is used to find the optimal policy for a threshold value a^* to minimize the *TAC*, which is defined as

Step 1: Fix the value of maximum bulk size 'b'and threshold value 'N';
Step 2: Select the value 'a' which will satisfy the following relation:

$$\text{TAC}(a^*) \leq TAC(a),\ 1 \leq a \leq N \tag{58}$$

Step 3: The value a^* is optimum, since it gives minimum *TAC*.

By following the steps outlined above, one may determine the best value of 'a' to minimize the *TAC* function. In the section that follows, numerical examples will be given to back up the preceding answer.

9. Numerical Illustration

Numerical justification for the theoretical findings of the proposed model is provided under the specified assumptions and notations (Table 2):

Table 2. Parameters and Notations.

Parameter	Distribution	Notations
Arrival rate	Poisson distribution	λ_1
First essential service	2-Erlang distribution	μ_1
Second essential service	2-Erlang distribution	μ_2
Vacation	Exponential distribution	ξ
Renewal	Exponential distribution	η
Setup time	Exponential distribution	α

The bulk size distribution of the arrival is geometric with a mean of 2.

Minimum server capacity	a
Maximum server capacity	b
Threshold value	N
Startup cost	Rs. 4
Holding cost per customer	Rs. 3
Operating cost per unit time	Rs. 5
Reward per unit time due to vacation	Rs. 1
Renewal cost per unit time	Rs. 2
Setup time cost per unit time	Rs. 0.50

9.1. *Results and Discussion*

Here, we cover the research that looks at how various factors affect performance metrics and how different metrics fare when subjected to set threshold values.

9.1.1. Impact of Arrival Rate on Performance Metrics

With the assumptions given in Table 2, from Table 3 and Figure 1, it is clear that if the arrival rate increases, the expected number of customers in the queue, expected duration of the busy period of the server, and expected waiting time of a customer in the queue increase whereas the expected duration of the dormant period decreases.

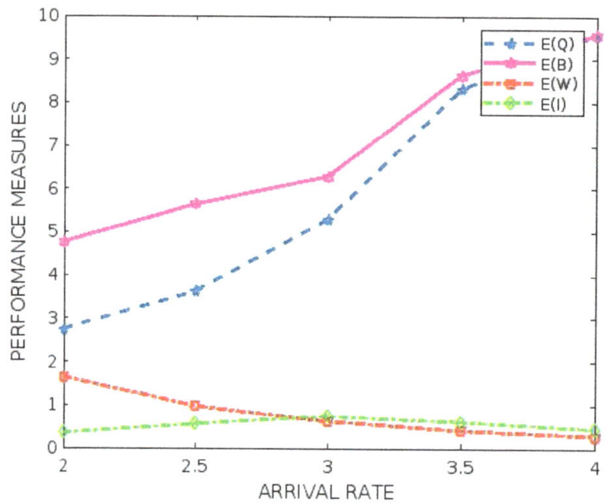

Figure 1. Arrival rate versus performance metrics.

Table 3. Arrival rate versus performance metrics.

λ_1	E(Q)	E(B)	E(I)	E(W)
3.0	3.7541	5.2123	2.5454	1.2212
3.4	4.5432	6.5216	2.1181	2.3321
4.0	5.6632	7.9934	1.5432	4.1254
4.5	7.1123	9.1211	1.1214	5.4313
5.0	8.8246	11.2321	0.5432	6.2242
5.6	9.6542	12.4532	0.3243	7.3232
6.0	10.4342	14.2321	0.1211	9.1214

E(Q)—Expected number of customers in the queue; E(B)—Expected duration of the busy period of the server; E(W)—Expected waiting time of a customer in the queue; E(I)—Expected duration of the dormant period. (For minimum server capacity $a = 2$, maximum server capacity $b = 4$, vacation rate $\xi = 10$, renewal rate $\eta = 8$, breakdown probability $\delta = 0.2$, feedback probability $\beta = 0.5$).

9.1.2. Impact of Breakdown Probability on Performance Metrics

The influence of performance metrics for various failure rates is shown in Table 4 and Figure 2. It can be seen that when the failure rate increases, the predicted inactive period duration and the estimated client waiting time in the queue will also increase.

Table 4. Breakdown of probability versus performance measures.

δ	E(Q)	E(B)	E(I)	E(W)
0.5	10.2343	8.5472	8.2231	9.1227
0.6	11.4532	9.2345	7.8535	11.2236
0.7	13.1231	11.4532	5.1232	13.5645
0.8	15.2941	12.6341	3.2212	15.6543
0.9	16.3987	13.9871	2.1545	16.6432

E(Q)—Expected number of customers in the queue; E(B)—Expected duration of the busy period of the server; E(W)—Expected waiting time of a customer in the queue; E(I)—Expected duration of the dormant period.

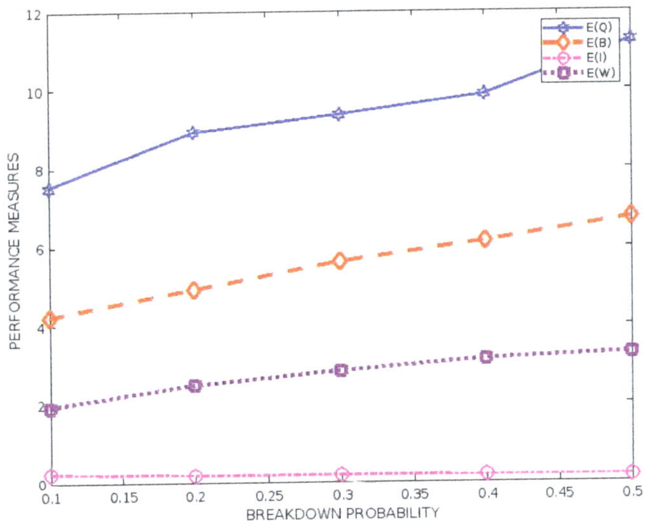

Figure 2. Breakdown probability vs. performance metrics.

9.1.3. Effects of Renewal Rate on Performance Measures

In Table 5 and Figure 3, the impact on performance metrics for various renewal rates is presented, and it is noted that the expected waiting time in the queue will be decreased whenever the renewal rate increases.

Table 5. Renewal ratio versus performance measures.

Renewal Rate	E(Q)	E(B)	E(I)	E(W)
2	6.932	6.6532	4.1534	5.2345
4	6.134	6.2543	5.6734	3.4564
6	5.513	5.2321	7.4765	1.5643
8	4.927	4.1431	8.2451	1.1457
10	3.623	2.9256	10.1543	0.4381

E(Q)—Expected number of customers in the queue; E(B)—Expected duration of the busy period of the server; E(W)—Expected waiting time of a customer in the queue; E(I)—Expected duration of the dormant period.

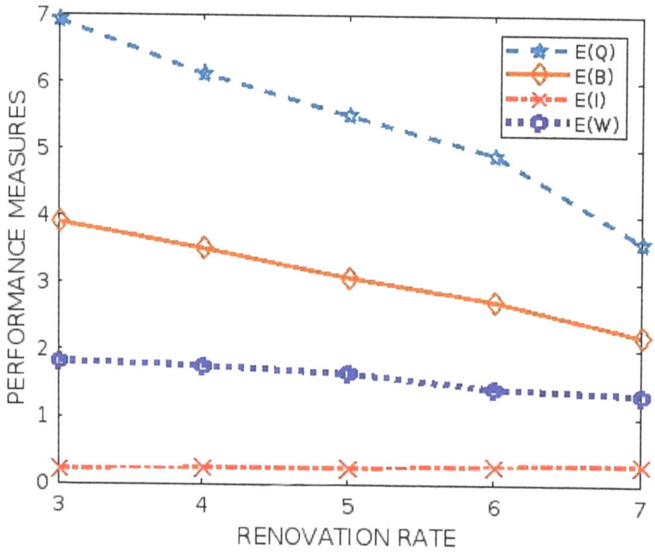

Figure 3. Renewal rate vs. performance metrics.

9.1.4. Effects of Threshold Values 'a' and 'N' on Total Average Cost

In Table 6 and Figure 4, the effects of the bulk size 'a' on the TAC with $b = 8$ are given. From Table 6 and Figure 5, one can see that, to minimize the overall cost the minimum bulk size 'a' should be fixed as 3. Similarly, Table 7 and Figures 5–7 suggest to fix the threshold value 'a' to minimize the total average cost for various arrival rates, service rates, and vacation rates, and to minimize the overall cost the minimum bulk size should be fixed at $a = 5$ and $N = 6$.

Table 6. Threshold Value 'a' vs. Total Average Cost.

a	E(Q)	E(B)	E(I)	TAC
2	1.3563	6.2874	2.8963	1.2753
3	1.4389	6.6421	3.7524	0.8754
4	1.5129	7.7943	4.7327	0.6798
5	1.8319	8.4862	5.5639	0.9875
6	2.0345	13.5782	5.8032	0.9234
7	2.2427	18.4592	7.6731	0.9875
8	2.8193	24.5728	8.6932	0.9109
9	3.6738	26.8432	9.4589	1.5098
10	3.8921	30.1732	10.5821	1.4326

E(Q)—Expected number of customers in the queue; E(B)—Expected duration of the busy period of the server; E(I)—Expected duration of the dormant period. Arrival rate $\lambda_1 = 2$; maximum server capacity b = 8, service rate of FES μ_1 = service rate of SES μ_2 = 2.0, vacation rate ξ = 1, break down probability $\delta = 3$, renewal rate $\eta = 4$, set up time $\alpha = 6$.

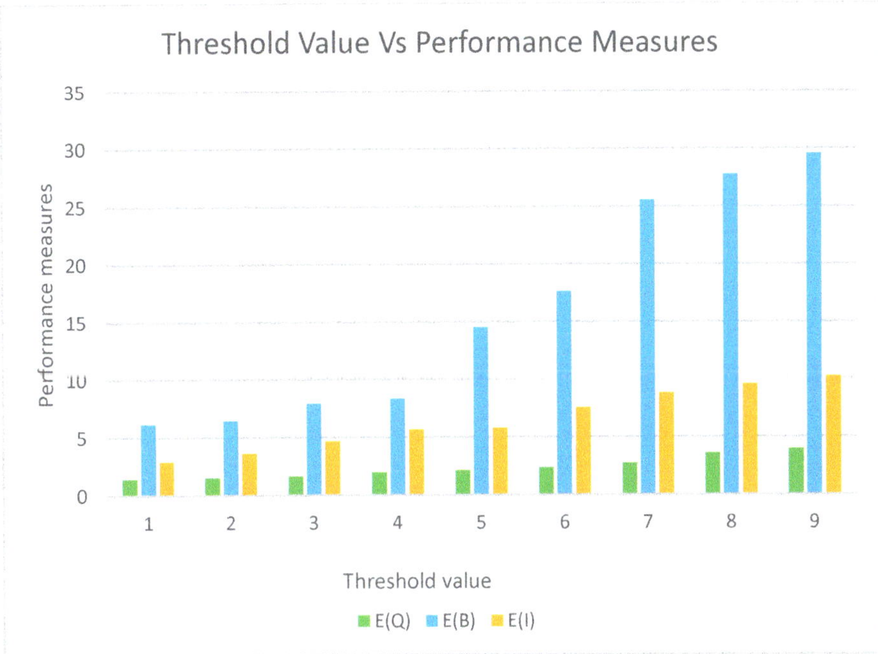

Figure 4. Threshold value '*a*' vs. Performance metrics.

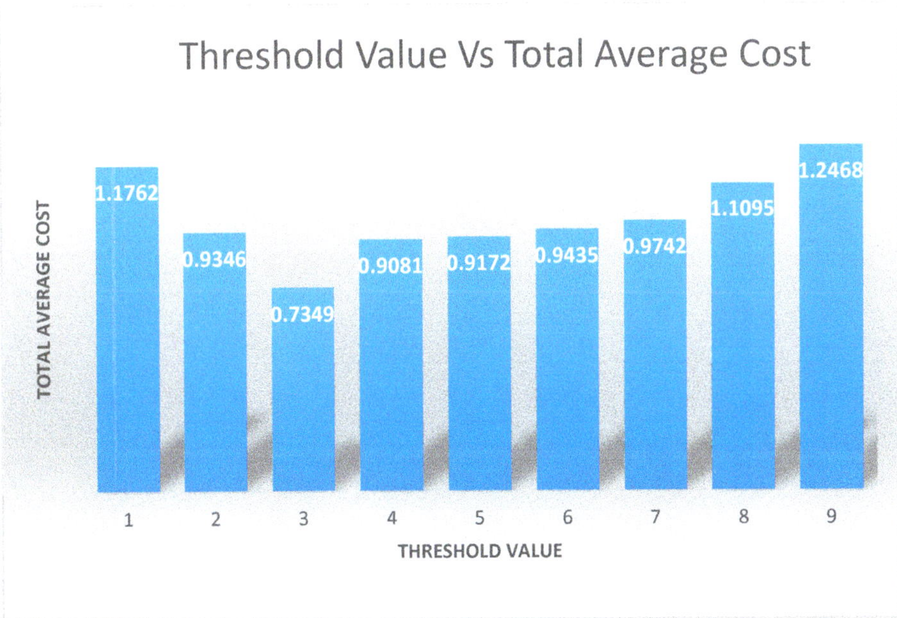

Figure 5. Threshold value '*a*' vs. TAC.

Table 7. Threshold value versus TAC.

Threshold value 'a' to start service	Threshold Value 'N' to Start Bulk Service								
a \ N	2	3	4	5	6	7	8	9	10
	TAC								
1	4.861	4.732	4.746	4.965	5.583	5.951	6.247	6.365	7.483
2		4.567	4.518	4.872	5.432	5.673	6.084	6.247	6.941
3			4.452	4.672	4.792	4.864	5.272	5.431	5.934
4				4.295	4.643	4.821	5.093	5.187	5.531
5					4.283	4.314	4.421	5.042	5.467
6						4.315	4.410	4.989	5.035
7							4.357	4.745	5.021
8								4.578	4.995
9									4.982

Minimum TAC occurs when a = 5 and N = 6.

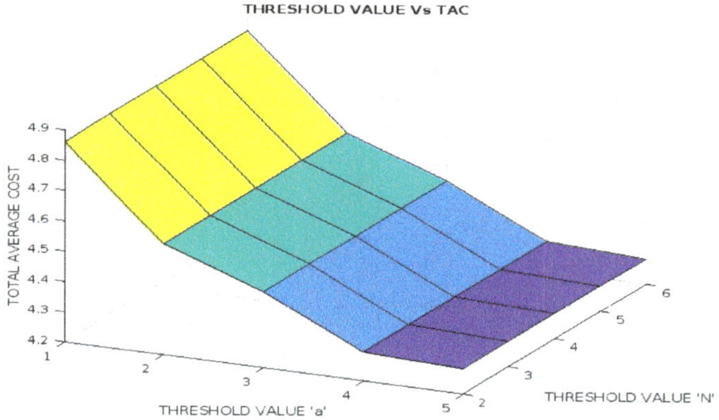

Figure 6. Threshold values 'a' and 'N' versus TAC.

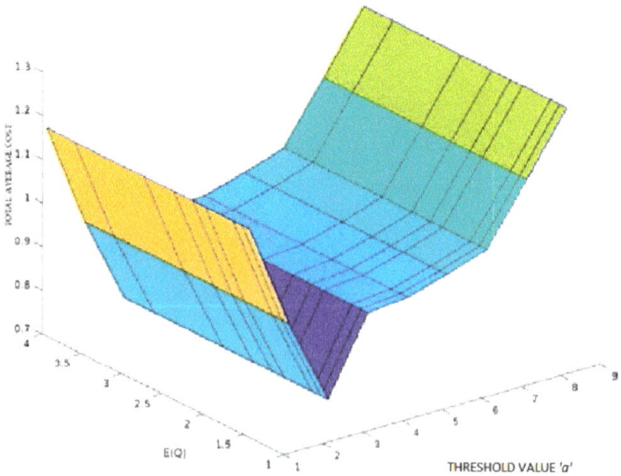

Figure 7. Threshold value vs. TAC for $\lambda = 2$, $b = 8$, $\mu_1 = \mu_2 = 2.0$, $\xi = 1$, $\gamma = 3$, $\eta = 4$, $\alpha = 6$.

9.2. Optimal Cost

Here, we take a look at a numerical example to see how the DRX mechanism might help LTE networks save power. Fixing the values for the thresholds and utilizing the acquired result to minimize the median cost of the entire system is possible. Table 7 shows the impact of different threshold values 'a' and 'N' on the TAC; setting a = 5 and N = 4.283 yields the lowest total average cost.

10. Conclusions

Here, we have examined two-phase bulk service with active Bernoulli feedback, vacation, and breakdown, as well as bulk arrival in bulk. By utilizing supplementary variable approaches under steady-state settings, we may derive the probability-generating function of the queue size at any given moment. To gauge performance, we estimate things like the number of customers expected to be in line, how long the server's busy phase will be, how long customers are expected to wait in line, and how long the dormant period will be. We provide concrete numerical examples to ensure that the analytical results are genuine. An application of the proposed queueing model in 4G/5G networks using the DRX mechanism has been given. Additionally, optimum cost analysis has been carried out to minimize the total average cost of the system and make better decisions to fix the threshold value for the service. The uniqueness of the considered model is in the sense that we have introduced an essential two-phase bulk service, renewal time, and two-level control policy for the bulk queueing system. All the introduced parameters are more useful for studying many real-time applications in network systems.

Author Contributions: Conceptualization, S.P.N. and S.D.L.; Data curation, S.P.N. and S.D.L.; Formal analysis, K.K., M.M. and S.D.L.; Investigation, S.P.N. and K.K.; Methodology, S.P.N.; Supervision, S.D.L.; Visualization, M.M. and S.D.L.; Writing—original draft, S.D.L. and S.P.N.; Writing—review and editing, K.K. and M.M. All authors have read and agreed to the published version of the manuscript.

Funding: This work was supported by the project SP2023/074 Application of Machine and Process Control Advanced Methods supported by the Ministry of Education, Youth and Sports, Czech Republic.

Data Availability Statement: The datasets used and/or analyzed during the current study are available from the corresponding author upon reasonable request.

Conflicts of Interest: The authors declare no conflicts of interest.

References

1. Tian, N.; Zhang, Z.G. *Vacation Queueing Models Theory and Applications*; International Series in Operations Research & Management Science; Springer: Boston, MA, USA, 2006; Volume 93, ISBN 978-0-387-33721-0.
2. Arumuganathan, R.; Jeyakumar, S. Steady state analysis of a bulk queue with multiple vacations, setup times with N-policy and closedown times. *Appl. Math. Model.* **2005**, *29*, 972–986. [CrossRef]
3. Jeyakumar, S.; Senthilnathan, B. Steady state analysis of bulk arrival and bulk service queueing model with multiple working vacations. *Int. J. Math. Oper. Res.* **2016**, *9*, 375–394. [CrossRef]
4. Baba, Y. The M/PH/1 queue with working vacations and vacation interruption. *J. Syst. Sci. Syst. Eng.* **2010**, *19*, 496–503. [CrossRef]
5. Haridass, M.; Arumuganathan, R. Analysis of a MX/G(a,b)/1 queueing system with vacation interruption. *RAIRO-Oper. Res.* **2012**, *46*, 305–334. [CrossRef]
6. Gao, S.; Liu, Z. An M/G/1 queue with single working vacation and vacation interruption under Bernoulli schedule. *Appl. Math. Model.* **2013**, *37*, 1564–1579. [CrossRef]
7. Tao, L.; Wang, Z.; Liu, Z. The GI/M/1 queue with Bernoulli-schedule-controlled vacation and vacation interruption. *Appl. Math. Model.* **2013**, *37*, 3724–3735. [CrossRef]
8. Pradhan, S.; Gupta, U.C. Modeling and analysis of an infinite-buffer batch-arrival queue with batch-size-dependent service: MX/Gn(a,b)/1. *Perform. Eval.* **2017**, *108*, 16–31. [CrossRef]
9. Madan, K.; Abu-Dayyeh, W.; Gharaibeh, M. Steady state analysis of two MX/Ma,b/1 queue models with random breakdowns. *Int. J. Inf. Manag. Sci.* **2003**, *14*, 37–51.
10. Jeyakumar, S.; Senthilnathan, B. A study on the behaviour of the server breakdown without interruption in a Mx/G(a,b)/1 queueing system with multiple vacations and closedown time. *Appl. Math. Comput.* **2012**, *219*, 2618–2633. [CrossRef]

11. Wu, W.; Tang, Y.; Yu, M. Analysis of an M/G/1 queue with N-policy, single vacation, unreliable service station and replaceable repair facility. *Opsearch* **2015**, *52*, 670–691. [CrossRef]
12. Niranjan, S.P.; Chandrasekaran, V.M.; Indhira, K. Stochastic modelling of a two phase bulk service queueing system with active bernoulli feedback, server loss and vacation. *Int. J. Pure Appl. Math.* **2017**, *115*, 433–445.
13. Sama, H.; Vemuri, V.; Talagadadeevi, S.; Bhavirisetti, S. Analysis of an N-policy MX/M/1 Two-phase Queueing System with State-dependent Arrival Rates and Unreliable Server. *Ingénierie Syst. Inf.* **2019**, *24*, 233–240. [CrossRef]
14. Rao, A.A.; Vedala, N.R.D.; Chandan, K. M/M/1 Queue with N-Policy Two-Phase, Server Start-Up, Time-Out and Breakdowns. *Int. J. Recent. Technol. Eng.* **2019**, *8*, 9165–9171. [CrossRef]
15. Enogwe, S.U.; Onyeagu, S.I.; Obiora-Ilouno, H.O. On single server batch arrival queueing system with balking, three types of heterogeneous service and Bernoulli schedule server vacation. *Math. Theory Model.* **2021**, *11*, 40.
16. GnanaSekar, M.M.N.; Kandaiyan, I. Analysis of an M/G/1 Retrial Queue with Delayed Repair and Feedback under Working Vacation policy with Impatient Customers. *Symmetry* **2022**, *14*, 2024. [CrossRef]
17. Niranjan, S.P. Managerial decision analysis of bulk arrival queuing system with state dependent breakdown and vacation. *Int. J. Adv. Oper. Manag.* **2020**, *12*, 351–376. [CrossRef]
18. Blondia, C. A queueing model for a wireless sensor node using energy harvesting. *Telecommun. Syst.* **2021**, *77*, 335–349. [CrossRef]
19. Merit, C.K.D.; Haridass, M. A simulation study on the necessity of working breakdown in a state dependent bulk arrival queue with disaster and optional re-service. *Int. J. Ad Hoc Ubiquitous Comput.* **2022**, *41*, 1–15. [CrossRef]
20. Deepa, V.; Haridass, M.; Selvamuthu, D.; Kalita, P. Analysis of energy efficiency of small cell base station in 4G/5G networks. *Telecommun. Syst.* **2023**, *82*, 381–401. [CrossRef]
21. Niranjan, S.P.; Chandrasekaran, V.M.; Indhira, K. Phase dependent breakdown in bulk arrival queueing system with vacation break-off. *Int. J. Data Anal. Tech. Strateg.* **2020**, *12*, 127–154. [CrossRef]
22. Ayyappan, G.; Deepa, T. Analysis of batch arrival bulk service queue with multiple vacation closedown essential and optional repair. *Appl. Appl. Math.* **2018**, *13*, 2.
23. Niranjan, S.P.; Komala Durga, B.; Thangaraj, M. Steady-State Analysis of Bulk Queuing System with Renovation, Prolonged Vacation and Tune-Up/Shutdown Times. In Proceedings of the 2nd International Conference on Mathematical Modeling and Computational Science, Surat, India, 5–6 February 2022; Peng, S.-L., Lin, C.-K., Pal, S., Eds.; Springer Nature: Singapore, 2022; pp. 35–48.
24. Nithya, R.P.; Haridass, M. Cost optimisation and maximum entropy analysis of a bulk queueing system with breakdown, controlled arrival and multiple vacations. *Int. J. Oper. Res.* **2020**, *39*, 279–305. [CrossRef]
25. Enogwe, S.; Obiora-Ilouno, O.; Enogwe, S.; Obiora-Ilouno, H. Effects of Re-neging, Server Breakdowns and Vacation on a Batch Arrival Single Server Queueing System with Three Fluctuating Modes of Service. *Open J. Optim.* **2020**, *9*, 105–128. [CrossRef]
26. Khan, I.; Paramasivam, R. Reduction in Waiting Time in an M/M/1/N Encouraged Arrival Queue with Feedback, Balking and Maintaining of Reneged Customers. *Symmetry* **2022**, *14*, 1743. [CrossRef]
27. Ammar, S.; Rajadurai, P. Performance Analysis of Preemptive Priority Retrial Queueing System with Disaster under Working Breakdown Services. *Symmetry* **2019**, *11*, 419. [CrossRef]
28. Hanukov, G.; Shoval, S. A Model for a Vacation Queuing Policy Considering Server's Deterioration and Recovery. *Mathematics* **2023**, *11*, 2640. [CrossRef]
29. Xing, R.; Cai, X.; Liu, Y.; Yang, Z.; Wang, Y.; Peng, B. Study on Queue Length in the Whole Process of a Traffic Accident in an Extra-Long Tunnel. *Mathematics* **2023**, *11*, 1773. [CrossRef]
30. Chaudhry, M.; Datta Banik, A.; Barik, S.; Goswami, V. A Novel Computational Procedure for the Waiting-Time Distribution (In the Queue) for Bulk-Service Finite-Buffer Queues with Poisson Input. *Mathematics* **2023**, *11*, 1142. [CrossRef]
31. Rece, L.; Vlase, S.; Ciuiu, D.; Neculoiu, G.; Mocanu, S.; Modrea, A. Queueing Theory-Based Mathematical Models Applied to Enterprise Organization and Industrial Production Optimization. *Mathematics* **2022**, *10*, 2520. [CrossRef]
32. Demircioglu, M.; Bruneel, H.; Wittevrongel, S. Analysis of a Discrete-Time Queueing Model with Disasters. *Mathematics* **2021**, *9*, 3283. [CrossRef]
33. Marcel, F. Neuts A General Class of Bulk Queues with Poisson Input. *Ann. Math. Stat.* **1967**, *38*, 759–770. [CrossRef]
34. Cox, D.R. The analysis of non-Markovian stochastic processes by the inclusion of supplementary variables. *Math. Proc. Camb. Philos. Soc.* **1955**, *51*, 433–441. [CrossRef]

mathematics

MDPI

Article

Simulation of Heuristics for Automated Guided Vehicle Task Sequencing with Resource Sharing and Dynamic Queues

Jonas F. Leon [1,2], Mohammad Peyman [3], Xabier A. Martin [3] and Angel A. Juan [3,*]

1 Department of Computer Science, Multimedia and Telecommunication, Universitat Oberta de Catalunya, 08018 Barcelona, Spain; jofule@uoc.edu
2 Spindox España S.L., 08021 Barcelona, Spain
3 Research Center on Production Management and Engineering, Universitat Politècnica de València, 03801 Alcoy, Spain; mpeyman@upv.es (M.P.); xamarsol@upv.es (X.A.M.)
* Correspondence: ajuanp@upv.es

Abstract: Automated guided vehicles (AGVs) stand out as a paradigmatic application of Industry 4.0, requiring the seamless integration of new concepts and technologies to enhance productivity while reducing labor costs, energy consumption, and emissions. In this context, specific industrial use cases can present a significant technological and scientific challenge. This study was inspired by a real industrial application for which the existing AGV literature did not contain an already well-studied solution. The problem is related to the sequencing of assigned tasks, where the queue formation dynamics and the resource sharing define the scheduling. The combinatorial nature of the problem requires the use of advanced mathematical tools such as heuristics, simulations, or a combination of both. A heuristic procedure was developed that generates candidate task sequences, which are, in turn, evaluated in a discrete-event simulation model developed in Simul8. This combined approach allows high-quality solutions to be generated and realistically evaluated, even graphically, by stakeholders and decision makers. A number of computational experiments were developed to validate the proposed method, which opens up some future lines of research, especially when considering stochastic settings.

Keywords: automated guided vehicles; heuristics; discrete-event simulation

MSC: 90-10; 90C59; 90B06

1. Introduction

Industry 4.0 presents great opportunities for improving productivity, but it also comes with plenty of technological challenges. These challenges mostly relate to the transformation of human-supervised processes into automated and machine-controlled processes, which, in turn, lead to distributed complex system coordination and connectivity issues [1]. In this context, the use of AGVs is becoming increasingly important, mainly due to the potential productivity enhancement and reduction in labor cost, energy consumption, and emissions [2]. Furthermore, AGVs are paradigmatic since their implementation requires the symbiotic integration of many of the Industry 4.0 key concepts and technologies, such as adaptive robotics, embedded systems, communication and networking, cloud systems, simulation, virtualization, data analytics, and artificial intelligence [3].

A great deal of research has been devoted to AGVs since they were initially introduced more than 25 years ago [4]. However, there are still open areas of development and specific use cases that pose a technological and scientific challenge. The case presented in this study was inspired by a real industrial application that was difficult to model following existing AGV problems found in the literature. The problem revolves around the dispatching, routing, and scheduling of tasks for multiple AGVs. However, these terms are not strictly equivalent [5]. In Vivaldini et al. [6] a possible distinction between them has been established: (i) dispatching is the process of selecting and assigning tasks to vehicles; (ii) routing is the selection of specific paths that each vehicle needs to execute in order to fulfill the assigned tasks; and (iii) scheduling is the definition of the arrival and departure times of the vehicles along the assigned routes for each one of its assigned tasks. Following these definitions, solving the scheduling problem assumes that the routing and dispatching problems have already been taken care of. Furthermore, in the present work, the scheduling is considered to be a consequence of the sequence in which the different tasks are carried out by the resources available at each point in time. This means that the queue formation dynamics and resource sharing are the key elements defining the schedule if handled by a sufficiently representative model. The problem presented in this form could be referred to as task sequencing, i.e., defining the order in which the (already assigned and planned) tasks are executed. The problem is trivial if the number of resources is infinite and the interaction between resources is neglected, but it becomes a true combinatorial challenge when the resources are constrained and the queue dynamics are accounted for. Hence, the coordination of multiple AGVs that are performing a given set of tasks, and that are considering also the interaction with other machines and the existence of resource sharing constraints, is a complex problem that can be modeled in many different ways. For instance, it could be modeled as a robotic task sequencing problem (RTSP) or as a resource-constrained scheduling problem (RCSP). Both the RTSP [7] and the RCSP [8] have been proven to be NP-hard. Thus, it is expected that any version that can be considered a particular case or combination of both problems is also NP-hard in nature. In other words, as the number of AGVs and workstations increases, capturing the interactions between the individual AGVs and workstations becomes nearly impossible using conventional mathematical methods, and it becomes necessary to resort to more advanced mathematical tools such as heuristics or simulation (or a combination of them).

In that sense, the use of algorithms and heuristics to find high-quality solutions in a reasonable time can be considered the preferred option to solve these types of problems, as opposed to exact procedures that aim for an optimal solution. The time it would take to find the optimal solution to a problem with such a vast solution space and the gap between the optimal solution found and the real optimal solution to the problem (e.g., considering the randomness present in the real system) makes heuristics a very sensible approach [9]. The approach followed in this study consists of identifying several algorithms typically used for sorting non-uniform tasks and resources, and then combining them in a heuristic procedure that generates candidate solutions for the task sequencing problem. Furthermore, to increase the fidelity of the proposed model, a discrete-event simulation model was developed in the Simul8 commercial software to evaluate the performance of the heuristic results. The use of simulators such as Simul8 can have many advantages in this context, such as the following: (i) aiding the graphical validation of results from stakeholders, especially technical personnel and decision makers; and (ii) facilitating the creation of complex and detailed models of real-life scenarios [10]. Without the simulation component, the evaluation of the candidate solutions obtained by the heuristic procedure is not possible due to the dynamic nature of the queues and shared resource availability (temporal or sequential dependencies).

There are many studies in the literature that, as reviewed in Section 2, approach scheduling or sequencing problems by disregarding or simplifying the complex interaction between the available resources, as well as by considering that the idealized solutions found can be executed in a realistic environment. The situation is even worse when the environment is stochastic, as is the case in all real-life industrial applications. Therefore, there is a gap in terms of scalable methodologies that can cope with those complex interactions and can be extended to more complicated settings where random variability is considered. Therefore, the main contribution of this paper is the development of a methodology that combines simulation and the use of simple heuristics to find high-quality solutions when the sharing of limited resources causes queuing and interactions. The effectiveness of the proposed methodology is proven, through various numerical experiments, to be more efficient than the NEH-based algorithm that uses the state-of-the-art NEH heuristic.

The rest of the paper is structured as follows: Section 2 reviews the relevant literature related to the problem studied. Afterward, Section 3 defines the problem precisely but also includes an example to clarify the concepts. The solving methodology is described in detail in Section 4, and the results are presented in Section 5 together with a brief discussion of the obtained results. Finally, Section 6 highlights the most important conclusions of the study and some future lines of research.

2. Literature Review

In this section, a brief literature review is conducted to present the current developments in the scientific community aimed at solving AGV task sequencing problems using heuristic and simulation methods.

2.1. AGVs in Industry 4.0

As mentioned in Section 1, the use of AGVs is increasingly regarded as an essential element in realizing the productivity improvements promised by the Industry 4.0 framework. The most basic challenge facing AGV technology is the efficient path planning for navigating manufacturing landscapes. Fransen and van Eekelen [11] discussed AGV control strategies and illustrated the use of the A* algorithm on a geometric graph to aid proficient path planning, thus influencing the flow layout within facilities. When multiple AGVs are used, traffic management strategies must be implemented to prevent collisions and ensure the smooth operation of AGVs. In this regard, Pratissoli et al. [12] proposed novel methods for coordinating a fleet of AGVs in an industrial setting, where they focused on developing complete traffic manager software based on a multi-level control architecture. Furthermore, the emergence of 5G connectivity has been identified as a technological trigger for AGV implementation, enhancing their collaborative capabilities via high-speed, low-latency networks. Vlachos et al. [13] used a case study to investigate the implications of AGVs integrated with the IoT in flexible manufacturing systems, depicting the technological synergy between AGVs and the IoT within a manufacturing enterprise. Also, Reis et al. [14] proposed a systematic literature review to identify the most relevant methodologies and technologies related to AGV position control, a critical aspect of manufacturing intralogistics and material handling, thereby aiding in defining optimal vehicle requirements and enhancing operational efficiency. For an overview of the current challenges and technological advances in AGVs, readers can refer to Oyekanlu et al. [15]. Conversely, for a survey on the design and control of AGV systems (flow layout, traffic management, vehicle requirements, etc.), readers can refer to Vis [4]. In the context of automated container terminals, Kim and Bae [16] introduced a dispatching method for AGVs to work with container cranes, enhancing efficiency by assigning future tasks and using simulation in various environments. Li et al. [17] tackled task assignment and sequencing for AGVs in manufacturing using a harmony search algorithm, which was tested in real-life scenarios. Zou et al. [18] employed a bee colony algorithm for a similar problem in a Chinese manufacturing company, focusing on a single depot like in our study.

2.2. Task Sequencing: Conceptual Clarifications and Evolution

Despite the extensive and often ambiguous terminology in its domain, scheduling, which is closely related to task sequencing, provides valuable insights for this work. As previously stated, terms such as dispatching, task scheduling, sequencing, and allocation are frequently used interchangeably in the literature [19]. Within the context of this study, it is crucial to underscore how shared resource availability influences task sequencing and scheduling. Since its introduction several decades ago [20], the RCSP has evolved into a well-studied optimization problem [21]. This problem involves scheduling a set of tasks or activities by assigning them specific execution times, aiming to minimize the total project duration or makespan while adhering to various constraints. These constraints are generally categorized based on the following: (i) the available resources required for completing different activities; and/or (ii) activity sequences (often referred to as precedence constraints) [22]. Due to its practical importance, the RCSP has been the focus of numerous studies. For instance, Hartman and Briskorn [23] surveyed RCSP and its extensions, highlighting the significance of efficient resource allocation for optimal scheduling solutions. Recent advances in computational techniques have encouraged the development of novel approaches to tackle the challenges posed by the RCSP. Notably, van der Beek et al. [24] introduced a hybrid differential evolution algorithm specifically tailored for the RCSP. This algorithm considers a flexible project structure along with the dynamics of resource consumption and production, showcasing the potential of evolutionary algorithms in navigating the complex challenges of resource allocation and task sequencing.

Equally pertinent to this study is reviewing the literature for the RTSP. The RTSP has undergone extensive study as it aims to optimize the sequence of tasks performed by robots in diverse industrial settings. Foundational work by Maimon [25] laid the groundwork, addressing the efficient utilization of robot task flexibility characteristics and providing a framework and classification for such problems. Over time, a plethora of approaches and methodologies have been proposed to address the challenges posed by the RTSP. For example, Suárez-Ruiz et al. [26] made a significant contribution by devising a method to optimize the sequence in which a robot visits multiple targets in industrial applications, resulting in fast RTSP solutions, which are especially beneficial in time-sensitive operations. Subsequently, Li et al. [27] introduced an efficient approach employing a decoupling strategy to determine an optimal sequence of collision-free motions for robots executing a set of repetitive tasks, thus emphasizing the continuous efforts to enhance efficiency and safety in robotic operations, particularly in environments where collision avoidance is critical. Furthermore, Chen et al. [28] investigated optimizing joint-space tour scheduling to align with manufacturing criteria for each task point visit, highlighting the significance of planning the sequence of robotic tasks in attaining operational excellence in industrial settings. Some authors have translated RTSP concepts to AGV applications, focusing on a single AGV unit. For instance, Li et al. [29] converted the RTSP into a traveling salesman problem, a common practice in robotics. They proposed a heuristic to reduce its complexity from $O(N^3)$ to $O(N^2)$ by utilizing auxiliary data structures. In another approach, Martin et al. [30] proposed a reactive solution for a dynamic RTSP, where the AGV resets after each task, akin to this study's application. They focused on task sequencing, using simulation to manage resource constraints, workstation availability, and queue dynamics, thus leading to effective scheduling.

Another significant problem family that extensively explores optimizing task sequences executed by robots is the multi-robot task allocation (MRTA) problem. Korsah et al. [31] presented a comprehensive taxonomy for MRTA, establishing a framework that aids in the efficient utilization of robot task flexibility characteristics. This taxonomy assists in understanding the features and complexity of MRTA problems, which have been extensively investigated in several studies. For example, Khamis et al. [32] studied multi-robot systems executing collective behaviors for tackling complex tasks. Similarly, Alshaboti and Baroudi [33] discussed state-of-the-art algorithms and strategies employed in tackling MRTA problems, providing insights into the evolving landscape of robot task allocation. Additionally, Chakraa et al. [34] reviewed optimization techniques for multi-robot task allocation problems, showcasing current methods and offering insights into future directions for optimizing task allocation among multi-robots.

2.3. Application of Discrete-Event Simulation

Most of the articles mentioned above employ simulation to varying extents to validate algorithms developed for their AGV-related problems. Simulation facilitates a better understanding of reality's complexity, reducing the necessity for the oversimplifications and unrealistic assumptions sometimes required in analytical models [35]. Discrete-event simulation, in particular, has proven to be a valuable tool for modeling AGV-based transport systems, such as AGV traffic management policies, or, as in the current study, AGV task dispatching/sequencing rules [36]. For example, in Inoue [37] a discrete-event simulation model was established to simulate AGV behavior and to identify the best control policy in a real factory use case. Similarly, bin Md Fauadi et al. [38] proposed a discrete-event simulation approach to determine vehicle requirements in a manufacturing environment. Notably, the authors emphasized simulation's role in accurately modeling queuing behavior when multiple AGVs interact. Also, Kühn et al. [39] introduced a two-stage genetic algorithm for generating sequencing heuristics in stochastic, decentralized, multi-project scheduling with limited resources. The algorithm emphasizes efficient heuristic generation with lower simulation efforts and uses deterministic values initially for robust solutions, followed by a more intensive computation stage incorporating stochastic values. The PyScOp framework facilitates this simulation and optimization process. Equally, Azimi and Sholekar [40] presented a novel approach to solving the multi-objective multi-mode resource-constrained project scheduling problem with stochastic duration. This approach employs a simulation-based optimization method, SIMSUM1, which integrates discrete-event simulation with a relaxation technique for binary decision variables. Given the advantages that discrete-event simulation offers in modeling multi-AGV scenarios, the use of commercial simulators can expedite model creation, ensure its validity, and simplify result communication to stakeholders.

Since the majority of the reviewed papers did not address the specific use of simulation software in our problem context, namely the complex interaction between shared resources, the purpose of this study is to fill this gap in the literature. To provide a novel approach in this area, we combined a heuristic algorithm with discrete-event simulation software. This combination is intended to improve problem-solving effectiveness in our particular problem scenario. While previous studies have utilized commercial simulation software like ARENA [41] or FlexSim [42] for warehouse AGV applications, Simul8 was selected for this research due to its capabilities and alignment with the study's objectives. Simul8 (www.simul8.com, accessed on 22 December 2023) is a commercial simulator renowned for its flexibility in modeling complex systems, where its focus is on being intuitive, fast, and effective. Although Simul8 has been successfully employed in other applications such as healthcare systems [43], supply chain optimization [44], or transportation [45], to the best of the authors' knowledge, it has not been previously utilized for AGV sequencing optimization.

3. Problem Description

In this section, the industrial case that inspired this study is presented. Subsequently, an illustrative example of the problem is provided to enhance comprehension of the application under consideration. Finally, the problem is formulated in mathematical terms.

3.1. Motivation and Industrial Context

The problem delineated in this study draws inspiration from a genuine industrial scenario at a manufacturing company in Spain. The company operates a production facility equipped with several AGVs responsible for collecting and transporting products between designated plant locations. Initially, the products awaiting processing are stored temporarily in a specific warehouse location, known as the depot. Then, these products are transported to various workstations, each dedicated to a distinct manufacturing process. Following the transportation of the product, the AGV stationed there travels back to the starting point to transport the next product. The number of AGVs available at the starting point remains fixed and are shared among the different streams of work. Visiting a workstation involves a travel time (to and from) and a processing time. Notice that each workstation has the capacity to process only one product at a time. Consequently, if an AGV intends to visit an already occupied workstation, it must wait in the queue until the station becomes available. Figure 1 provides a schematic representation of the aforementioned industrial scenario. The primary objective of the company is to establish the sequence for the execution of various tasks by the AGVs to minimize the total production time, commonly referred to as the makespan.

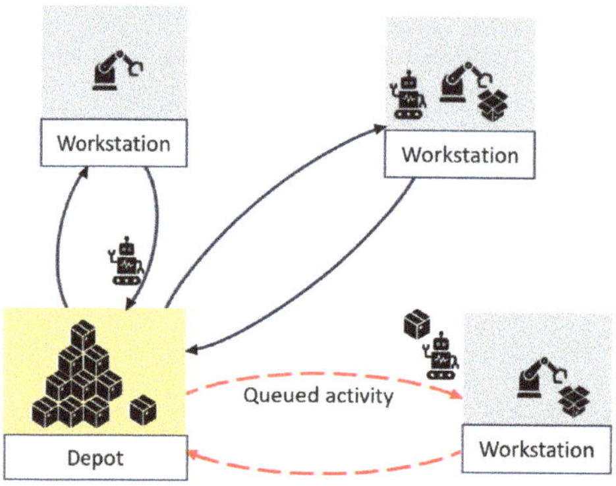

Figure 1. Schematic representation of the different elements present in the problem.

In this case study, one should differentiate between scheduling and sequencing, as outlined in Sections 1 and 2. The task allocation to workstations and AGVs is predetermined by the company. Each task is already assigned to a specific location and AGV. This means that the products designated for processing are predetermined, along with their respective travel and processing times. All the products to be processed are assumed to be available at the start time. The problem can be likened to uniform machine scheduling, but with a unique aspect: the resources are limited and shared among the different tasks to be executed (i.e., each AGV can only handle one task at a time). This characteristic creates a variant of the resource-constrained scheduling problem previously discussed in Section 2. Additionally, typical assumptions for such scheduling problems are incorporated, such as the absence of preemption (tasks cannot be interrupted) and considering resources as renewable (AGVs can perform another task once they finish the current task). The approach in this study is deterministic, implying fixed processing times for each AGV when handling a job at a specific workstation.

3.2. An Illustrative Numerical Example

Consider a scenario where there are five tasks allocated across three distinct workstations, with the assignment of tasks to workstations already predetermined. All three workstations have equal processing times. Specifically, task 1 is designated for workstation 1, tasks 2 and 4 for workstation 2, and tasks 3 and 5 for workstation 3. In this setup, there are two available AGVs. AGV A is responsible for tasks 1, 2, and 3, while AGV B handles tasks 4 and 5. The illustration of this scenario is depicted on the left side of Figure 2.

Let us consider that, for the sake of simplicity, the travel time is negligible compared to the processing time in the workstations; thus, it is not considered. In the simplest scenario with infinite resources, where there are no constraints on the AGVs, tasks can be executed whenever the workstations are available. In such cases, scheduling becomes straightforward as the sequence remains unchanged, and a first-in-first-out (FIFO) approach suffices. The total makespan is determined by the maximum number of tasks within a workstation, given they share the same processing time. This situation is depicted in the timeline (a) in Figure 2, illustrating a total makespan of two times the workstation processing time.

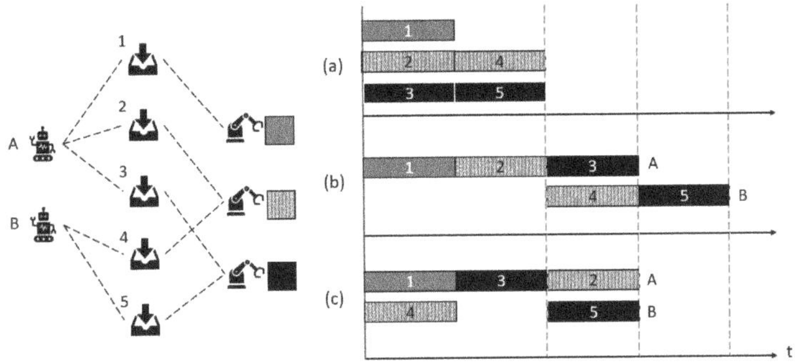

Figure 2. Illustrative example of the problem. In case (**a**), no resource constraint is considered; in case (**b**), the resource constraints are active, and the task sequence is {1, 2, 3, 4, 5}; and, in case (**c**), the resource constraints are active, and the task sequence is {1, 4, 3, 2, 5}.

When resource sharing constraints are taken into account, as shown in timelines (b) and (c) of Figure 2, the task sequence becomes crucial in determining the total makespan. In timeline b), if the task sequence {1, 2, 3, 4, 5} remains unchanged, tasks 1, 2, and 3 are executed sequentially as AGV A becomes available. Task 4 can occur concurrently with task 3 since both AGV B and the corresponding workstation are available. Task 5 is the final activity after AGV B becomes free. This results in a total makespan of four times the workstation processing time, which is twice as long as the situation with infinite resources. The resource constraint causes tasks to queue until the assigned resource is available. As the sequence is strictly adhered to, rearranging tasks can improve the total makespan.

In timeline (c) of Figure 2, the task execution order was altered to {1, 4, 3, 2, 5}. Here, tasks 1 and 4 can be performed concurrently because they are allocated to different AGVs and workstations. Following this, task 3 is executed, and although AGV B is free, the workstation is occupied, causing task 5 to queue and be executed simultaneously with task 2. This sequence change optimizes the makespan, reducing it to only three times the workstation processing time.

3.3. Generic Formulation for the Sequencing Problem with Shared Resources

Let $M = \{m_1, m_2, \ldots, m_M\}$ be the set of workstations such that workstation $m_k \in M$ has an associated processing time p_k, which could be deterministic or, in the most generic version of the problem, stochastic. Let R be the set of available resources such that AGV $r_j \in R = \{r_1, r_2, \ldots, r_R\}$. The set of tasks can be defined as the binary relation T such that the following applies:

$$T \subset R \times M = \{(r_j, m_k) \mid r_j \in R, m_k \in M\}, \tag{1}$$

with task $t_i \in T = \{t_1, t_2, \ldots, t_T\}$. The goal of the RCSP is to produce the totally ordered set $S(T, \leq)$ such that the total makespan C_{max} is minimized. The total makespan can be defined as follows:

$$C_{max} = max\Big(E(t_i) + p_k\Big), \quad \forall t_i \in S, \tag{2}$$

where $E(t_i)$ denotes the start time of a given task. The total makespan is, therefore, calculated as the maximum start time plus its corresponding processing time p_k for all the tasks in S. The activities carried out are constrained by the available resources and workstations. The current activity, $C(S, t) \subset T$, for a given sequence S at time t, is a subset of the set of tasks T that have to comply with both the resource constraint

$$\sum_{\forall t_i \in C(S,t)} \#r_j \leq 1, \tag{3}$$

and the workstation constraint

$$\sum_{\forall t_i \in C(S,t)} \#m_k \leq 1, \tag{4}$$

thus meaning that the number of times (represented by the symbol '#') that the resource r_j or the workstation m_k appears in the subset of current activities, C is less or equal than 1. In other words, a resource or a workstation can only be used once at any given point in time t.

4. Methods and Methodology

In this section, the methodology employed to address the problem introduced in Section 3 is delineated and the sequential steps and their principal components are detailed. Additionally, the various heuristic algorithms developed in this study and the instances developed for the computational experiments are described.

4.1. A Two-Step Method for Sequencing Tasks

To tackle the problem described in Section 3, a two-step process integrating heuristics and simulation was adopted. During the first step, the heuristic component aims to generate high-quality candidate sequences, minimizing the total makespan by ordering tasks efficiently. On the second step, the performance of the proposed sequence is evaluated. It is important to note that evaluating each sequence entails considering the intricate and dynamic queuing resulting from the idle time of AGVs when traveling to occupied workstations. As evidenced in the simplified example provided in Section 3.2, minor alterations in the sequence significantly impact task interferences. This complexity amplifies with an increasing number of tasks, and it becomes nearly impossible to handle by traditional methods for big instances or when stochastic variables are present. Hence, the proposal is to model the queuing phenomenon directly within Simul8. This simulation software is apt for managing complex queuing scenarios, thereby allowing for a robust evaluation of the interaction between shared resources. Moreover, utilizing Simul8 enables the easy creation of a stochastic version of the problem by introducing stochastic processing times instead of fixed processing times. Figure 3 visually illustrates the described methodology.

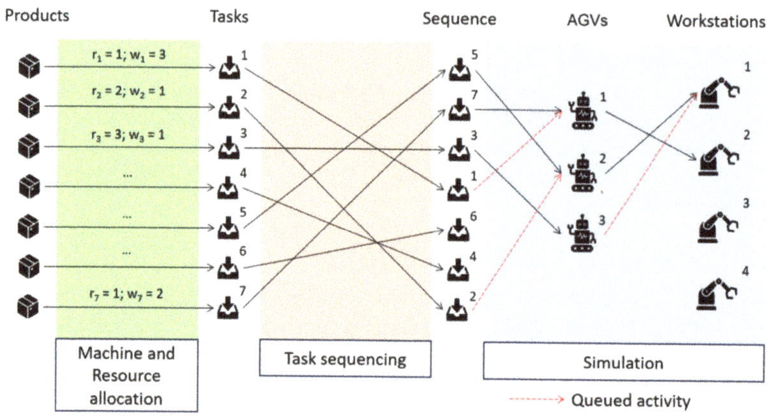

Figure 3. Schematic representation of the proposed solving methodology involving the task sequencing heuristic and Simul8 simulation of the dynamic queues.

The initial phase illustrated in Figure 3, involving the assignment of workstations and AGVs to tasks, is considered external to the core problem and is assumed as an input. Task-specific information (traveling and processing times, as well as AGV-to-workstation assignments) is encapsulated within the problem instances, which are detailed further below in Section 4.3. Essentially, the company predefines both task-to-workstation and task-to-AGV assignments. Subsequently, the task sequencing begins (the first step of the method), which make use of the heuristic algorithms outlined in Section 4.2, by focusing on determining the order of task execution. After that, at the second step of the method, the simulation component evaluates the optimized sequence, considering the dynamic queue formations as the simulation progresses and the resources are shared between the different streams of tasks. Figure 4 depicts the implementation of one of the problem instances in Simul8. It must be highlighted that the simulation strictly follows the optimized sequence, and it automatically manages the shared AGV availability depending on the dynamically generated queues.

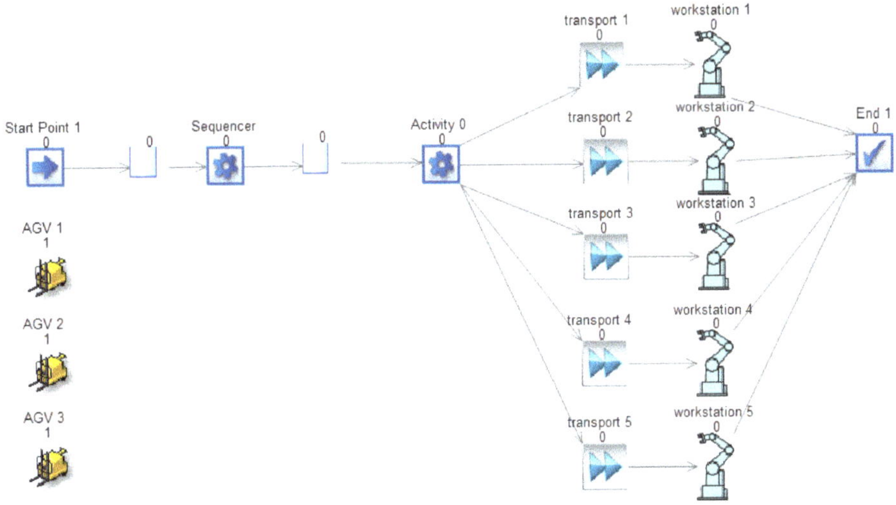

Figure 4. Screenshot of the Simul8 model for the instances with three AGVs and five workstations. The simulation model follows the sequence and automatically manages the queues for both workstations and AGVs.

4.2. *Algorithm Combination and the NEH-Based Benchmark*

To derive efficient task sequences minimizing the total makespan, several well-known sequencing algorithms were combined in this study to generate a number of efficient sequencing heuristics for ordering the given tasks. As elucidated in Section 1, the application of heuristics is well founded due to the impracticality of finding an optimal solution given the simplifications considered along with the inherent complexity of the problem. The heuristic algorithms were devised using the information available within the instances, including the number of workstations, AGVs, tasks, traveling and processing times for each task, and task-specific workstation and AGV allocations. The partial sequencing algorithms considered in this study were the following:

- Most loaded resource first (MLRF): This algorithm sorts AGVs, prioritizing the most loaded AGV first based on either the total processing time the AGV is engaged or the number of times it is required by a task. This study used total processing time for sorting.
- Less loaded resource first (LLRF): Similar to MLRF, LLRF sorts AGVs from lower workload to higher workload.
- Shortest processing time first (SPTF): This algorithm prioritizes tasks with the shortest processing times, sorting workstations from the least to the greatest processing time for tasks.
- Longest processing time first (LPTF): Contrary to SPTF, LPTF sorts workstations in reverse order, from lower to higher processing times.

These were referred to as partial sequencing algorithms because each one of them orders resources (i.e., AGVs) or workstations but not tasks, which are the specific combination of an AGV and a workstation, with its corresponding travel and process time. These algorithms can be viewed as individual components that can be integrated into a comprehensive heuristic procedure that generates candidate solutions for the task sequencing problem while considering shared resources. The heuristic procedure initiates by arranging the AGVs and workstations. This process involves employing the partial algorithms discussed earlier, such as sorting AGVs (MLRF and LLRF) and workstations (SPTF and LPTF). The combination of these sorting algorithms gives rise to four distinct heuristics: (i) MLRF/LPTF, (ii) MLRF/SPTF, (iii) LLRF/SPTF, and (iv) LLRF/LPTF. After organizing the AGVs and workstations, the tasks are incorporated into the final sequence through a round-robin approach. This involves commencing from the top-ranked workstation and AGV, selecting a workstation from the sorted list, and then choosing the first AGV from the corresponding list. If the pairing is not among the tasks to be performed, the next AGV is examined. This process continues until all tasks are accommodated in the final candidate sequence. Algorithm 1 showcases the MLRF/LPTF version of the heuristic. To derive other versions of the heuristic, modifications in lines 4 to 5 are required, while the rest of the procedure remains consistent. The details of the heuristic process are provided in a graphical manner in Figure 5.

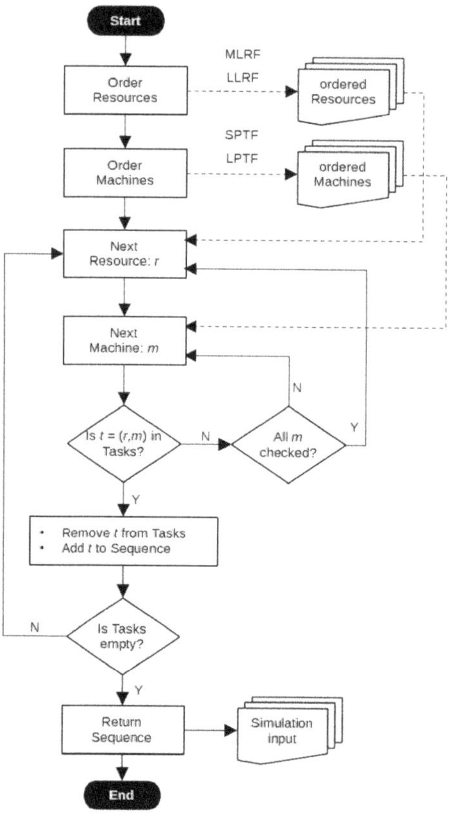

Figure 5. Schematic of the heuristic followed to generate the candidate solutions, i.e., the task sequences that were used as simulation inputs.

In order to measure the performance of our solving methodology, we provide a benchmark algorithm that uses the state-of-the-art NEH heuristic to serve as a reference baseline for comparison purposes [46]. Algorithm 2 outlines the main steps of the denoted NEH-based algorithm. Initially, the list of tasks to schedule was divided into several sub-problems based on their workstation–AGV combination. In other words, tasks with equal workstation and AGV allocation were grouped together. Each of these sub-problems were solved independently using the well-known NEH heuristic without considering resource sharing. Once a sub-sequence was generated for each sub-problem, the final sequence of tasks was built-up, combining each sub-sequence into the final task sequence. Specifically, the sub-sequences were first sorted by their number of tasks in descending order, and one task from each sub-sequence was added to the final sequence until all tasks were added to the sequence.

Algorithm 1 MLRF/LPTF algorithm.

Input: Tasks = $\{t_i : i \leq T\}$, Resources = $\{r_j : j \leq R\}$, Machines = $\{m_k : k \leq M\}$
Output: Sequence

```
for Tasks do
    (r_j, m_k) ← t_i
    r_j.load ← sum(m_k.processTime)          ▷ Calculate total workload per resource
Resources ← orderBy(r_j.load, desc)          ▷ From max. to min.
Machines ← orderBy(m_k.processTime, desc)    ▷ From max. to min.
m ← first(Machines)
while Tasks ≠ ∅ do
    r ← next(Resources)                      ▷ Using Round-Robin
    t ← (r, m)
    if t ∈ Tasks then
        Sequence ← add(t)
        Tasks ← remove(t)
        m ← next(Machines)
    else
        for Machines do
            m ← next(Machines)               ▷ Using Round-Robin
            t ← (r, m)
            if t ∈ Tasks then
                Sequence ← add(t)
                Tasks ← remove(t)
return Sequence
```

Algorithm 2 NEH-based algorithm.

Input: Tasks = $\{t_i : i \leq T\}$, Resources = $\{r_j : j \leq R\}$, Machines = $\{m_k : k \leq M\}$
Output: Sequence

```
Combinations ← ∅
for t ∈ Tasks do                                      ▷ Split tasks into combinations
    Combinations(t.machine, t.resource) ← add(t)
SubSequences ← ∅
for c ∈ Combinations do                               ▷ Solve Combinations using NEH
    SortedTasks ← orderBy(c.totalTimes, desc)
    s ← HeuristicNEH(SortedTasks)
    SubSequences ← add(s)
SortedSequences ← orderBy(SubSequences.length, desc)
while SortedSequences ≠ ∅ do                          ▷ Combine Sub-Sequences
    for s ∈ SortedSequences do
        if s ≠ ∅ then
            t ← removeFirst(s)
            Sequence ← add(t)
return Sequence
```

4.3. Computational Experiment Instances

The computational experiments were conducted on a Windows 10 operating system, utilizing an i7-4500U CPU 2.40 GHz with 6 GB RAM. All algorithms were implemented using Python v3.8.10. Simul8 2022 version 29.0 was employed for the simulation model. To evaluate the efficacy of the various heuristic algorithms developed for AGV task scheduling, multiple problem instances were generated. Table 1 presents all instances used in this study along with their key characteristics. An instance is defined by the following factors: the number of workstations, the number of AGVs available, the number of tasks to be performed, the travel and processing times for each task, and the allocation of tasks to workstations and AGVs. In the following section, both the AGV travel time and the workstation process time will be referred to as "processing time". As a matter of fact, two distinct instance types were considered for each workstation–AGV–task combination regarding processing time. The first type features processing times, derived from a uniform random distribution, tightly centered around an average value, resulting in instances with low variability in processing times (LVPT). In contrast, the second type showcases a broader range between minimum and maximum processing times, leading to instances with high variability in processing times (HVPT). Similarly, for assigning tasks to workstation–AGV combinations, two instance types were created. The first type ensures a balanced assignment, resulting in low variability in the task assignment (LVTA) to each workstation–AGV combination. Conversely, the second type introduces an unbalanced assignment, causing some workstation–AGV combinations to handle more work than others, thereby leading to high variability in task assignments (HVTAs). Combining these characteristics results in the following four distinct instance types for assessing the performance of the algorithms: (i) low variability in processing times and low variability in task assignment (LVPT/LVTA); (ii) high variability in processing times and low variability in task assignment (HVPT/LVTA); (iii) low variability in processing times and high variability in task assignment (LVPT/HVTA); and (iv) high variability in processing times and task assignment (HVPT/HVTA).

Table 1. Instances for the computational experiments.

Instance	Workstations	AGVs	Tasks	Type
$m5r3t100$_01	5	3	100	LVPT/LVTA
$m5r3t100$_02	5	3	100	HVPT/LVTA
$m5r3t100$_03	5	3	100	LVPT/HVTA
$m5r3t100$_04	5	3	100	HVPT/HVTA
$m5r3t200$_01	5	3	200	LVPT/LVTA
$m5r3t200$_02	5	3	200	HVPT/LVTA
$m5r3t200$_03	5	3	200	LVPT/HVTA
$m5r3t200$_04	5	3	200	HVPT/HVTA
$m10r5t300$_01	10	5	300	LVPT/LVTA
$m10r5t300$_02	10	5	300	HVPT/LVTA
$m10r5t300$_03	10	5	300	LVPT/HVTA
$m10r5t300$_04	10	5	300	HVPT/HVTA
$m10r5t600$_01	10	5	600	LVPT/LVTA
$m10r5t600$_02	10	5	600	HVPT/LVTA
$m10r5t600$_03	10	5	600	LVPT/HVTA
$m10r5t600$_04	10	5	600	HVPT/HVTA
$m20r10t1200$_01	20	10	1200	LVPT/LVTA
$m20r10t1200$_02	20	10	1200	HVPT/LVTA
$m20r10t1200$_03	20	10	1200	LVPT/HVTA
$m20r10t1200$_04	20	10	1200	HVPT/HVTA

5. Results and Discussion

This section presents the numerical results obtained from the computational experiments, followed by an analysis and discussion of the obtained results. Table 2 includes the output of the simulation for each instance and for each of the heuristic algorithms considered. The first column identifies the instances, while subsequent columns show the total makespan required to complete all tasks within the instance. First, we present the results obtained from the NEH-based approach, reflecting the reference baseline to be used for comparison purposes. Following this, the rest of the columns in the table display the results for the various combinations of sequencing algorithms. Additionally, the average makespan is computed for each set of instances. Finally, the percentage gaps with respect to the NEH-based approach is provided as per the following:

$$Gap[\%] = \frac{C^{i}_{max} - C^{NEH}_{max}}{C^{NEH}_{max}} \times 100, \tag{5}$$

where C_{max} is the total makespan for each one of the i = {MLRF/LPTF, MLRF/SPTF, LLRF/SPTF, LLRF/LPTF} algorithms considered. At this point, it is of relevance to focus on those situations in which the sharing of resources results in inefficiencies for a given task sequence. The inefficiencies in the sequence occur when a task is supposed to start its processing but it has to first queue (a) because there is no AGV available for transportation or (b) because the workstation to which it is traveling is already occupied by a previous task. Let consider the case in which the resources are not shared among different AGV–workstation pairs, or in which there are sufficiently abundant resources to be shared between workstations. In the context of this study, these types of situations are considered as inefficiency-free scenarios. In these cases, the NEH-based approach is expected to perform extremely well and minimize the total makespan for the different sizes and types of instances. However, for the instances analyzed, the NEH-based approach yields the highest total makespan across almost all cases since it lacks a dedicated strategy for minimizing the overall makespan when resources are shared. It can be observed that all approaches presented in this work obtain better solutions than the NEH-based approach, as can be seen by the lower makespan values and negative percentage gaps. It should be noticed that the more negative the gap is, the more substantial the improvement in the makespan relative to the NEH-based strategy. This is attributed to the improved sequence, which minimizes the possible inefficiencies and, in turn, decreases the overall sequence makespan. Apart from the obvious increment in makespan as the size of the instance increases (a larger number of tasks requires more time for completion), the algorithm performance tends to improve with larger instances. For scenarios involving more AGVs, workstations, and tasks, the algorithm consistently yields better solutions in comparison to the baseline. This trend might be attributed to the limited potential for improvement in smaller instances, where altering task sequencing has minimal impact due to less scope for enhancement.

Regarding the different types of instances, it is noteworthy that the ones that exhibit significant variability in task assignment (HVTA) result in an imbalanced usage of the system resources (the AGVs and workstations), meaning that some resources tend to have more tasks assigned to them than other resources. In turn, a lower number of interactions between the AGVs and workstations occurs in the system, and the NEH-based algorithm is able to obtain solutions that have an acceptable performance. On the other hand, instances with low variability in task assignment (LVTA) tend to result in a higher number of interactions between shared resources, in which the proposal algorithm performs better, as observed in the comparatively larger percentage gaps. One extreme case of this situation is depicted in the results obtained for the instance *m5r3t100_04*, which had a high variability in processing times and task assignment. Notably, the NEH-based approach outperformed our proposed algorithms, obtaining percentage gaps between 4.09% and 7.42%. After a comprehensive examination of the instance in the simulation, we observed that most tasks were assigned to a particular workstation–AGV combination. Subsequently, the number of interactions due to the sharing of resource was significantly low. Thus, the NEH heuristic was able to construct a high-quality sequence for that combination that minimized the makespan, and, in turn, built a better task sequence than our proposed methods.

The observed pattern suggests that our proposed algorithms are less effective when high variability is present in task assignment, meaning that the resources are not uniformly shared but assigned in an unbalanced way, as described in Section 4.3. Interestingly, this phenomenon is not encountered in the largest set of instances. This can be attributed to the increase in the number of tasks compared to the increase in number of AGVs and workstations. As the number of tasks increases, the variability in task assignment tends to be mitigated due to a higher number of tasks available for sequencing. Hence, the interaction between resources tend to take place regardless of the level of variability in task assignment. These results point toward a promising scalability of our proposed methodology, especially when dealing with a substantial number of tasks in an environment with shared resources. Additionally, it appears that the algorithm performance also diminishes in instances characterized by high variability in processing times (HVPT). This could be explained by the inefficiencies imposed by exceptionally large processing times for certain workstations, leading to unavoidable queues and subsequently reducing the efficacy of sequence alterations. The boxplot depicted in Figure 6 illustrates the average percentage gaps observed for the MLRF/LPTF, MLRF/SPTF, LLRF/SPTF, and LLRF/LPTF strategies in comparison to the NEH-based approach. As indicated in Section 4.2, the NEH-based approach was selected as the reference baseline for assessing other strategies, as its performance can be considered at the state-of-the-art level, at least in scenarios without resource sharing interactions. Hence, the NEH-based heuristic can help when evaluating the relative performance of alternative strategies. Notice that the average percentage gap consistently fell below zero, indicating an improvement in the average makespan compared to the NEH-based approach across all instances, where the average percentage gaps ranged between −16.82% and −19.49%. The large gap with respect to the NEH-based approach suggests that the improvement could be due to the round-robin sequencing rather than due to the combination of different sorting algorithms for the AGVs and workstations. The conclusion is that, for situations in which resource sharing becomes critical for the application, the balancing of resources is more important than the quality of the sequencing for a given stream of work. In the case presented, the combination of simple sequencing strategies outperforms the NEH algorithm when naively used in a context in which resources are limited and have to be shared among different streams of work.

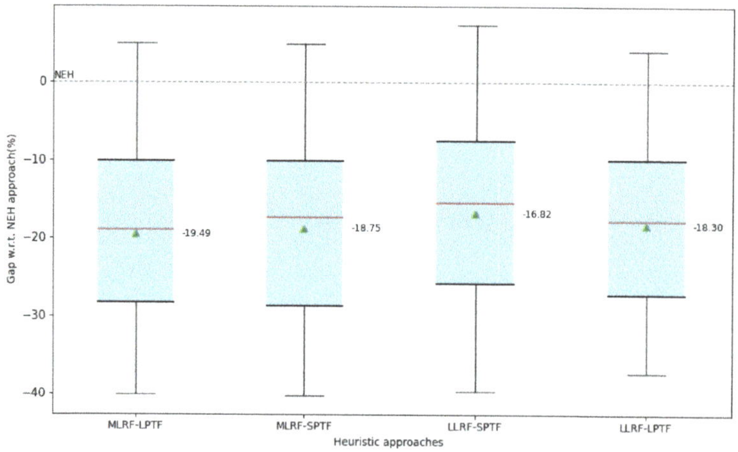

Figure 6. Boxplot of the gaps of different heuristic approaches with respect to the NEH approach. The red line indicates the median and the green triangle the mean of the data set.

Table 2. Results of the computational experiments in terms of the total makespan and percentage gap with respect to the NEH strategy.

Instance	NEH	MLRF/LPTF	Gap (%)	MLRF/SPTF	Gap (%)	LLRF/SPTF	Gap (%)	LLRF/LPTF	Gap (%)
*m*5*r*3*t*100_01	6594	5248	−20.41%	5377	−18.46%	5480	−16.89%	5310	−19.47%
*m*5*r*3*t*100_02	6838	5674	−17.02%	6061	−11.36%	6414	−6.20%	5536	−19.04%
*m*5*r*3*t*100_03	8644	8125	−6.00%	8115	−6.12%	8568	−0.88%	8277	−4.25%
*m*5*r*3*t*100_04	8688	9121	4.98%	9115	4.91%	9333	7.42%	9043	4.09%
Average:	7691	7042	−9.61%	7167	−7.76%	7448.75	−4.14%	7041.50	−9.67%
*m*5*r*3*t*200_01	13,818	9752	−29.43%	10,090	−26.98%	10,405	−24.70%	9946	−28.02%
*m*5*r*3*t*200_02	14,761	11,016	−25.37%	11,509	−22.03%	11,895	−19.42%	11,350	−23.11%
*m*5*r*3*t*200_03	16,896	14,528	−14.02%	14,623	−13.45%	15,048	−10.94%	14,921	−11.69%
*m*5*r*3*t*200_04	17,236	15,986	−7.25%	16,410	−4.79%	16,607	−3.65%	16,402	−4.84%
Average:	15,677.75	12,820.50	−19.02%	13,158	−16.81%	13,488.75	−14.68%	13,154.75	−16.91%
*m*10*r*5*t*300_01	14,966	11,249	−24.84%	10,613	−29.09%	11,866	−20.71%	10,918	−27.05%
*m*10*r*5*t*300_02	14,719	11,393	−22.60%	11,786	−19.93%	12,243	−16.82%	12,226	−16.94%
*m*10*r*5*t*300_03	24,557	22,198	−9.61%	22,438	−8.63%	22,589	−8.01%	22,453	−8.57%
*m*10*r*5*t*300_04	23,817	21,690	−8.93%	21,828	−8.35%	22,546	−5.34%	21,905	−8.03%
Average:	19,514.75	16,632.50	−16.49%	16,666.25	−16.50%	17,311	−12.72%	16,875.50	−15.15%
*m*10*r*5*t*600_01	36,203	23,095	−36.21%	22,665	−37.39%	22,094	−38.97%	24,633	−31.96%
*m*10*r*5*t*600_02	36,759	26,424	−28.12%	25,766	−29.91%	25,414	−30.86%	26,826	−27.02%
*m*10*r*5*t*600_03	53,791	47,427	−11.83%	47,565	−11.57%	47,684	−11.35%	47,628	−11.46%
*m*10*r*5*t*600_04	54,801	49,184	−10.25%	48,980	−10.62%	49,037	−10.52%	49,149	−10.31%
Average:	45,388.50	36,532.50	−21.60%	36,244	−22.37%	36,057.25	−22.93%	37,059	−20.19%
*m*20*r*10*t*1200_01	52,242	31,338	−40.01%	31,198	−40.28%	31503	−39.70%	32,768	−37.28%
*m*20*r*10*t*1200_02	54,533	38,646	−29.13%	38,945	−28.58%	37,442	−31.34%	37,821	−30.65%
*m*20*r*10*t*1200_03	75,115	45,027	−40.06%	45,039	−40.04%	47,707	−36.49%	47,524	−36.73%
*m*20*r*10*t*1200_04	78,231	54,280	−30.62%	55,022	−29.67%	55,259	−29.36%	54,306	−30.58%
Average:	65,030.25	42,322.75	−34.95%	42,551	−34.64%	42,977.75	−34.22%	43,104.75	−33.81%

In detail, the approaches that give priority to the most loaded resource (MLRF/LPTF and MLRF/SPTF) seem to give as good or even better results compared to the other two approaches. This can be attributed to the way the studied benchmark instances are specified, as the number of AGVs is always lower than the number of workstations. Thus, the most important resource to take into account when generating an improved sequence of tasks is to consider the process times in the AGVs in order to prioritize the most loaded ones. Moreover, the strategies that prioritize workstations with longer processing times (LPTF) also tend to perform very well since they prevent excessive workstation occupancy during the later stages of task processing. Thus, sequences favoring the LPTF strategy over SPTF exhibit lower percentage gaps, underscoring its effectiveness across nearly all instances. The MLRF/LPTF algorithm emerges as the most effective sequencing heuristic for addressing the proposed problem. As already discussed, its superiority primarily stems from the fact that it strategically places the most heavily utilized AGVs and most loaded workstations at the beginning of the sequencing, thereby mitigating potential queue formations and inefficiencies that might arise later in the process.

6. Conclusions

This study addressed the complex challenge of optimizing task sequencing within manufacturing environments. The primary objective was to minimize the total production time, also known as the makespan, by determining the most efficient order for executing tasks assigned to AGVs and workstations. The methodology proposed in this study employed a two-step process integrating heuristic algorithms and simulation techniques. The heuristics were designed to generate high-quality candidate sequences considering resource utilization, task assignment, and processing times. Simul8, a discrete-event simulation software, was utilized to model the complex queuing dynamics arising from the AGV task sequencing, providing a robust evaluation framework for the proposed sequencing strategies. From the developed heuristic algorithms, MLRF/LPTF emerged as a superior strategy for task sequencing. This algorithm strategically prioritized the most loaded AGVs and workstations with the highest processing times, resulting in substantial improvements in the makespan compared to the default sequencing strategy, which was based on the well-known NEH algorithm. The performance of the proposed algorithms demonstrated consistent enhancements, especially for larger instances, emphasizing their effectiveness in improving AGV task sequencing efficiency in the context of limited and shared resources. Nonetheless, the analysis revealed a correlation between the variability in the task assignment and processing times, as well as in the algorithms' performance. Instances characterized by high variability exhibited reduced improvement potential due to dominating factors such as non-uniformly load machines with very long processing times, thus limiting the algorithms' effectiveness.

Building upon the insights gained from this study, several research lines emerge. A future line of research that naturally extends from this study involves the development of a stochastic version of the presented problem. This stochastic behavior can be achieved by transforming the fixed task/activity process times into random variables selected from specific probability distributions, such as log-normal or Weibull distributions. This direction benefits from the methodology established in this study, where the evaluation of the final scheduling utilizes a discrete-event simulator like Simul8. Leveraging such a simulator enables the realistic simulation of dynamic queues resulting from stochastic processing times. Furthermore, enhancing the interaction between the algorithmic component and simulation could allow for more integrated simulation–optimization frameworks, often referred to as simheuristics [35,47]. This integration holds promise for efficiently deriving high-quality and robust solutions that consider the stochastic nature inherent in warehouse and production processes. Another research line could involve extending the constructive heuristics into biased-randomized algorithms [48] capable of providing enhanced results, and also utilizing the simulation developed in this study as an environment for a reinforcement learning agent. Such an agent could learn optimal sequencing policies by being dynamically based on the current production state. By adapting to queues and resource sharing in a changing environment, the agent could propose improved sequencing strategies over time. Finally, investigating the scalability and applicability of the developed heuristic algorithms to diverse industrial scenarios could be an area for further investigation.

Author Contributions: Conceptualization, J.F.L. and A.A.J.; methodology, J.F.L.; validation, J.F.L., M.P. and X.A.M.; writing—original draft preparation, J.F.L., M.P. and X.A.M.; writing—review and editing, J.F.L. and A.A.J.; supervision, J.F.L. and A.A.J. All authors have read and agreed to the published version of the manuscript.

Funding: This work was supported by the European Commission (AIDEAS HORIZON-CL4-2021-TWIN-TRANSITION-01-07-101057294 and SUN HORIZON-CL4-2022-HUMAN-01-14-101092612), Simul8, Spindox, AGAUR (2020-DI-116), and the Spanish Ministry of Science and Innovation (PRE2020-091842).

Data Availability Statement: The data presented in this study are available on request from the corresponding author.

Conflicts of Interest: Author J.F.L. was employed by the company Spindox España S.L. The remaining authors declare that the research was conducted in the absence of any commercial or financial relationships that could be construed as a potential conflict of interest.

References

1. Klingenberg, C.O.; Borges, M.A.V.; Antunes, J.A.d.V. Industry 4.0: What makes it a revolution? A historical framework to understand the phenomenon. *Technol. Soc.* **2022**, *70*, 102009. [CrossRef]
2. Bechtsis, D.; Tsolakis, N.; Vlachos, D.; Iakovou, E. Sustainable supply chain management in the digitalisation era: The impact of Automated Guided Vehicles. *J. Clean. Prod.* **2017**, *142*, 3970–3984. [CrossRef]
3. Salkin, C.; Oner, M.; Ustundag, A.; Cevikcan, E. A Conceptual Framework for Industry 4.0. In *Industry 4.0: Managing The Digital Transformation*; Ustundag, A., Cevikcan, E., Eds.; Springer Series in Advanced Manufacturing; Springer International Publishing: Cham, Switzerland, 2018; pp. 3–23.
4. Vis, I.F.A. Survey of research in the design and control of automated guided vehicle systems. *Eur. J. Oper. Res.* **2006**, *170*, 677–709. [CrossRef]
5. Ruiz, R. Scheduling Heuristics. In *Handbook of Heuristics*; Martí, R., Pardalos, P.M., Resende, M.G.C., Eds.; Springer International Publishing: Cham, Switzerland, 2018; pp. 1197–1220.
6. Vivaldini, K.C.T.; Rocha, L.F.; Becker, M.; Moreira, A.P. Comprehensive Review of the Dispatching, Scheduling and Routing of AGVs. In Proceedings of the CONTROLO'2014—Proceedings of the 11th Portuguese Conference on Automatic Control, Porto, Portugal, 21–23 July 2014 ; Moreira, A.P.; Matos, A.; Veiga, G., Eds.; Lecture Notes in Electrical Engineering; Springer: Cham, Switzerland, 2015; pp. 505–514.
7. Alatartsev, S.; Stellmacher, S.; Ortmeier, F. Robotic Task Sequencing Problem: A Survey. *J. Intell. Robot. Syst.* **2015**, *80*, 279–298. [CrossRef]
8. Blazewicz, J.; Lenstra, J.K.; Kan, A.H.G.R. Scheduling subject to resource constraints: Classification and complexity. *Discret. Appl. Math.* **1983**, *5*, 11–24. [CrossRef]
9. Pinedo, M.L. Modeling and Solving Scheduling Problems in Practice. In *Scheduling: Theory, Algorithms, and Systems*; Pinedo, M.L., Ed.; Springer International Publishing: Cham, Switzerland, 2016; pp. 431–458.
10. Leon, J.F.; Marone, P.; Peyman, M.; Li, Y.; Calvet, L.; Dehghanimohammadabadi, M.; Juan, A.A. A Tutorial on Combining Flexsim with Python for Developing Discrete-Event Simheuristics. In Proceedings of the 2022 Winter Simulation Conference (WSC), Singapore, 11–14 December 2022; pp. 1386–1400.
11. Fransen, K.; van Eekelen, J. Efficient path planning for automated guided vehicles using A*(Astar) algorithm incorporating turning costs in search heuristic. *Int. J. Prod. Res.* **2023**, *61*, 707–725. [CrossRef]
12. Pratissoli, F.; Battilani, N.; Fantuzzi, C.; Sabattini, L. Hierarchical and Flexible Traffic Management of Multi-AGV Systems Applied to Industrial Environments. In Proceedings of the 2021 IEEE International Conference on Robotics and Automation (ICRA), Xi'an, China, 30 May–5 June 2021; pp. 10009–10015.
13. Vlachos, I.; Pascazzi, R.M.; Ntotis, M.; Spanaki, K.; Despoudi, S.; Repoussis, P. Smart and flexible manufacturing systems using Autonomous Guided Vehicles (AGVs) and the Internet of Things (IoT). *Int. J. Prod. Res.* **2022**, 1 –22. [CrossRef]
14. Reis, W.P.N.d.; Couto, G.E.; Junior, O.M. Automated guided vehicles position control: A systematic literature review. *J. Intell. Manuf.* **2023**, *34*, 1483–1545. [CrossRef]
15. Oyekanlu, E.A.; Smith, A.C.; Thomas, W.P.; Mulroy, G.; Hitesh, D.; Ramsey, M.; Kuhn, D.J.; Mcghinnis, J.D.; Buonavita, S.C.; Looper, N.A.; et al. A Review of Recent Advances in Automated Guided Vehicle Technologies: Integration Challenges and Research Areas for 5G-Based Smart Manufacturing Applications. *IEEE Access* **2020**, *8*, 202312–202353. [CrossRef]

16. Kim, K.H.; Bae, J.W. A Look-Ahead Dispatching Method for Automated Guided Vehicles in Automated Port Container Terminals. *Transp. Sci.* **2004**, *38*, 224–234. [CrossRef]
17. Li, G.; Li, X.; Gao, L.; Zeng, B. Tasks assigning and sequencing of multiple AGVs based on an improved harmony search algorithm. *J. Ambient. Intell. Humaniz. Comput.* **2019**, *10*, 4533–4546. [CrossRef]
18. Zou, W.Q.; Pan, Q.K.; Meng, T.; Gao, L.; Wang, Y.L. An effective discrete artificial bee colony algorithm for multi-AGVs dispatching problem in a matrix manufacturing workshop. *Expert Syst. Appl.* **2020**, *161*, 113675. [CrossRef]
19. Hari, S.K.K.; Nayak, A.; Rathinam, S. An Approximation Algorithm for a Task Allocation, Sequencing and Scheduling Problem Involving a Human-Robot Team. *IEEE Robot. Autom. Lett.* **2020**, *5*, 2146–2153. [CrossRef]
20. Dike, S.H. Project scheduling with resource constraints. *IEEE Trans. Eng. Manag.* **1964**, *EM-11*, 155–157. [CrossRef]
21. Ding, H.; Zhuang, C.; Liu, J. Extensions of the resource-constrained project scheduling problem. *Autom. Constr.* **2023**, *153*, 104958. [CrossRef]
22. Van Eynde, R.; Vanhoucke, M. Resource-constrained multi-project scheduling: Benchmark datasets and decoupled scheduling. *J. Sched.* **2020**, *23*, 301–325. [CrossRef]
23. Hartman, S.; Briskorn, D. A survey of variants and extensions of the resource-constrained project scheduling problem. *Oper. Res. Manag. Sci.* **2011**, *51*, 67.
24. van der Beek, T.; Souravlias, D.; van Essen, J.; Pruyn, J.; Aardal, K. Hybrid differential evolution algorithm for the resource constrained project scheduling problem with a flexible project structure and consumption and production of resources. *Eur. J. Oper. Res.* **2023**, *313* , 92–111. [CrossRef]
25. Maimon, O. The robot task-sequencing planning problem. *IEEE Trans. Robot. Autom.* **1990**, *6*, 760–765. [CrossRef]
26. Suárez-Ruiz, F.; Lembono, T.S.; Pham, Q.C. Robotsp—A fast solution to the robotic task sequencing problem. In Proceedings of the 2018 IEEE International Conference on Robotics and Automation (ICRA), Brisbane, Australia, 21–25 May 2018; pp. 1611–1616.
27. Li, D.; Wang, Q.; Zou, W.; Su, H.; Wang, X.; Xu, X. An Efficient Approach for Solving Robotic Task Sequencing Problems Considering Spatial Constraint. In Proceedings of the 2022 IEEE 18th International Conference on Automation Science and Engineering (CASE), Mexico City, Mexico, 20–24 August 2022; pp. 60–66.
28. Chen, C.H.; Chou, F.I.; Chou, J.H. Optimization of robotic task sequencing problems by crowding evolutionary algorithms. *IEEE Trans. Syst. Man Cybern. Syst.* **2021**, *52*, 6870–6885. [CrossRef]
29. Li, H.; Liu, S.Y.; Huang, Y.W.; Chen, Y.Q.; Fu, Z.H. An Efficient 2-opt Operator for the Robotic Task Sequencing Problem. In Proceedings of the 2019 IEEE International Conference on Real-time Computing and Robotics (RCAR), Irkutsk, Russia, 4–9 August 2019; pp. 124–129.
30. Martin, X.A.; Hatami, S.; Calvet, L.; Peyman, M.; Juan, A.A. Dynamic Reactive Assignment of Tasks in Real-Time Automated Guided Vehicle Environments with Potential Interruptions. *Appl. Sci.* **2023**, *13*, 3708. [CrossRef]
31. Korsah, G.A.; Stentz, A.; Dias, M.B. A comprehensive taxonomy for multi-robot task allocation. *Int. J. Robot. Res.* **2013**, *32*, 1495–1512. [CrossRef]
32. Khamis, A.; Hussein, A.; Elmogy, A. Multi-robot task allocation: A review of the state-of-the-art. In *Cooperative Robots and Sensor Networks 2015*; Springer, Cham, Switzerland , 2015; pp. 31–51.
33. Alshaboti, M.; Baroudi, U. Multi-robot task allocation system: Fuzzy auction-based and adaptive multi-threshold approaches. *SN Comput. Sci.* **2021**, *2*, 1–11. [CrossRef]
34. Chakraa, H.; Guérin, F.; Leclercq, E.; Lefebvre, D. Optimization techniques for Multi-Robot Task Allocation problems: Review on the state-of-the-art. *Robot. Auton. Syst.* **2023**, p. 104492. [CrossRef]
35. Leon, J.F.; Li, Y.; Peyman, M.; Calvet, L.; Juan, A.A. A Discrete-Event Simheuristic for Solving a Realistic Storage Location Assignment Problem. *Mathematics* **2023**, *11*, 1577. [CrossRef]
36. López, J.; Zalama, E.; Gómez-García-Bermejo, J. A simulation and control framework for AGV based transport systems. *Simul. Model. Pract. Theory* **2022**, *116*, 102430. [CrossRef]
37. Inoue, K. Discrete-Event Simulation for Autonomous Guided Vehicle. *IFAC Proc. Vol.* **2001**, *34*, 87–92. [CrossRef]
38. bin Md Fauadi, M.H.F.; Li, W.L.; Murata, T.; Prabuwono, A.S. Vehicle requirement analysis of an AGV system using discrete-event simulation and data envelopment analysis. In Proceedings of the 2012 8th International Conference on Computing Technology and Information Management (NCM and ICNIT), Seoul, Republic of Korea, 24–26 April 2012; Volume 2, pp. 819–823.
39. Kühn, M.; Schmidt, T.; Völker, M. Simulation-Based Optimization Approach for Efficient Generation of Sequencing Heuristics for Solving the Stochastic Resource-Constrained Scheduling Problem. In *Proceedings of the Simulation in Produktion und Logistik*; Kassel University Press: Kassel, Germany, 2019; pp. 403–412.
40. Azimi, P.; Sholekar, S. A simulation optimization approach for the multi-objective multi-mode resource constraint project scheduling problem. *Int. J. Ind. Eng. Prod. Res* **2021**, *32*, 37–45.
41. Kesen, S.E.; Baykoç, O.F. Simulation of automated guided vehicle (AGV) systems based on just-in-time (JIT) philosophy in a job-shop environment. *Simul. Model. Pract. Theory* **2007**, *15*, 272–284. [CrossRef]
42. Chen, J.C.; Chen, T.L.; Teng, Y.C. Meta-model based simulation optimization for automated guided vehicle system under different charging mechanisms. *Simul. Model. Pract. Theory* **2021**, *106*, 102208. [CrossRef]
43. Viana, J.; Brailsford, S.C.; Harindra, V.; Harper, P.R. Combining discrete-event simulation and system dynamics in a healthcare setting: A composite model for Chlamydia infection. *Eur. J. Oper. Res.* **2014**, *237*, 196–206. [CrossRef]

44. Mensah, P.; Merkuryev, Y.; Longo, F. Using ICT in Developing a Resilient Supply Chain Strategy. *Procedia Comput. Sci.* **2015**, *43*, 101–108. [CrossRef]
45. Wales, J.; Marinov, M. Analysis of delays and delay mitigation on a metropolitan rail network using event based simulation. *Simul. Model. Pract. Theory* **2015**, *52*, 52–77. [CrossRef]
46. Nawaz, M.; Enscore, E.E., Jr.; Ham, I. A heuristic algorithm for the m-machine, n-job flow-shop sequencing problem. *Omega* **1983**, *11*, 91–95. [CrossRef]
47. Hatami, S.; Calvet, L.; Fernández-Viagas, V.; Framinan, J.M.; Juan, A.A. A simheuristic algorithm to set up starting times in the stochastic parallel flowshop problem. *Simul. Model. Pract. Theory* **2018**, *86*, 55–71. [CrossRef]
48. Dominguez, O.; Juan, A.A.; Faulin, J. A biased-randomized algorithm for the two-dimensional vehicle routing problem with and without item rotations. *Int. Trans. Oper. Res.* **2014**, *21*, 375–398. [CrossRef]

mathematics

Article

REFS-A Risk Evaluation Framework on Supply Chain

István Mihálcz and Zsolt T. Kosztyán *

Department of Quantitative Methods, Institute of Management, Faculty of Business and Economics, University of Pannonia, Egyetem u. 10., 8200 Veszprem, Hungary; istvan.mihalcz@uniturn.hu
* Correspondence: kzst@gtk.uni-pannon.hu

Abstract: Large, powerful corporations were formerly solely and exclusively responsible for supplies, manufacturing, and distribution; however, the supply chain has undergone significant transformations over the last half-century. Almost all supply chain processes are currently outsourced, owing to the initiatives of cutting-edge, contemporary businesses. According to a compilation of studies, analysts, and news sources, the level of risk associated with modern supply chains is considerably higher than the majority of supply chain managers believe. Supply chain vulnerabilities continue to pose a substantial obstacle for a great number of organizations. Neglecting to adequately address these risks—encompassing natural disasters, cyber assaults, acts of terrorism, the credit crisis, pandemic scenarios, and war—could result in substantial reductions in metrics such as profitability, productivity, revenue, and competitive advantage. Unresolved concerns persist with respect to the risk assessment of the supply chain. The purpose of this article is to propose a framework for risk evaluation that can be efficiently applied to the evaluation of hazards within the supply chain. This research study significantly enhances the existing knowledge base by offering supply chain managers a pragmatic tool to evaluate their processes, regardless of the mathematical foundations or the variety of variables utilized in risk assessment. The outcomes of multiple aggregation methods are compared using a case study from an automotive EMS production; the conclusions are validated by risk and FMEA specialists from the same factory.

Keywords: supply chain; FMEA; new FMEA; risk evaluation framework; TREF; fuzzy FMEA

MSC: 26A48

1. Introduction

In the past decade, numerous organizations have incurred expenses amounting to hundreds of millions of dollars or euros due to unforeseen disruptions and weaknesses in their supply chains. At the heart of these problems is the absence of dependable mechanisms to identify and effectively mitigate the escalating supply chain risks that result from increased global interconnectedness. As a consequence, the evaluation of supply chain risk is progressively gaining importance. There has been an exponential increase in the quantity of risk analysis papers published since the beginning of the century [1]. Considering the number of scholarly articles dedicated to the most widely used risk analysis techniques and pragmatic implementations of FMEA in diverse domains, the supply chain would rank last on this list [1]. Notwithstanding this, a multitude of concerns pertaining to the FMEA methodology continue to be unresolved in the recently published FMEA (released in [2]). In regard to supply chain risk analysis, uncharted territories still remain.

The evaluation and selection of suppliers are critical components of the supply chain. Dickson established the initial classification system in 1966 [3], and Cheraghi subsequently revised it in 2011 [4]. Huang et al. [1] published a systematic literature review in 2021 that demonstrates the exponential growth of risk analysis publications over the past two decades. Keyword analysis reveals that "FMEA", "system", "risk evaluation", "criticality analysis", and "failure mode" have risen to prominent positions. Similar findings were published by Liu et al. [5] in 2013. It can be concluded that the FMEA continues to be the most widely utilized tool for risk assessment; however, it is presently employed in conjunction with alternative evaluation approaches [1,5].

Multiple authors [6–8] have examined the reasons behind the limited use of FMEA and other risk analysis methods in the supply chain. The researchers conducted an analysis and successfully identified the main factors: the main difficulty impeding wider deployment appears to arise from a lack of understanding of how to apply FMEA within a supply chain environment.

Numerous scholarly articles have highlighted the limitations of the FMEA [5,9–11]. As a result, the FMEA was revised through a collaborative effort between AIAG and VDA. The AIAG-VDA FMEA 1st Edition, a novel FMEA framework, was published in the year 2019 [2]. The recent update to the system includes the addition of a chapter titled "Monitoring and System Response". In this update, the Risk Priority Number (RPN) has been replaced with Action Priority Tables. Furthermore, a comprehensive approach consisting of seven steps, namely: planning, structure analysis, function analysis, failure analysis, risk analysis, optimization, and documentation of results has been implemented. The utilization of the Severity (S), Occurrence (O), and Detection (D) scales persists, and it is advisable for the team to evaluate them in a manner consistent with a conventional FMEA. The utilization of the Action Priority Level, which is determined based on the values of the S, O, and D components from a designated Action Priority (AP) Table, has replaced the use of RPN. The suggested table for AP levels is derived from the values assigned to the components S, O, and D. However, it is subject to modification based on factors such as the nature of the business, the specific process, or the industry involved. The AP table delineates the instances in which the organization is authorized to initiate action, as opposed to the responsibility falling upon the FMEA Team. No action is required for Low AP levels, while any lack of action for Medium AP levels should be adequately justified. In the case of High AP levels, immediate action must be taken to mitigate the risk. This suggests that instead of relying on the RPN value, the actions are selected based on the specific values of the factors. Regrettably, as demonstrated in Table A6, the current system is incapable of accurately discerning the actual amount of risk.

It may be inferred from the existing body of research that the supply chain industry uses **risk analysis methods** that closely resemble those employed in various other domains. The authors exclusively employ the FMEA [12–14] assessment technique, or a modified version of FMEA with factors limited to 5 levels instead of 10 [15]. Alternatively, they utilize mixed evaluation techniques such as Fuzzy-FMEA [11,16–19], Fuzzy-AHP [20,21], FMEA-ANP [22], or Fuzzy Bayesian-based FMEA [14]. Fuzzy FMEA [19] is considered the second most often utilized risk analysis technique, following the FMEA method. The three membership functions commonly utilized in Fuzzy FMEA are triangular, trapezoidal, and Gaussian [23–25].

The conventional approach for assessing supply chain risk predominantly involves employing the FMEA framework, which incorporates three key **factors:** Severity, Occurrence, and Detection. A limited number of authors argue against the adequacy of three factors and instead propose the utilization of models that incorporate either four (expense, time, flexibility, and quality) [26] or five (likelihood, consequence of time/delay, consequence of additional expense, consequence of damage to quality, and visibility) [27] factors. In the present case, commonly employed variables were assessed, namely Visibility and Consequence, with the latter being determined by the provider's delay, the cost associated with the supplier, and the quality of the given components.

In the context of supply chain risk analysis, **new factors** have emerged, such as Quality, Time, Cost [14,26], Intensity [13], Consequence [8], Effect, Cause, Measure [28], and others.

The multiplication aggregation function remains the most commonly employed way for analyzing the usage of aggregation functions [6–8,21,28]. The second approach integrates Fuzzy analysis with FMEA [11,16,17,20].

Organizations, irrespective of their business, are clearly susceptible to both internal and external threats that might disrupt their supply chain. This document provides a limited selection of illustrative examples instead of a comprehensive collection of all possible failures. A preliminary example was created at the manufacturing facility where the case study was conducted and is represented by the subsequent enumeration. The framework integrates perspectives obtained from comprehensive industry expertise, audit results from both internal and external sources, instructor lectures during educational sessions, analysis of current events, and customer queries. Similar works published by subsequent authors [29–32] further contributed to the expansion of our knowledge and were duly incorporated into our knowledge base.

Internal supply chain interruption can potentially arise due to:

- Instances of internal operational disruptions;
- Instances of significant management, staff, and operational procedure changes;
- Instances of failure to implement contingency plans in response to problems;
- Instances of inadequate implementation of cybersecurity policies and controls leading to cyberattacks and data breaches;
- Instances of non-compliance with labor laws or environmental standards;
- Instances of unavailability of products to meet customer demands (attributable to inventory issues, ERP system malfunctions, human errors, etc.).

The external supply chain risk might arise due to factors such as:

- Unpredictable or misunderstood consumer demand;
- Delays in the transportation and distribution of commodities, encompassing many types such as components, finished products, and raw materials;
- The potential risks posed by terrorism, armed conflict, economic or political penalties, as well as social, governmental, and economic challenges;
- The management of supplier risk includes concerns regarding the physical infrastructure and regulatory compliance of a supplier;
- Natural disasters, such as tornadoes, hurricanes, floods, droughts, landslides, and earthquakes;
- Human errors occur at all levels and in all locations.

The above list serves as an exemplification of the types of factors that ought to be taken into account; nevertheless, they should be considered in light of the region's past supply chain issues, trends, and potential challenges.

In summary, a pertinent, functional, and adaptable instrument for performing supply network risk assessment is currently non-existent. It is imperative that supply chain managers and risk analysts have easy access to this instrument, considering the aforementioned activities and global developments that have an impact on the supply chain. The forthcoming instrument ought to enhance its efficacy in discerning credible threats, encompass a more extensive spectrum of risk factors surpassing the present three boundaries, and uphold a degree of user-friendliness comparable to that of the conventional FMEA methodology.

To put constraints aside, it is frequently necessary to monitor a great number of factors; thus, a risk evaluation framework was developed in accordance with these concepts. It was also considered that numerous authors attempted to utilize alternative aggregation methods, such as Euclidean, multiplicative, additive, median, or other functions. Alternatively, they attempted to integrate FMEA with AHP, ANP, TOPSIS, or other methodologies, frequently employing Fuzzy logic. Combining the aforementioned, the TREF method was developed [33,34] in response to these articles. TREF now was expanded to include a Fuzzy-FMEA function with multiple factors. The issue at hand pertains to the optimal aggregating function. This is an attempt to be answered in the article.

This article in Section 1 conducts an extensive literature review on techniques for managing risks in supply chains and provides a concise overview of the many types and levels of factors that are taken into account. Section 2 of the article explores further methods of aggregating several risk factors, namely more than three, by expanding on the commonly used Failure Mode and Effects Analysis (FMEA) as a fundamental framework. The framework is improved by integrating the Fuzzy-FMEA methodology. Furthermore, this study undertakes a comparative analysis of various risk analysis methodologies within the context of the flexible TREF-based risk evaluation framework. The techniques are graded using the TOPSIS algorithm in the following manner. Section 3 provides a clear set of instructions for effectively putting the concept into practice. Section 4 presents a case study that examines the analysis of supply chain risks in an automotive manufacturing service organization as a Tier 2 supplier. Section 5 provides an exposition of the findings obtained from this case study.

2. Mathematical Background

Several authors acknowledged in the preceding chapter that three factors are insufficient for a comprehensive risk assessment. As the number of factors increases, the aggregation function becomes more intriguing. The same limitations that are evident in the FMEA become apparent when employing multiplicative aggregation, which is the same logic as the aggregation function in the FMEA. As a result, the research investigates the criteria that define an aggregation function, the various types of aggregation functions that can be employed, and the benefits and drawbacks of these functions in the context of risk assessment.

2.1. Aggregation Functions Criteria

In the study conducted by the authors in [35–37], various aggregating functions were examined. Aggregation functions necessitate several conditions [38,39], including validity, monotonicity, sensitivity, symmetricity, linearity, scale fit, and scale endpoint identity.

- Validity: Consider the manner in which the risk emanates from the constituents.

$$F : \mathbb{I}^n \to \mathbb{R}; \quad x \in \mathbb{I}^n; \quad a, b \in \mathbb{R}; \quad F(x) = a, \text{ and } \quad F(x) = b \Rightarrow a = b \tag{1}$$

- Monotonicity: refers to the property of a function where it exhibits non-decreasing behavior, meaning that it yields a non-negative reaction to any increase in its arguments. In other words, the function does not reduce its output value when any input value is increased.

$$F : \mathbb{I}^n \to \mathbb{R} \quad x, x' \in \mathbb{I}^n, \quad x \geq x' \Rightarrow F(x) \geq F(x') \tag{2}$$

  The membership functions and the defuzzification function employed in this study exhibit monotonic characteristics.
- Sensitivity refers to the degree of responsiveness or reactivity exhibited in a certain context. In the specific scenario of rigorous monotonicity, sensitivity pertains to the extent to which a change in one variable directly and consistently influences a change in another variable.

$$F : \mathbb{I}^n \to \mathbb{R} \quad i \in [n] \quad F(x) \neq F(x + \lambda) \quad x \in \mathbb{I}, \quad \lambda \neq 0 \quad x + \lambda \in \mathbb{I} \tag{3}$$

- The property of symmetricity, also known as commutativity, is true when the components or elements of a distribution follow a symmetric distribution. In such cases, the distribution of the aggregated values also exhibits symmetry. This property is also observed in the Fuzzy functions employed.

$$F : \mathbb{I}^n \to \mathbb{R} \quad F(x) = F(|x|) \tag{4}$$

- Linearity refers to the property where, in the scenario of components or factors adhering to a uniform distribution, the resulting distribution of the aggregated values will also exhibit uniformity.

- Scale fitting: The aggregate processes should be conducted using the scale values that have been applied. This criterion is also met as the range of each factor is identical.
- Scale endpoint identity: In order to adhere to the boundary criteria, the endpoints of the scales were modified to fall within the interval [1, 10]. This adjustment was important as it ensured that each factor's potential values were defined within the same range.

2.2. Risk Aggregation Functions

Definition 1. *Let* $\mathbf{f} = [f_1, f_2, \ldots, f_n]^T$, $(n \geq 3, n \in \mathbb{N})$ *be the vector representing the set of risk factors. Let* $r = S(\mathbf{f})$ *represent the* ***resulting risk value****, where S is a monotonous aggregation function. The* ***risk aggregation protocol*** *(RAP) is denoted as* $(\mathbf{f}, S)$.

Remark 1. *It is commonly assumed that the risk factors* f_i *and* f_j*, where* $(i \neq j)$ *are independent of one another. Nevertheless, the proposed RAP does not need its independence.*

According to the provided definition, the quantity of factors, including severity, detection, incidence, cost, and others, is denoted by the variable $n \in \{3, 4, 5, \ldots\} \in \mathbb{N}$. The risk ranking numbers, denoted as $f_i \in \{1, 2, \ldots, 10\}$ are related to factor i. This input will be employed by aggregation functions to evaluate each risk case.

Several instances of aggregation functions S are as follows, along with their respective output ranges:

- $S_1(\mathbf{f}) = \prod_{i:=1}^{n} f_i$ is the geometric mean of risk factors. If n = 3, and the factors are severity, occurrence, and detection, we have the original RPN (risk priority number) from the FMEA. $S_1(\mathbf{f}) \in [1, 10^n] \in \mathbb{N}$
- $S_2(\mathbf{f}) = Median(\{\mathbf{f}\})$ is the median of risk factors. $S_2(\mathbf{f}) \in [1, 10] \in \mathbb{N}$
- $S_3(\mathbf{f}) = \frac{1}{n} \sum_{i:=1}^{n} f_i$ is the average of risk factors. $S_3(\mathbf{f}) \in [1, 10] \in \mathbb{R}^+$
- $S_4(\mathbf{f}) = \sqrt{\sum_{i:=1}^{n} f_i^2}$ is the generalized n-dimensional radial distance of risk factors. $S_4(\mathbf{f}) \in \left[\sqrt{n}, 10\sqrt{n}\right] \in \mathbb{R}^+$
- $S_5(\mathbf{f})$ = Aggregation of Fuzzy membership functions based on rule base. In this case, the output function range depends on the defuzzyfication function established by user, and can be in any prespecified range.

The utilization of risk analysis inside the supply chain is not as prevalent as it ideally should be, primarily due to a lack of competence among purchasing, procurement, and logistics managers, as stated in the preceding chapter. The risk assessment framework, known as [33], has undergone an expansion to incorporate a fuzzy module. This addition has been implemented to effectively address the issue at hand.

2.3. Implementation of Fuzzy

The methodology employed in the previously disclosed fuzzy aggregation function will not be altered. Fuzzy logic comprises three distinct phases, with the initial one being **Fuzzyfication/Fuzzyfier**. In this phase, the factors (crisps) are converted into fuzzy input variables in the form of membership functions. The subsequent process, **Inference**, produces output fuzzy variables by utilizing the fuzzy rule base to ascertain which control actions ought to be executed in light of the fuzzy input variables. This constituent could potentially be considered an aggregation protocol. In the concluding phase, **Defuzzyfication/Defuzzifier**, the produced output is transformed back into genuine output variables, namely the value and/or risk level.

2.3.1. Fuzzyfication/Fuzzyfier

Initially, it is necessary to define the input fuzzy variables by employing the input membership functions. This implies that fuzzy membership functions should be used to convert each risk factor into an input fuzzy variable. The designation for these values is "crisps". A multitude of linguistic variables influence the number of membership functions associated with a given variable. Typically, Fuzzy FMEA utilizes three to seven linguistic variables [40,41]. It is possible to incorporate additional variables; however, in the given context, the rule base became exceedingly intricate. In the beginning, the input fuzzy variables must be defined through the utilization of input membership functions. Accordingly, each risk factor should be converted into an input fuzzy variable utilizing fuzzy membership functions. These qualities are referred to as "crisps". The number of membership functions attributed to a specific variable is influenced by an abundance of linguistic variables. Fuzzy FMEA generally employs between three and seven linguistic variables [40,41]. Although it is feasible to include further variables, doing so would have rendered the rule base significantly complex in the given context.

At the beginning and end of the interval, the sigmoid function was implemented:

$$\mu(x,a,b)_{sigu} = \begin{cases} 0, \ x \le a \\ \frac{1}{1+e^{a(x-b)}}, & \text{any other case} \end{cases} \tag{5}$$

$$\mu(x,a,b)_{sigd} = \begin{cases} 1 - \frac{1}{1+e^{a(x-b)}}, \ x \le a \\ 0, & \text{any other case} \end{cases} \tag{6}$$

where a is the steepness of function, and b is the inflection point.

For each range within the interval, the bell/splay function is applied:

$$\mu(x,a,b,c)_{spl} = \frac{1}{1+\left|\frac{x-b}{a}\right|^{2c}} \tag{7}$$

where b is the center of function, a is the width of curve and c is the steepness of function.

Both the splay and bell are Gaussian membership functions that were selected due to their smoothness, non-zero value at all point intervals, continuous differentiability, and mathematical and computational tractability [25].

As illustrated in Figure 1, for $n = 5$ (5 linguistic levels), in accordance with its original score or crisp, each component is converted into the sum of n membership functions.

$S_i(\mathbf{f_i}) = \sum_{i:=1}^{n} \mu_i(x)$, $x \le 10$ and $x \in \mathbb{R}^+$, other variables of membership functions are constants (a, b, c).

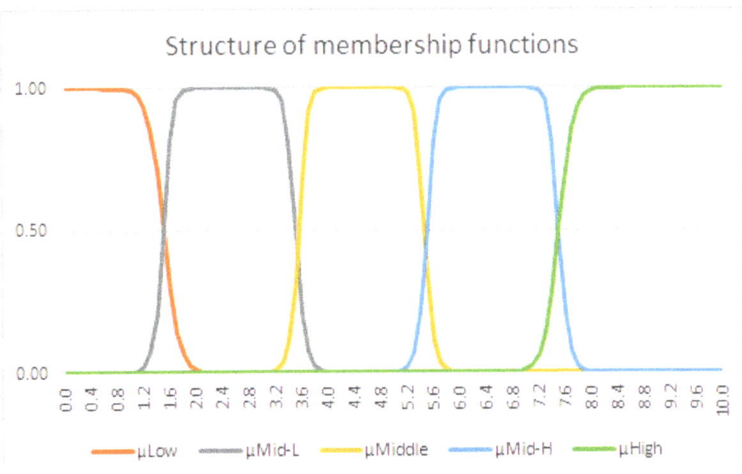

Figure 1. The structure of Fuzzy membership functions for each factor.

Each factor will have its own sum of membership functions, noted $S_i(\mathbf{f_i})$, $f_i \in \{1, 2, \ldots, 10\} \in \mathbb{N}$, representing the ranking of risk converted in a number.

2.3.2. Fuzzy Rule Base

An analogy can be drawn between the sum of the fuzzy membership functions and the accumulation of factors comprising the fuzzy rule base. The literature also contains considerable variation regarding the selected aggregation method for fuzzy sets: only sums, products, maximal functions, or the Mamdani Fuzzy Inference (MFI) are employed due to the more comprehensible and intuitive nature of their rule bases. The MFI functions optimally in expert system applications in which the norms are established based on the expertise possessed by human beings. The input of this aggregation consists of fuzzy sets, and the output is also a fuzzy set. The output is determined by the center of mass or gravity, and the rule basis is a simple IF-THEN structure. An instance of this can be described as follows:

$$W_i(\mathbf{S_i}) = S_1(\mathbf{f_i}) \otimes S_2(\mathbf{f_j}) \otimes \ldots \otimes S_n(\mathbf{f_n}) \tag{8}$$

where $\otimes$ is the aggregation protocol.

2.3.3. Defuzzyfication

The final phase entails the transformation of the amount of risk from a fuzzy state to a crisp state. In this phase, the determination of risk level will be achieved by converting the membership functions in real numbers. Several viable defuzzification strategies, including:

- Center of gravity of area—see Figure 2;
- Bisector of area refers to a vertical line that partitions a fuzzy set into two sub-regions of equivalent area. The phenomenon in question may exhibit alignment with the center of gravity, however this correlation is not universally observed;
- Mean of Max level;
- Largest of Max—the max value of the highest output membership function;
- Max—the max limit value achieved by any output function;
- Smallest of Max—the lowest value of the highest output membership function;
- Low—is the lowest value achieved by any output function.

The computation of the center of gravity of the membership function is performed, considering the factor's value, and subsequently, the results are aggregated.

$$x_i = \frac{\int \mu_C(x)x dx}{\int \mu_C(x) dx} \tag{9}$$

$\int \mu_C(X)dx$ represents the measure of the region enclosed by the membership function C. If the parameter μ_C is established based on multiple discrete membership functions, the center of gravity can be mathematically represented as the summation of these functions.

$$x_i = \frac{\sum_{i=1}^{N} \mu_C(x_i)x_i}{\sum_{i=1}^{N} \mu_C(x_i)} \tag{10}$$

In actuality, it is feasible to explicitly determine the center of gravity of membership functions by clearly describing the functions. The following diagram presents a visual representation of the methodologies employed in the calculation of accurate output (Figure 2).

The case study detailed in Section 4 employs the center of gravity methodology.

It can be asserted that the chosen and implemented fuzzy function, which includes the defuzzification process with the exception of sensitivity, satisfies every one of the six criteria previously outlined as prerequisites for an aggregate function. Given that the input values consist of natural numbers ranging from [1, 10], this aspect becomes relatively inconsequential (Section 2.1).

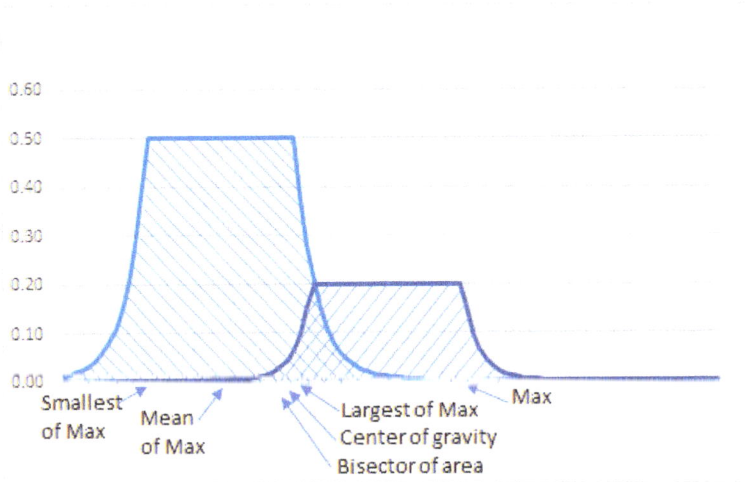

Figure 2. Used defuzzyfication methods to obtain the final output value.

2.4. Evaluating the Results of Used Aggregation Functions

Two approaches appeared viable for comparing the outcomes produced by the aggregating functions. One is when the range of output arguments of functions is set to be identical; this is typically resolved by multiplying the values by a constant. This was promptly abandoned due to the potential complexity that the behavior of the functions would have introduced to the situation. An alternative approach entails comparing the output values generated by distinct aggregating functions in the same order in which they assign equivalent risks. This methodology will be further implemented, elucidated in the validation methodology, and will be applied in the case study.

2.4.1. Rank Correlation

The Spearman's rank correlation coefficient is a statistical measure that quantifies the strength and direction of the association between two variables:

$$r_s = 1 - \frac{6\sum_{i=1}^{N}(R_{X_i} - R_{Y_i})^2}{N(N^2 - 1)} \tag{11}$$

where R_{X_i} and R_{Y_i} represent the ranks of the first and second variables, respectively. The sign and magnitude of the value both fall within the range of $[-1; +1]$.

2.4.2. TOPSIS (Technique for Order Preference by Similarity to Ideal Solution)

The application of a multi-criteria decision analysis technique will be employed to evaluate a set of alternatives and ascertain the ranking of the risk analysis models implemented. The TOPSIS method chooses the alternative that has the shortest geometric distance from a positive ideal solution and the greatest geometric distance from a negative ideal solution [42].

Let A represent the pairwise comparison matrix for factors as follows:

$$A = \begin{pmatrix} a_{11} & \dots & a_{1n} \\ \dots & \dots & \dots \\ a_{n1} & \dots & a_{nn} \end{pmatrix} \tag{12}$$

where a_{ij} are the judgement scores, considering $a_{ij} = 1/a_{ji}$, and $a_{ii} = 1$. This matrix is normalized with:

$$k_{ij} = \frac{a_{ij}}{\sum_{j=1}^{n} a_{ij}} \tag{13}$$

The local weight resulting:

$$w_i = \sum_{j=1}^{n} \frac{k_{ij}}{n} \tag{14}$$

The variables h_i are used to represent the risk incidents, where i ranges from 1 to n. Similarly, the variables f_j are employed to designate the TOPSIS evaluation criteria, with j ranging from 1 to m. The variable x_{ij} represents the numerical results of the alternative h_i with respect to the criteria f_j.

The formula for the normalized decision matrix can be expressed as follows:

$$d_{ij} = \frac{x_{ij}}{\sqrt{\sum_{j=1}^{m} x_{ij}^2}} \tag{15}$$

The weighted normalized decision matrix elements can be generated as follows:

$$V_{ij} = w_i \times d_{ij} \tag{16}$$

The ideal best solution V_j^+ and ideal worst solution V_j^- are determined by aggregating the highest and lowest values of each criterion.

For beneficial criteria:

$$V_j^+ = max[V_{ij}] \quad V_j^- = min[V_{ij}] \tag{17}$$

For non-beneficial criteria:

$$V_j^+ = min[V_{ij}] \quad V_j^- = max[V_{ij}] \tag{18}$$

Euclidian distances are measured from the ideal best (S_i^+) and ideal worst (S_i^-) values:

$$S_i^+ = \sqrt{\sum_{j=1}^{m} (V_{ij} - V_j^+)^2} \quad S_i^- = \sqrt{\sum_{j=1}^{m} (V_{ij} - V_j^-)^2} \tag{19}$$

The performance score (relative closeness to the ideal solution) can be calculated:

$$P_i = \frac{S_i^-}{S_i^+ + S_i^-} \tag{20}$$

The ranked options are subsequently arranged in descending order as the final step.

This methodology is suitable for pairwise correlation analysis, specifically when the number of variables being compared does not exceed seven. Implementing this strategy gets problematic in situations where there are more than ten hazards, which is a frequently seen phenomenon in real-world scenarios. An illustration depicting the initial use of the Technique for Order of Preference by Similarity to Ideal Solution (TOPSIS) may be observed in the [43] context.

When evaluating a case that involves more than seven significant individual hazards, it is recommended to engage a team of experts who possess comprehensive expertise regarding the consequences associated with each risk. The individuals possess the capability to produce a matrix that facilitates the rating of effects, dangers, and impacts, alongside another matrix that enables the evaluation of results. One can utilize RSTUDIO to input both matrices and calculate their ranks using the TOPSIS algorithm [44]. This methodology will be represented in Section 4 Step 6 & 7 and in the case study (Section 5).

3. Designing Steps for Practical Implementation and Validation

This chapter elucidates the practical application of the aforementioned theory. It is crucial to highlight that risk analysis is a qualitative approach that necessitates the involvement of a qualified team or teams. This team should include representatives from all areas of risk and the respective departments responsible for analyzing and evaluating them. Certain industries, like the automotive sector, have a competitive edge due to their reliance on specialized teams who collaborate closely through the entire product life cycle, from design to mass production to end-of-life.

Figure 3 illustrates the steps of evaluation, which are utilized in both the subsequent analysis of the theoretical framework and the case study.

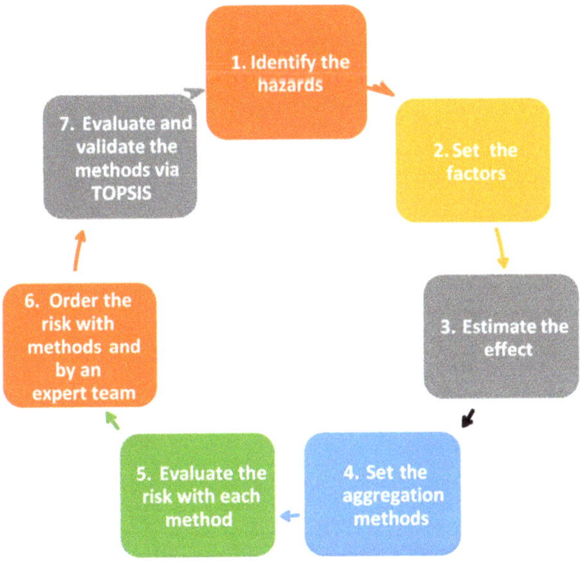

Figure 3. Determination of the appropriate risk evaluation method.

Step 0—Forming the Team: An assemblage of experts with specialized knowledge in logistics, quality management, risk assessment, evaluation, and mitigation, including all relevant departments such as finance/controlling or others, should be formed. Many firms already own risk assessment teams, such as the FMEA team in the automotive sector, which is mandated by the IATF16949:2016 [45] QMS standard. It is crucial that this team demonstrate dedication and possess the appropriate expertise to thoroughly test, assess, and validate the risk strategy. The team composition should be adaptable, so that additional experts from different departments may join based on the analysis conducted. Although referred to as Step 0, this essentially serves as the foundation of the evaluation approach.

Step 1—Hazards identification: This step is a comprehensive gathering of all supply chain concerns, encompassing claims, losses, and delays. It also involves analyzing news from a related business sector, including potential future events. It is imperative to consider the heightened vulnerability to cyber-attacks, dissemination of misinformation, potential conflicts, and climate fluctuations within the logistical network. If the business has conducted prior risk analyses, those should also be included in this gathering. Each input should be taken into consideration.

Step 2—Factors setting: The list from Step 1 should be used to identify the most accurate factors that describe the risk of organization, department, or process. This phase is exceptionally challenging. The factors included in the FMEA, namely detectability, severity, and occurrence, serve as a solid foundation. However, if there are other elements within these that can enhance our ability to precisely characterize the associated risk, they should be incorporated. In addition to the three previously mentioned factors, supply chains also utilize various other elements such as quality, time, cost, intensity, consequence, effect, cause, and measure. The quantity of factors is contingent upon the intricacy of the business or logistic procedures, traffic patterns, business affiliations, and other pertinent considerations (ex. sustainability, energy saving, ...). It is imperative to assess these factors on a case-by-case basis for each company, as the level of risk may vary depending on factors such as geographical location, supply chain network pattern, technological infrastructure, workforce availability and expertise, environmental conditions, core technological capabilities, political/economical/regional stability, etc. If a novel component can enhance the risk analysis from the perspective of the organization's functioning, it is recommended to utilize it. It is important to note that the elements should be linked to specific levels, which are ideally defined by the organization. However, it is recommended that the number of levels should be an even number. Typically, 10 levels are employed, although there is flexibility to differ from this standard.

Step 3—Risk assessment: In this section, we determine the levels of the factors for each risk. The FMEA manual contains specific guidelines for the Severity, Detector, and Occurrence settings in the level settings. For instance, if human detection is involved, the Detectability value must not be lower than 6. Similarly, in manufacturing, if certain areas or parameters are designated as SC (Significant Characteristic) or CC (Critical Characteristic) the Severity value must not be lower than 7. Such regulations can also be implemented for novel factors, particularly once the organization has gained proficiency in their utilization.

Step 4—Set aggregation methods: This step involves the selection of the aggregating functions that we intend to utilize for the purpose of analysis.

The standard FMEA will be utilized as a fundamental framework and point of comparison. Due to the inclusion of three levels (L, M, and H) in the revised FMEA, it is important to note that these levels serve solely as indicators for subsequent evaluation and are not intended for the purpose of risk prioritization. Due to this rationale, the analysis will not incorporate the new FMEA.

In the preceding FMEA, the term used to refer to this was Risk Priority Number (RPN). Organizations established a certain RPN level that necessitated action to decrease the risk. In the context of ISO9001:2015 [46], this threshold is typically regarded as the midpoint within the range of factors, resulting in a value of 125 for three factors ($5^3 = 125$). In the automotive industry, companies individually define this limit, which generally falls around 100 or lower, as determined by management. Moreover, when the most severe and imperceptible process flaw is amalgamated with a significantly low occurrence score, the Risk Priority Number (RPN) will amount to 100 ($1 \times 10 \times 10$), a value that falls below the commonly employed action criterion threshold by several firms. The implementation of the updated FMEA methodology will yield a slightly more accurate outcome. However, its effectiveness remains inadequate, as the risk level was merely the result of implementing risk mitigation measures. If individuals are not justified, it is imperative that they become justified.

Every organization has the autonomy to make a decision regarding whether to accept, mitigate, or acknowledge specific hazards. Based on the aforementioned information, the management of the company or the risk assessment team of experts can ascertain the specific aspects that accentuate the level of risk.

Section 2 provided a detailed presentation of numerous aggregation functions. However, it is possible to introduce additional aggregation functions that adhere to the criteria of aggregation functions.

Step 5—Evaluate the risk with each method: The risk level can be assessed by utilizing each of the selected aggregating functions.

Step 6—Order the results via TOPSIS method and by the experts: This pertains to the arrangement of outputs resulting from aggregating functions. This step comprises two components: the application of the TOPSIS algorithm for ordering and the ordering process conducted by the expert team members.

The determination of the ranking by the TOPSIS method, employing the weight technique. Upon doing risk analysis using the aforementioned six risk analysis functions, the resulting risk values are calculated and subsequently arranged in a certain order. This process enables the risk analysis functions to be compared with one another, marking the completion of Step 6.

Step 7—Evaluation and validation: The assessment of outcomes carries considerable significance at this phase, and requires meticulous and strategic preparation. The risk evaluation expert team was asked to form a committee including the most experienced individuals to assign incidents, disregarding the rankings already published or the outcomes of the risk assessment. This indicates that the indicated persons have a deficiency in understanding the output values of TOPSIS ranking and the results of the aggregation functions.

This committee will make a ranking effect matrix (see as example Table A7) and the impact matrix (see also an example Table A9) using their respective scores. The precision of these matrices is of utmost importance as it exerts a substantial influence on the final result. This implies that the perspectives of a specific cohort of specialists with substantial expertise in evaluating the relative effects of each approach should be considered.

The validation of the method involves comparing the results of the committee with the ranking made via TOPSIS. If it coincides, that will be the best aggregation function that can be used by the organization.

The risk assessment is conducted using individuals, thereby yielding qualitative data. Applying any aggregating function to these values yields a qualitative outcome, irrespective of the mathematical functions used to rank the data, such as AHP, TOPSIS, etc. Nevertheless, by conducting the same comparison using the most seasoned experts from the risk analysis team and employing the aforementioned comparative mathematical tools, the outcome should be identical. The occurrence of human error can be mitigated by conducting this study again with the group. Using this method, the most appropriate aggregating function for risk analysis within the organization.

4. Case Study

The experimental study is focused on an electronic manufacturing services (EMS) supplier. Conducting testing within the comprehensive supply chain offers several advantages owing to the central location of this EMS (see Figure 4).

In certain instances, manufacturers (S_x) or, in extreme circumstances, direct customers (C_x) are occasionally chosen as the source for larger quantities of raw materials or components, despite the customary practice of EMS firms to procure them via distributors (D_x). This holds particularly true in cases when the design of the final product is still undergoing development or when it becomes imperative to conduct tests on updated components. To facilitate the installation of these units by original equipment manufacturers (OEMs), the EMS delivers the goods to direct customers (C_x). Subsequently, these customers engage in further processes, such as the development of more intricate modules, testing, and programming.

Under some circumstances, the EMS may also provide the carmaker with goods directly, as indicated by the EMS-O_x connection in Figure 4. The instances of S_x and D_x have been simplified in the EMS. They are treated as a single node or "location" because the EMS communicates with them through their Distribution Centers or Offices, even though they consist of several factories/locations. Various logistical groups play a crucial role in facilitating the transportation of products between different nodes throughout the process. This case study offers a comprehensive opportunity to analyze a wide range of supply chain issues.

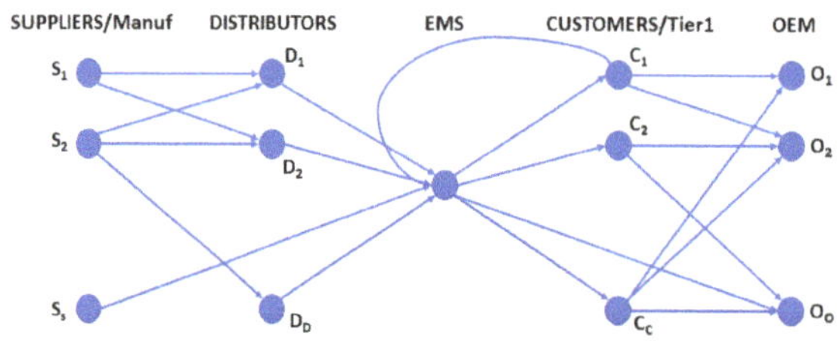

Figure 4. The supply chain map of the EMS company.

The automotive industry places significant importance on the availability of raw materials for manufacture, ensuring that they are provided at the appropriate time, quantity, and quality. Additionally, the industry recognizes the need for problem-free production, which is not the focus of this study, and the timely and accurate delivery of products to customers. Any departure from this stipulation leads to supplementary costs or a decrease in revenue.

A team of professionals specializing in logistics, quality management, risk assessment, finance/controlling, and FMEA was assembled within the EMS firm. The primary objective of this team was to conduct comprehensive testing, analysis, and validation of the entire approach.

Step 1—Hazards identification: The present study conducted an exhaustive analysis of various supply chain concerns, including claims, losses, and delays, spanning a period of four years. Subsequently, a comprehensive inventory of risks was compiled. In this particular case, a total of 20 unique concerns were identified.

Step 2—Factors setting: The criteria for evaluating each factor, specifically Occurrence, Severity, and Detection, are presented in Tables A1, A2, and A3, respectively. These tables may be found in the Appendix A.

Step 3—Risk assessment: The findings of the FMEA analysis, considering the aforementioned criteria, are presented in Table A6. The result was generated by employing both the previous FMEA standard, which solely considered the initial three factors (Occurrence, Severity, and Detectability), and the present FMEA standard which includes the AP (Action Priority) levels.

Table A6 illustrates three factors that are insufficient in appropriately highlighting the true level of threat. This is the reason why certain authors and researchers have started incorporating supplementary variables (such as performing analysis with four or five components).

The upper echelons of management within this EMS company were engaged in consultation, resulting in the selection of two more factors, namely control and cost.

The cost refers to the estimated financial impact incurred due to errors or inefficiencies in handling or logistics. Within the realm of literature, this particular element is commonly referred to as "Value".

The second factor is the Control factor, which assesses the feasibility and effectiveness of controlling, preventing, or mitigating a process, and determines the extent to which it can be achieved. Please refer to Tables A4 and A5 for a comprehensive overview of the established evaluation criteria pertaining to the supplementary components.

Step 4—Set aggregation methods: The present set of factors include Severity, Occurrence, Detectability, Cost, and Control. The next step involves the selection of the aggregating functions that we intend to utilize for the purpose of analysis. The standard FMEA will be utilized as a fundamental framework and point of comparison. Additional aggregating functions that will be employed encompass Multiplication, Average, Sum, and Euclidean Distance, augmented with Fuzzy. These functions consist of five elements and are all encompassed inside the TREF technique. All of these topics are addressed in Section 2.2.

The fuzzyfication function, depicted in Figure 1, is consistent across all five failure factors, namely severity, occurrence, detectability, cost, and controllability. With the exception of the initial and final functions, each function possesses a range in which its value is non-zero, and the midpoint is denoted. The variable $Midk$ represents the midpoint, while k denotes the number of linguistic variables utilized to describe each failure. In all instances, the membership function takes on values inside the range of 0 to 1. Here, A_k represents the count of non-zero elements in kS, kO, and kD. The variables S, O, D, Cs, and Cn are used to denote the severity, occurrence, detection, cost, and controllability, respectively.

Step 5—Evaluate the risk with each method: The risk level can be determined by employing each of the six aggregating functions.

Step 6—Order the results via TOPSIS method and by the experts: The outcomes of the aggregation functions are presented in this order, employing two distinct methods: TOPSIS and the expert group.

The determination of the ranking by the TOPSIS method, employing the weight technique. The symbol k_i represents the average value of the membership function, with i denoting the factors S, O, D, Cs, and Cn. Upon doing risk analysis using the aforementioned six risk analysis functions, the resulting risk values are calculated and subsequently arranged in a certain order. This process enables the risk analysis functions to be compared with one another, marking the completion of Step 6. The ranking outcomes are displayed in Table 1 below:

Table 1. A detail from the ranking matrix composed from the standard FMEA, TREF Multiplicative, Tref Average, TREF Median, TREF Distance, and TREF Fuzzy functions—the last 5 evaluations were made using 5 factors.

No	R. FMEA	R. TREF Multi	R. TREF Aver	R. TREF Medi	R. TREF Dist	R. TREF Fuzzy
1	1	15	15	17	14	17
2	2	17	17	18	17	8
3	3	18	18	19	18	9
4	5	13	14	14	16	7
5	4	19	19	20	19	16
6	19	20	20	16	20	20
7	18	16	16	15	15	13
8	9	7	7	7	7	15
9	10	5	5	5	4	2
10	6	1	1	2	1	3
11	11	6	6	6	5	11
12	7	3	3	3	6	14
13	12	14	13	13	12	12

The subsequent results are presented herein upon inputting all the data into R's TOPSIS analysis program [44] with uniform weights, while considering the assessment of impacts (see Table 2):

Table 2. Ranking of methods using TOPSIS without considering the weights.

Alt. Row	Name	Score	Rank
1	FMEA	0.6308374	1
2	TREF Multi	0.4312619	4
3	TREF Aver	0.4338759	3
4	TREF Medi	0.4414542	2
5	TREF Dist	0.4132224	5
6	TREF FMEA	0.2516496	6

To illustrate the potential outcome in the absence of an expert-established importance matrix, a random impact matrix was employed, yielding the following result (see Table A8). The highest rank (6) gives the best result.

Step 7—Evaluation and validation: The ranking effect matrix (Table A7) and the impact matrix (Table A9) were generated by expert members using their respective scores.

Table 3 displays the outcomes obtained from employing the matrices indicated earlier as weight and impact in the TOPSIS analysis program implemented in R [44].

Table 3. Ranking of methods using TOPSIS with weights.

Alt. Row	Name	Score	Rank
1	FMEA	0.5959322	1
2	TREF Multi	0.5529383	3
3	TREF Aver	0.5538219	2
4	TREF Medi	0.5418204	4
5	TREF Dist	0.5364203	5
6	TREF FMEA	0.1567300	6

In this scenario, the highest rank also yields the most optimal outcome.

This ordering is the same as the ordering made by experts.

The observation reveals that both the ordering obtained with the random impact matrix (refer to Table 2) and the ordering generated with the weighted impact matrix (refer to Table 3) indicate optimal aggregation function no. 6, namely the TREF FMEA.

5. Discussion and Result

The ranking of the several aggregation approaches, ranging from the riskiest (method 1) to the safest (method 6), is provided in Table 3. The finding that the basic FMEA with only three variables ranks as the riskiest is not unexpected, as experts emphasize the significance of two additional factors, namely Cost and Control, which are deemed highly important and justified.

The ranking of the remaining five risk aggregation methods, which consider five factors as input and employ multiplicative, average, median, modified Euclidean distance, and fuzzy functions, is very interesting.

The utilization of the frequency perspective in the assessment process can prove to be useful. The Crystal Ball (https://www.oracle.com/applications/crystalball/, accessed on 24 November 2023) application developed by Oracle, which is an add-in for Microsoft Excel, was employed for this purpose. For the examination of three variables, specifically for the conventional FMEA, the trial number was established at 10,000. In this particular case, the sensitivity for each element was 33.3%. In the case of evaluating five factors, the trial numbers were set to 100,000 to achieve equal sensitivity for each element, with each factor accounting for 20% of the total.

The figures that were generated to illustrate the distribution of frequencies and values are presented in Figure 5.

A comprehensive summary of the simulations conducted using Oracle's Crystal Ball is provided in Table 4.

Table 4. Characteristics of different aggregation methods for 5 factors including the standard FMEA with 3 factors.

Item	FMEA	TREF Multi	TREF Aver	TREF Median	TREF EucDist	TREF Fuzzy
Factors	3	5	5	5	5	5
Skewness	1.66	3.34	−0.0025	−0.003	−0.32	3.28
Kurtosis	5.77	18.84	2.36	2.37	3.02	17.91
Min	1	1	1	1	2	8
Max	1000	100,000	10	10	22	77,348

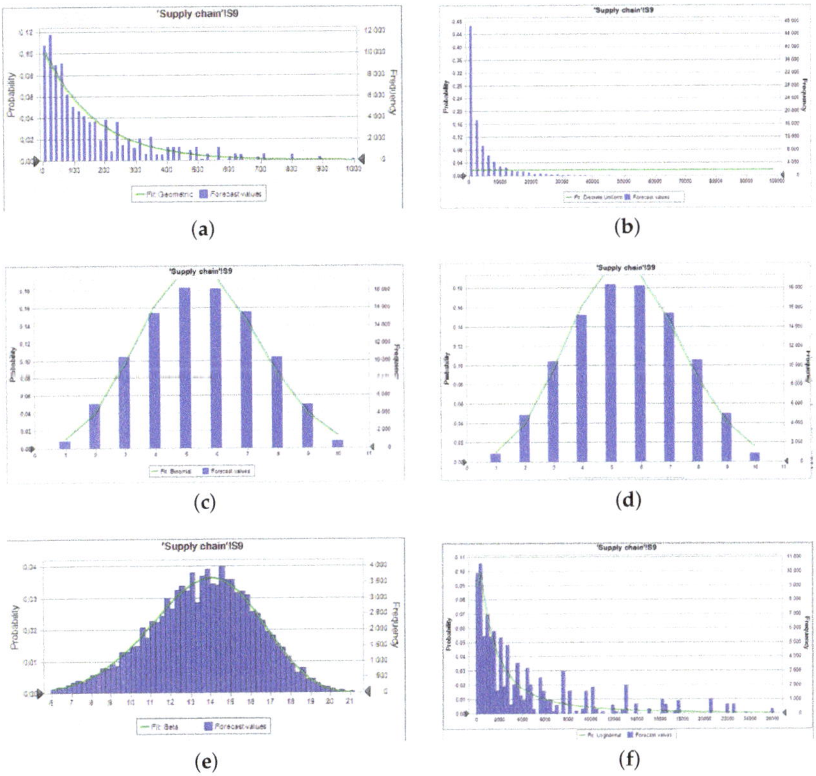

Figure 5. Results—Frequency. (**a**) Standard FMEA frequency/values distribution. (**b**) TREF multiplication frequency/values distribution. (**c**) TREF average frequency/values distribution. (**d**) TREF median frequency/values distribution. (**e**) TREF Euclidean distance frequency/values distribution. (**f**) TREF fuzzy frequency/values distribution.

The Skewness in Table 4 pertains to the absence of symmetry in the dataset, whereas the Kurtosis assesses whether the data exhibit heavy (positive values) or light (negative values) tails relative to a normal distribution.

Upon examination of the simulation figure (Figure 5), it is evident that:

- The results obtained via the **Multiplication Aggregation Method,** as depicted in Figure 5b, exhibit a level of comparability to those obtained from a conventional FMEA. However, it should be noted that the former method involved the consideration of five components, whereas the latter method typically considers three components. The linearity of the Multiplication technique and the standard FMEA is commendable. Consequently, the outcome for a scenario including n factors will yield a range of $[1, 10^n] \in \mathbb{N}$ for each factor, where the range of each factor is $[1, 10] \in \mathbb{N}$. The concerns of FMEA are equally relevant in this particular case.
- The input range and output range for the **Average aggregate** in Figure 5c are identical, spanning from 1 to 10. This method demonstrates strong linearity. The presence of extreme values can pose challenges in some scenarios. In that case, if one factor attains its maximum value and the remaining factors maintain low values, the resulting output will nevertheless fall below the midpoint of the output range. In this particular scenario, the presence of low-value components effectively mitigates the impact of any extreme values, hence impeding the identification and analysis of potential risks.

- The **Median aggregation** yields the lowest Skewness score, as depicted in Figure 5d, suggesting that the data exhibits a high degree of symmetry. The Kurtosis score of our dataset is rather low, suggesting a moderate level of customization in the data. This situation bears a resemblance to the Average aggregation approach.
- The linearity is only average and the computation is challenging in the case of the **Euclidean distance (generalized) aggregate** (see Figure 5e). Interpretation is challenging in n-dimensional space where $n > 3, n \in \mathbb{N}$. In the case of n factors, the output will be $[\sqrt{n}, 10\sqrt{n}] \in \mathbb{R}^+$ for each factor's range of values of $[1, 10] \in \mathbb{N}$. The linearity of the Euclidean distance (generalized) aggregate is only average, and its computation is problematic, as depicted in Figure 5e.
- The outcome data for the **Fuzzy aggregation method** (refer to Figure 5f), which is determined by the used membership and defuzzification functions, exhibit similarities to those of the TREF Multiplication. However, it is important to note that the output consists of just five primary groups (see Figure 1).

In conclusion, it is important to acknowledge that aggregations utilizing multiplication approaches, such as FMEA, generalized TREF Multiplication, and TREF Fuzzy with respect to defuzzification, yield the most unfavorable distribution. However, their significant contributions become essential in situations when elements exhibit elevated levels of risk.

The reason for arranging each output in decreasing order was to ensure that this pattern was accurately represented. The comparative analysis of rank modifications for various aggregation functions is illustrated in Figure 6.

The present graphic depiction of Alluvian representation serves to emphasize the discrepancies in ordering through the comparison of an initial state and a subsequent state. The depiction, however, commences with the conventional outcomes of the FMEA as a refference, considering the sequential Risk Priority Number (RPN) or output values. Subsequently, it demonstrates the alteration in prioritization of the aforementioned risk subsequent to the implementation of the novel aggregate function. The final diagram encompasses a triple figure that visually represents the transition from the conventional FMEA to the enhanced FMEA incorporating risk levels. This diagram enables readers to discern the differences between the two approaches. Additionally, the diagram includes the TREF Multiplicative, which functions as a comprehensive representation of various components. Please refer to Figure 6e for further details.

The comparison between the conventional FMEA and the TREF Fuzzy method depicted in Figure 6b holds significant importance in this study as it demonstrates the optimal results achieved by the utilization of the TREF Fuzzy aggregation function, as indicated in Table 3. The outcome was validated by the team of experts.

Outcome: The results obtained from this approach have been implemented, following the PDCA model (see Figure 3), and are presently under close scrutiny. If a new type of failure or unforeseen outcomes arise, the analysis will be repeated. After a period of six months of usage, no variation has been seen.

Remark: The purpose of this paper is to provide a comprehensive guide for the identification of risks connected with Supply Chain Management (SCM). Its objective is to facilitate a thorough understanding of various risk variables and their corresponding significance. This document imposes some limitations, with the exception of donations. The process of prioritizing risks is contingent upon the thorough examination, evaluation, and distinctive perspectives that have surfaced pertaining to the manufacturing facility in question, and at the specific moment of the expert's deliberation. Consequently, a hasty method has the potential to significantly undermine the precision and reliability of the investigation.

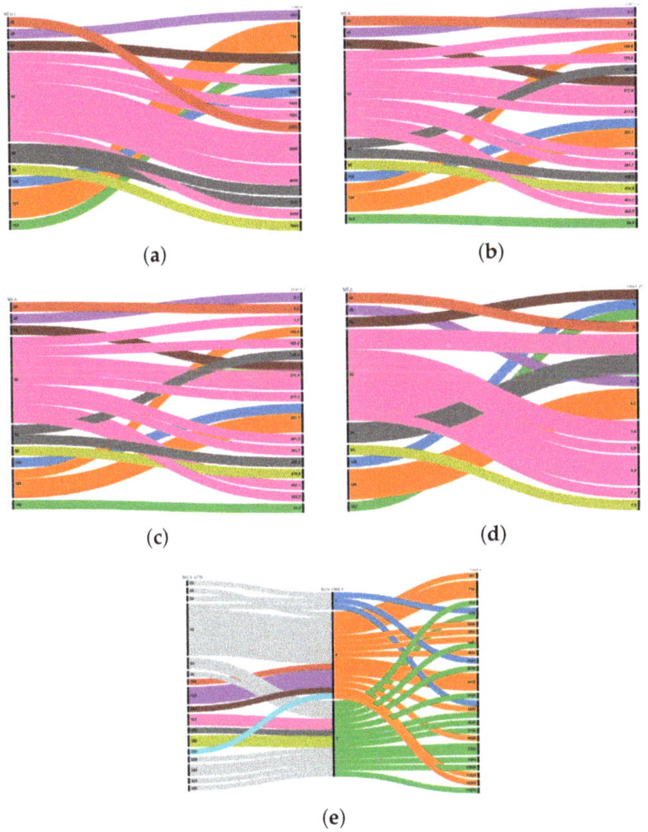

Figure 6. Results—Alluvian representation of original FMEA ranking with the used 5 TREF functions. (**a**) FMEA with TREF Multiplication. (**b**) FMEA with TREF Fuzzy. (**c**) FMEA–TREF Median. (**d**) FMEA–TREF Average. (**e**) FMEA–New FMEA–TREF Multiplicative.

6. Summary

On the basis of the data in Tables 3 and 4, and Figure 6b it is possible to conclude that the introduction of the two new factors substantially prolonged the identification of actual risks, i.e., risks that cause substantial damage emerged. The methodology that was demonstrated, as well as explained in the Case Study, is readily implementable by SCM decision-makers. This aids them in identifying the fundamental risks that require preparation and consequently facilitates the identification of such risks. The comprehensive exposition of the method's implementation steps in the case study renders them universal, and applicable to sectors and industries beyond supply chain management.

Author Contributions: Conceptualization, Z.T.K.; methodology, Z.T.K. and I.M.; validation, Z.T.K.; formal analysis, I.M.; investigation, I.M.; data curation, I.M.; visualization, I.M.; writing, I.M.; supervision, Z.T.K.; founding acquisition, Z.T.K.; validation, Z.T.K. All authors have read and agreed to the published version of the manuscript.

Funding: This work has been implemented by the TKP2021-NVA-10 project with the support provided by the Ministry of Culture and Innovation of Hungary from the National Research, Development and Innovation Fund, financed under the 2021 Thematic Excellence Programme funding scheme.

Data Availability Statement: The majority of the data is presented in the article. The complete data collection is available upon request from the authors.

Conflicts of Interest: The authors declare no conflict of interest. The funders had no role in the design of the study; in the collection, analyses, or interpretation of data; in the writing of the manuscript; or in the decision to publish the results.

Abbreviations

The following abbreviations are used in this manuscript:

AP	Action Priority, the term used in the new
AHP	Analytical Hierarchy Process
AIAG	Automotive Industry Action Group, is a not-for-profit association created to develop recommendations and a framework for the improvement of quality in the North American automotive industry
ANP	Analytical Network Process
ERP	Enterprise Resource Planning
FMEA	Failure Mode and Effect Analysis
MFI	Mamdani Fuzzy Inference
OEM	Original Equipment Manufacturers, refers to the car companies in this article
QMS	Quality Management System (ISO9001, IATF16949, etc.)
PDCA	Plan, Do, Check, and Act—the basis of any continuous improvement model
RPN	Risk Priority Number
SCM	Supply Chain Management
TOPSIS	Technique for Order Preference by Similarity to the Ideal Solution
TREF	Total Risk Evaluation Framework, is a generalized risk evaluation tool
Tier X	Suppliers in the automotive industry are organized in sequential levels called Tiers. The number X means how far are they from the OEM
VDA	Verband der Automobilindustrie, is the German Association of the Automotive Industry

Appendix A

Table A1. Criteria for evaluating the frequency of Occurrence of logistic defects at incoming.

Probability of Occurrence	Occurrence Definition	Score
Never	Never	1
Unlikely	Once a year	2
Very low	Once a month	3
Low	Once a week	4
Medium	Once a day	5
Medium high	Daily 2–4 time	6
Important	Daily 5–10 time	7
Very important	Once in an hour	8
Very very important	Hourly 2–4 time	9
Extremely important	Hourly more than 6 time	10

Table A2. Criteria for evaluating the severity of the logistic failure defects.

Severity of Failure	Severity Ranking	Score
No discernible effect	No discernible effect	1
Slight inconvenience in logistic process	Alarm at SCM	2
Can cause short stops	Red alarm at SCM	3
Can cause considerable stops in process	Can cause written remark	4
Small stops at Tier1	Warning from Tier1	5
Several small stops at Tier1	Escalation by Tier1	6
Serious stops at Tier1	Red alarm at Tier1	7
Delay at final customer	Escalation start from final customer	8
Small stops at final customer	Emergency at final customer	9
Serious stop at final customer	Stop final customer	10

Table A3. Criteria for assessing the detection of defects.

Probability of Detection	Detection Effect	Score
Automatic detection	No effect	1
Extremely Easy detection	Easy to detect	2
Very high probability	Small delays	3
High probability	Detected delays	4
Medium	Late deliveries	5
Little	Several late deliveries	6
Very little	Line stops	7
Hard to detect	Several line stops	8
Extremely high	Customer stop	9
Undetectable	End customer stop	10

Table A4. Criteria for evaluating the cost of logistic defects.

Probability of Cost	Cost Definition	Score
Never	No cost	1
Very small	Non-significant	2
Small	Tens of €	3
Low	Hundreds of €	4
Medium low	1–2k€	5
Medium	2–5k€	6
Significant	5–10k€	7
High	10–25k€	8
Very High	25–100k€	9
Extremely high	Over 100k€	10

Table A5. Criteria for evaluating the controllability of logistic defects.

Probability of Control	Control Definition	Score
Fully controlled	No attention required	1
Exceedingly simple to control	Needs small attention	2
Simple to control	Attention	3
Gap in control	Easy re-planning	4
Several gaps in control	Re-planning	5
Serious gaps in control	Fast reaction	6
Difficult to control	Several fast reactions	7
Very difficult to control	Difficult	8
Partially out of control	Very difficult	9
Completely out of control	Impossible	10

Table A6. A detail from the standard and new FMEA analysis results for 3 factors.

No	Process	Sub-Process	Failure mode	Effect	O	S	D	RPN	AP
1	handling	at supplier	damaged	stop prod/cust	2	9	9	162	H
2	handling	during transp	damaged	stop prod/cust	2	9	7	126	M
3	handling	during uploading	damaged	stop prod/cust	2	9	7	126	M
4	handling	during downloading	damaged	stop prod/cust	2	9	7	126	M
5	handling	delay(nat.hol)	delay in production	stop cust or delay	1	7	7	49	M
6	transport	delay traffic	delay in production	stop cust or delay	1	9	6	54	M
7	transport	delay disaster	delay in production	stop cust or delay	1	10	6	60	M
8	transport	accident	delay in production	stop cust or delay	1	10	6	60	M
9	mat.ordering	order mistake	stop production	stop customer	1	10	6	60	M
10	IT system	IT failure	system error	stop customer	1	10	6	60	M
11	WH	mat.ordering	mat shortage at reseller or supply	stop customer	1	10	6	60	M
12	WH	mat.ordering	mat. shortage market situ	stop customer	1	10	6	60	M
13	WH	mat.ordering	distrib WH issue	stop customer	1	10	6	60	M

Table A7. Ranking of effect by experts from EMS company.

No	C1	C2	C3	C4	C5	C6	C7	C8	C9	C10	C11	C12	C13	C14	C15	C16	C17	C18	C19	C20
C1	1	4.5	4	5	1	0.33	2	1	7.5	7	3	1.5	2.5	0.83	6	3.5	8.5	5.5	6.5	0.5
C2	0.22	1	0.83	1.2	0.25	0.17	0.33	0.25	3	2.5	0.5	0.33	0.5	0.2	1.5	0.67	4	2	2.5	0.25
C3	0.25	1.2	1	1.5	0.29	0.18	0.4	0.29	3.5	3	0.67	0.33	0.5	0.2	2	0.83	4.5	1.5	2.5	0.2
C4	0.2	0.83	0.67	1	0.22	0.15	0.4	0.29	3.5	3	0.67	0.33	0.5	0.2	2	0.83	4.5	1.5	2.5	0.2
5C	1	4	3.5	4.5	1	0.5	15	1.2	7	6.5	2.5	1	2	0.5	5.5	3	7.5	5	6	0.67
C6	3	6	5.5	6.5	2	1	3.5	2.5	9	8.5	4.5	3	4	1	7.5	5	9.5	7	8	1
C7	0.5	3	2.5	3	0.67	0.29	1	0.83	6.5	5	1.3	0.9	1.2	0.4	4	1.5	6.5	3.5	4.5	0.33
C8	1	4	3.5	4	0.83	0.4	1.2	1	6.5	6	2	1.2	1.5	0.67	5	2.5	7.5	4.5	5.5	0.5
C9	0.13	0.33	0.29	0.4	0.14	0.11	0.15	0.15	1	0.8	0.22	0.17	0.2	0.13	0.15	0.25	2	0.5	0.83	0.12
C10	0.14	0.4	0.33	0.5	0.15	0.12	0.2	0.17	1.25	1	0.25	0.18	0.22	0.13	0.83	0.29	3	0.67	0.91	0.13
C11	0.33	2	1.5	2	0.4	0.22	0.77	0.5	4.5	4	1	0.67	0.91	0.29	3	1.2	5	2.5	3.5	0.25
C12	0.67	3	3	3.5	1	0.33	1.11	0.83	6	5.5	1.5	1	1.2	0.5	0.22	2	6.5	4	5	0.4
C13	0.4	2	2	2.5	0.5	0.25	0.83	0.67	5	4.5	1.1	0.83	1	0.33	3.5	1.2	5.5	3	4	0.29
C14	1.2	5	5	5.5	2	1	2.5	1.5	8	7.5	3.5	2	3	1	6.5	4	8.5	6	7	0.83
C15	0.17	0.67	0.5	0.67	0.18	0.13	0.25	0.2	6.5	1.2	0.33	4.5	0.29	0.15	1	0.4	2	0.83	1.2	0.14
C16	0.29	1.5	1.2	1.5	0.33	0.2	0.67	0.4	4	3.5	0.83	0.5	0.83	0.25	2.5	1	5	2	3	0.22
C17	0.12	0.25	0.22	0.29	0.13	0.11	0.15	0.13	0.5	0.33	0.2	0.15	0.18	0.12	0.5	0.2	1	0.4	0.67	0.11
C18	0.18	0.5	0.67	0.77	0.2	0.14	0.29	0.22	2	1.5	0.4	0.25	0.33	0.17	1.2	0.5	2.5	1	1.2	0.15
C19	0.15	0.4	0.4	0.56	0.17	0.13	0.22	0.18	1.2	1.1	0.29	0.2	0.25	0.14	0.83	0.33	1.5	0.83	1	0.13
C20	2	4	5	6	1.57	1	3	2	8.5	8	4	2.5	3.5	1.2	7	4.5	9	6.5	7.5	1

Table A8. Random evaluation of impacts in all risk cases.

No	C1	C2	C3	C4	C5	C6	C7	C8	C9	C10	C11	C12	C13	C14	C15	C16	C17	C18	C19	C20
Eval	+	−	+	−	+	−	+	−	+	−	+	−	+	−	+	−	+	−	+	−

Table A9. Evaluation of impacts in all risk cases based on ranking matrix.

No	C1	C2	C3	C4	C5	C6	C7	C8	C9	C10	C11	C12	C13	C14	C15	C16	C17	C18	C19	C20
Eval	−	+	+	+	−	−	−	−	+	+	−	−	−	+	−	+	+	+	+	−

References

1. Huang, J.; You, J.X.; Liu, H.C.; Song, M.S. Failure mode and effect analysis improvement: A systematic literature review and future research agenda. *Reliab. Eng. Syst. Saf.* **2020**, *199*, 106885. [CrossRef]
2. AIAG-VDA. *Failure Mode and Effects Analysis–FMEA Handbook*, 1st ed.; Automotive Industry Action Group: Southfield, MI, USA, 2016; Volume 1.
3. Dickson, W.G. An analysis of vendor selection systems and decisions. *J. Purch.* **1966**, *2*, 5–20. [CrossRef]
4. Cheraghi, S.H.; Dadashzadeh, M.; Subramanian, M. Critical Success Factors For Supplier Selection: An Update. *J. Appl. Bus. Res.* **2011**, *20*, 91–108 [CrossRef]
5. Liu, H.C.; Liu, L.; Liu, N. Risk evaluation approaches in failure mode and effects analysis: A literature review. *Expert Syst. Appl.* **2013**, *40*, 828–838. [CrossRef]
6. Curkovic, S.; Scannell, T.; Wagner, B. Using FMEA for Supply Chain Risk Management. *Mod. Manag. Sci. Eng.* **2013**, *1*, 251–256.
7. Curkovic, S.; Scannell, T.; Wagner, B. *ManagingSupply Chain Risk, Integrating with Risk Management*; CRC Press: Boca Raton, FL, USA, 2016.
8. Vodenicharova, M. Opportunities for the applications of FMEA Model in logistics processes in Bulgarian enterprises. *Logist. Sustain. Transp.* **2017**, *8*, 31–41. [CrossRef]
9. Lolli, F.; Ishizaka, A.; Gamberini, R.; Rimini, B.; Messori, M. FlowSort-GDSS–A novel group multi-criteria decision support system for sorting problems with application to FMEA. *Expert Syst. Appl.* **2015**, *42*, 6342–6349. [CrossRef]
10. Malekitabar, H.; Ardeshir, A.; Sebt, M.H.; Stouffs, R.; Teo, E.A.L. On the calculus of risk in construction projects: Contradictory theories and a rationalized approach. *Saf. Sci.* **2018**, *101*, 72–85. [CrossRef]
11. Wu, X.; Wu, J. The Risk Priority Number Evaluation of FMEA Analysis Based on Random Uncertainty and Fuzzy Uncertainty. *Complexity* **2021**, *2021*, 8817667. [CrossRef]
12. Ewa Kulinska, D.M.; Dendera-Gruszka, M. New Application of FMEA Analysis in the Heavy Industry Supply Chain. *Eur. Res. Stud. J.* **2021**, *24*, 600–616 . [CrossRef]
13. Ebadi, A.; Keyghobadi, A.R.; Motadel, M.R.; Yeganegi, M.R. The Analysis of Sustainable Supply Chain Risks Based on the FMEA Method in the Oil and Gas industry and Factors Affecting Risk Management. *Pet. Bus. Rev.* **2020**, *4*, 95–116. [CrossRef]
14. Indrasari, L.D.; Vitasmoro, P.; Pariyanto, A.Y.T. FMEA Approach to Risk Factors as a Factor in Implementing Green Supply Chain Management (Study in PT. Gresik Cipta Sejahtera). *J. Phys. Conf. Ser.* **2021**, *1858*, 012069. [CrossRef]

15. Aleksic, B.; Djekic, I.; Miocinovic, J.; Memisi, N.; Smigic, N. Application of FMEA Analysis in the Short Cheese Supply Chain. *Meat Technol.* **2020**, *61*, 161–173. [CrossRef]
16. Mustaniroh, S.A.; Murod, F.A.I.K.; Silalahi, R.L.R. The risk assessment analysis of corn chips supply chain using Fuzzy FMEA. *IOP Conf. Ser. Earth Environ. Sci.* **2020**, *475*, 012052. [CrossRef]
17. Trenggonowati, D.L.; Bahauddin, A.; Ridwan, A.; Wulandari, Y. Proposed Action of Supply Chain Risk Mitigation Air Compressor Type L Unloading ¼ HP Using The Fuzzy–FMEA and Fuzzy–AHP Method in PT. XYZ. *J. Innov. Technol.* **2021**, *2*, 10–17. [CrossRef]
18. Lu Lu, R.Z.; de Souza, R. Enhanced FMEA for supply chain risk identification. In Proceedings of the Hamburg International Conference of Logistics (HICL), Hamburg, Germany, 13–14 September 2018; Hamburg University of Technology (TUHH): Hamburg, Germany, 2018; pp. 311–330. . [CrossRef]
19. Petrović, D.V.; Tanasijević, M.; Milić, V.; Lilić, N.; Stojadinović, S.; Svrkota, I. Risk assessment model of mining equipment failure based on fuzzy logic. *Expert Syst. Appl.* **2014**, *41*, 8157–8164. [CrossRef]
20. Trenggonowati, D.L.; Ulfah, M.; Arina, F.; Lutfiah, C. Analysis and strategy of supply chain risk mitigation using fuzzy failure mode and effect analysis (fuzzy fmea) and fuzzy analytical hierarchy process (fuzzy ahp). *IOP Conf. Ser. Mater. Sci. Eng.* **2020**, *909*, 012085. [CrossRef]
21. Canbakis, S.K.; Karabas, M.; Kilic, H.S.; Koseoglu, S.; Unal, E. A risk assessment model for supply chains. *Pressacademia* **2018**, *7*, 122–125. [CrossRef]
22. Zammori, F.; Gabbrielli, R. ANP/RPN: A multi criteria evaluation of the Risk Priority Number. *Qual. Reliab. Eng. Int.* **2011**, *28*, 85–104. [CrossRef]
23. Ling, W.K. *Nonlinear Digital Filters*; Elsevier Ltd.: Boston, MA, USA, 2004.
24. Kubler, S.; Robert, J.; Derigent, W.; Voisin, A.; Traon, Y.L. A state-of the-art survey & testbed of fuzzy AHP (FAHP) applications. *Expert Syst. Appl.* **2016**, *65*, 398–422. [CrossRef]
25. Johanyák, Z.; Kovács, S. On the right selection of the fuzzy membership function. *GAMF J.* **2004**, *19*, 73–84.
26. Zhu, Q.; Golrizgashti, S.; Sarkis, J. Product deletion and supply chain repercussions: Risk management using FMEA. *Benchmarking Int. J.* **2020**, *28*, 409–437. [CrossRef]
27. Wan, C.; Yan, X.; Zhang, D.; Qu, Z.; Yang, Z. An advanced fuzzy Bayesian-based FMEA approach for assessing maritime supply chain risks. *Transp. Res. Part E Logist. Transp. Rev.* **2019**, *125*, 222–240. [CrossRef]
28. Dendera-Gruszka, M.; Kulińska, E. Supply Chain FMEA Risk Analysis for the Heavy Industry Sector. In *Risk Management and Assessment*; IntechOpen: London, UK, 2020. [CrossRef]
29. Salamai, A.; Hussain, O.K.; Saberi, M.; Chang, E.; Hussain, F.K. Highlighting the Importance of Considering the Impacts of Both External and Internal Risk Factors on Operational Parameters to Improve Supply Chain Risk Management. *IEEE Access* **2019**, *7*, 49297–49315. [CrossRef]
30. Roscoe, S.; Eckstein, D.; Blome, C.; Goellner, M. Determining how internal and external process connectivity affect supply chain agility: A life-cycle theory perspective. *Prod. Plan. Control.* **2020**, *31*, 78–91. [CrossRef]
31. Srivastava, M.; Rogers, H. Managing global supply chain risks: Effects of the industry sector. *Int. J. Logist. Res. Appl.* **2022**, *25*, 1091–1114. [CrossRef]
32. Mohammed, A.; Jabbour, A.B.L.d.S.; Diabat, A. COVID-19 pandemic disruption: A matter of building companies' internal and external resilience. *Int. J. Prod. Res.* **2023**, *61*, 2716–2737. [CrossRef]
33. Kosztyán, Z.T.; Csizmadia, T.; Kovács, Z.; Mihálcz, I. Total risk evaluation framework. *Int. J. Qual. Reliab. Manag.* **2020**, *37*, 575–608. [CrossRef]
34. Kovács, Z.; Kosztyán, Z.T.; Csizmadia, T. TREF–Total Risk Evaluation Framework: Integrált kockázatmenedzsment-szemléletű keretrendszer kifejlesztése és bevezetése egy magyarországi termelővállalatnál. *Vezetéstudomány/Bp. Manag. Rev.* **2014**, *45*, 71–82. [CrossRef]
35. Kovács, Z.; Csizmadia, T.; Mihálcz, I.; Kosztyán, Z.T. A vállalati kockázatkezelésben használt aggregálófüggvények jellemzése. *Statisztikai Szle.* **2022**, *100*, 821–853. [CrossRef]
36. Calvo, T.; Kolesárová, A.; Komorníková, M.; Mesiar, R. Aggregation Operators: Properties, Classes and Construction Methods. In *Aggregation Operators*; Physica-Verlag HD: Heidelberg, Germany, 2002; pp. 3–104. [CrossRef]
37. Grabisch, M.; Marichal, J.L.; Mesiar, R.; Pap, E. Aggregation functions: Means. *Inf. Sci.* **2011**, *181*, 1–22. [CrossRef]
38. Grabisch, M.; Marichal, J.L.; Mesiar, R.; Pap, E. *Aggregation Functions (Encyclopedia of Mathematics and Its Applications)*; Cambridge University Press: Cambridge, UK, 2009; Volume 127, pp. 428–453.
39. Zahedi Khameneh, A.; Kilicman, A. Some Construction Methods of Aggregation Operators in Decision-Making Problems: An Overview. *Symmetry* **2020**, *12*, 694. [CrossRef]
40. Kozarević, S.; Puška, A. Use of fuzzy logic for measuring practices and performances of supply chain. *Oper. Res. Perspect.* **2018**, *5*, 150–160. [CrossRef]
41. Cardiel-Ortega, J.J.; Baeza-Serrato, R. Failure Mode and Effect Analysis with a Fuzzy Logic Approach. *Systems* **2023**, *11*, 348. [CrossRef]
42. Chakraborty, S. TOPSIS and Modified TOPSIS: A comparative analysis. *Decis. Anal. J.* **2022**, *2*, 100021. [CrossRef]
43. Bognár, F.; Hegedűs, C. Analysis and Consequences on Some Aggregation Functions of PRISM (Partial Risk Map) Risk Assessment Method. *Mathematics* **2022**, *10*, 676. [CrossRef]

44. Yazdi, M.M. TOPSIS Method for Multiple-Criteria Decision Making (MCDM). R Package. Available online: https://rdrr.io/cran/topsis/man/topsis.html (accessed on 24 November 2023).
45. *IATF16949-2016*; Quality Management System Requirements for Automotive Production and Relevant Service Parts Organizations; AIAG: Southfield, MI, USA, 2016. Available online: https://www.aiag.org/quality/iatf-16949-2016 (accessed on 1 December 2023).
46. *ISO9001-2015*; Quality Management Systems—Requirements; ISO: Geneva, Switzerland, 2015. Available online: https://www.iso.org/standard/62085.html (accessed on 1 December 2023).

mathematics

Article

Model and Algorithm for a Two-Machine Group Scheduling Problem with Setup and Transportation Time

Yu Ni, Shufen Dai, Shuaipeng Yuan *, Bailin Wang and Zhuolun Zhang

School of Economics and Management, University of Science and Technology Beijing, No. 30, Xueyuan Road, Haidian District, Beijing 100083, China; daisf@ustb.edu.cn (S.D.); wangbl@ustb.edu.cn (B.W.); b2114136@ustb.edu.cn (Z.Z.)

* Correspondence: yuansp@ustb.edu.cn

Abstract: This paper investigates a two-machine group scheduling problem with sequence-independent setup times and round-trip transportation times, which is derived from the production management requirements of modern steel manufacturing enterprises. The objective is to minimize the makespan. Addressing limitations in prior studies, we consider a critical but largely ignored transportation method, namely round-trip transportation, and restricted transporter capacity between machines. To solve this problem, a mixed-integer programming model is first developed. Then, the problem complexity is analyzed for situations with both single and unlimited transporters. For the NP-hard case of a single transporter, we design an efficient two-stage heuristic algorithm with proven acceptable solution quality bounds. Extensive computational experiments based on steel plant data demonstrate the effectiveness of our approach in providing near-optimal solutions, and the maximum deviation between our algorithm and the optimal solution is 1.38%. This research can provide an operable optimization method that is valuable for group scheduling and transportation scheduling.

Keywords: group scheduling; transportation time; mathematical model; heuristic algorithm

MSC: 90B35; 90C59; 90-10

1. Introduction

Recent years have witnessed a surge of interest in tackling combinatorial optimization problems in various real-world industrial contexts, such as the steel manufacturing companies referenced in [1–3] and the manufacturing industry mentioned in [4,5]. This work investigates a two-machine group scheduling problem, where both the sequence independence setup times between groups and the transportation times between machines are considered. This problem is derived from the production management requirement of the tube processing workshop in iron and steel enterprises. Tube processing occurs after the hot rolling stage and includes two production stages: tube cutting and tube processing. In the cutting machine, each long tube is cut into several short tubes, and a certain setup time is required while switching tubes. Because the number of tubes in the cutting machine changes and the processing time is relatively long, the cutting process (CP) is the core link of the entire process flow. After cutting, the short tubes are trans-ported to the tube-processing stage by a transporter. Limited by the processing environment and tubes' properties, the number and capacity of transporters between machines are finite, and the transportation process is limited by the availability of the transporters. Specifically, for any tube, it can be transported only if the transporter has transported the previous tube to next machine and returned. If we take the long tubes at the cutting stage as the group of the short tubes after the CP, then the whole process can be abstracted into a two-machine group scheduling problem with setup times and round-trip transportation times. To achieve the goals of streamlined production and management, this scheduling problem needs to fully consider the constraints of transportation capacity between machines.

The round-trip transportation method and limited transportation capacity between machines make this problem significantly different to classical scheduling group problems. To the best of our knowledge, no relevant research on this problem has been published, resulting in significant limitations of existing achievements in practical applications. Therefore, we are motivated to investigate this type of problem in this work. We first develop a mixed-integer linear programming model with the objective of minimizing the makespan, and then prove that there is a polynomial optimal algorithm for the case that the number of transporters is unlimited. When there is only one transporter, it is proved that the problem is a strong NP-hard problem, and a heuristic algorithm with an upper bound of 3 is proposed. Finally, a simulation experiment based on actual production data is performed and it is verified that the algorithm has a good solution effect. We believe that our research in this work can further narrow the gap between theoretical results of group scheduling and practical applications.

The rest of this paper is organized as follows. Section 2 reviews the literature relevant to this study. Section 3 describes the studied problem and the developed model. Section 4 presents the characteristics of the problem. The designed algorithms are shown in Section 5. Computational results are presented in Section 6. Section 7 concludes our work and suggests areas for future study.

2. Literature Review

Classical scheduling problems have been studied by many scholars from different perspectives. For example, Tian et al. studied a single-machine parallel-batch scheduling problem with non-identical job sizes under time-of-use electricity prices [6]. The objective was to minimize the total energy consumption. To solve the problem, they proposed three mathematical programming models and designed a column-generation algorithm. Chen et al. [7] investigated an energy-oriented scheduling problem arising from hot rolling production in the steel enterprises. The problem was first modeled as a vehicle routing problem with special constraints, and then solved via a knowledge-based NSGA-II algorithm. Zhao et al. [8] addressed an energy-efficient flowshop scheduling problem with the objective of minimizing total energy consumption and total tardiness. A hyper-heuristic Q-learning technique was developed. Tian et al. [9] studied a remanufacturing system scheduling problem with lot-streaming production mode. They formulated the problem as a multi-objective mathematical model aimed at simultaneously minimizing the total energy consumption and makespan. A hybrid optimization algorithm combing the fruit fly optimization algorithm and simulated annealing mechanism was developed. For comprehensive research on scheduling problems, the reader can refer to Dauzère-Pérès et al. [10] and Strusevich [11].

Due to their practical relevance, group scheduling problems have also received much attention in this academic field over the past decade. Lin and Ying [12] investigated a no-wait flowshop group scheduling problem with sequence-dependent setup times. They first established the problem's strong NP-hardness and subsequently formulated a linear programming model with the objective of reducing the makespan. To address this complex problem, they proposed a two-stage metaheuristic algorithm. Costa et al. [13] investigated a flowshop group scheduling with blocking constraints, and developed a parallel genetic algorithm based on adaptive and parallel computing techniques. Recently, Zhao et al. [14] extracted a flowshop group scheduling problem with batch processing characteristics from the steel industry. A mixed-integer linear programming model and a memetic algorithm were formulated to minimize the total number of delayed jobs and the total setup times. Pan et al. [15] explored a distributed flowshop group scheduling problem with the objective of minimizing the makespan. They constructed a mixed-integer linear programming model and proposed a cooperative co-evolutionary algorithm. Building upon Pan's work, Wang et al. [16] further refined the problem by focusing on tardiness. Their improved iterative greedy algorithm demonstrated promising results in minimizing total tardiness. Neufeld et al. [17] provided a comprehensive overview of the current research status about the flow-shop group scheduling problem.

There are few related studies on the group scheduling problem considering transportation times between machines. Liou and Hsieh [18] proposed a hybrid particle swarm and genetic algorithm based on the classic flowshop environment and presented two lower bounds of the optimal solution through theoretical analysis. For the same problem, Ahmadizar and Shahmaleki [19] formulated a mixed-integer linear programming model with the goal of minimizing the total completion time. A genetic algorithm embedding problem specific rules was proposed. Yuan et al. [20] investigated a flowshop group scheduling problem with round-trip transportation times. A mixed-integer linear programming model and an improved differential evolution algorithm were developed with the objective of minimizing makespan.

Although there is a large body of work in the field of group scheduling, most of the studies have focused on the setup time constraint, and only a few studies have considered the transportation process between machines simultaneously. Even for those that have, a fundamental assumption has been that no constraint exists on the availability of transporters between machines, and only one-way transportation time was investigated. That is, once a job is processed on the current machine, it can be transported to the next machine in real time. However, this ideal scenario does not fully align with the realities of industrial settings. As a result, the existing results fall short of addressing the practical requirements of industrial applications, such as the abovementioned tube-processing method in modern iron and steel enterprises. To our knowledge, we are the first to study the group scheduling problem, where the number and capacity of the transporters between machines is limited.

3. Problem Description and Mathematical Model

3.1. Problem Description

The two-machine group scheduling problem with sequence independence setup and transportation times can be summarized as follows: There are g groups to be processed on two machines, and each group has $n_i (1 \leq i \leq g)$ jobs. Each job may be processed on at most one machine at a time, and each machine can process at most one job at a time. The jobs in the same group must be processed continuously without any interruption by the jobs of other groups. Especially, each group requires a sequence-independent setup time on both machines. A round-trip transportation time is required for moving the jobs from the first machine to the second machine. Each transporter must complete a round-trip before the next job can be transported. Different jobs might have different transportation times. In addition, it is assumed that the capacity of the transporter is 1. The objective is to minimize the makespan.

This scheduling problem needs to determine the sequence of groups, and the sequence of jobs within each group so that the makespan is the minimum. If we use GT to denote a group scheduling with intermediate transportation, where x is the number of available transporters and y is the single transport capacity per transporter, then the scheduling problem in this paper can be described as $F2|GT|V(x,1)|C_{\max}$.

3.2. Notations and Model

Notations used in this work are defined below.

g: The number of groups.

G_i: Group index, $i = 1, 2, \ldots, g$.

n_i: The number of jobs in group G_i.

J_{il}: Job index in group G_i, $l = 1, 2, \ldots, n_i$.

M_k: Machine index, $k = 1, 2$.

s_{ilk}: Start time of the job J_{il} on machine M_k.

p_{ilk}: Processing time of the job J_{il} on machine M_k.

c_{ilk}: Completion time of the job J_{il} on machine M_k.

st_{ik}: Setup time of group G_i on machine M_k.

It can be easily demonstrated that the $C_{\max}$ will be greater than z if any of the aforementioned conditions are not met. Suppose that the 3-partition problem has no solution, which implies that there exists a T_i such that $\sum_{a_j \in T_i} a_j \neq b$, or, equivalently, a T_w such that $\sum_{a_j \in T_w} a_j > b$. Consequently, $C_{w1} > 17b/4$, indicating that there is some idle time for transporter while transporting jobs in group G_w, which violates the above condition 2. As previously discussed, this situation is untenable. □

5. Solving Algorithm

5.1. Optimality Analysis

Because the problem $F2|GT|V(1,1)|C_{\max}$ has strong NP-hard characteristics, we can only construct heuristic algorithm by analyzing the characteristics of the problem. In this section, the properties of the optimal solution are analyzed first, and then a heuristic algorithm with upper bound of 3 is proposed.

Lemma 1. *In any optimal scheduling, the sequence of jobs on the two machines is identical, and the order of transportation is also the same.*

Proof. The above lemma can be proved by standard theory of interchange of jobs; there is no further detail to provide. □

From the above lemma, it can be observed that the two sub-problems of the groups sequence and the jobs sequence within each group satisfy the characteristics of the permutation flowshop. For the first sub-problem, it is equivalent to $TF2|prmu|V(1,1)|C_{\max}$, and for the other one, due to the overlapping of the processing times between the groups, it is necessary to introduce the following two definitions.

Definition 1 (Extension). *The difference between the completion time of the group G_i on the two machines is called extension, denoted as B_i. The calculation formula is $B_i = C_{i2} - C_{i1}$.*

Definition 2 (Indentation). *The maximum extension of a group can be provided for its tight front group without changing its own completion time. and the calculation formula is $A_i = max(C_{i1} + t_1, c_{i(n_i-1)2}) - \sum_{l=1}^{n_i-1} p_{il2} - st_{i2}$. It is shown as the shadow part of Figure 2.*

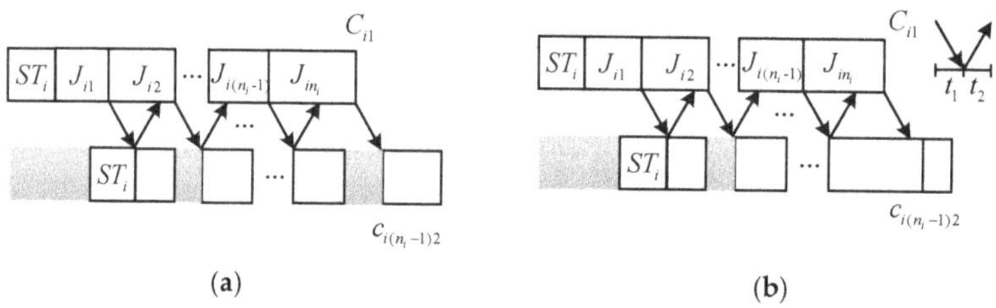

Figure 2. Classification of the indentation for (**a**) $C_{i1} + t_1 > c_{i(n_i-1)2}$ and (**b**) $C_{i1} + t_1 \leq c_{i(n_i-1)2}$.

5.2. Heuristic Algorithm

Figure 2 indicates that the overlap time changes with the location change in the scheduling sequence. Therefore, we can propose the following two-stage heuristic algorithm (Algorithm 1) based on the value of extension and indentation.

Algorithm 1: Two-stage heuristic algorithm

for i = 1 **to** g
  for l = 1 **to** n_i
    $N_1 \leftarrow \{J_{il}|p_{il1} <= t_1 + t_2\}$.
    $N_2 \leftarrow \{J_{il}|p_{il1} > t_1 + t_2\}$.
  end
  $S_1 \leftarrow$ Sort the sequence according to the SPT rule of p_{il2} for jobs in N_1.
  $S_2 \leftarrow$ Sort the sequence according to the SPT rule of p_{il1}, p_{il2} for jobs in N_2.
  $\pi_i \leftarrow [S_1, S_2]$ /* π_i is the job sequence in group G_i */
  /* Calculate A_i and B_i according to the π_i */
  $A_i \leftarrow \max(C_{i1} + t_1, c_{i(n_i-1)2}) - \sum_{l=1}^{n_i-1} p_{il2} - st_{i2}$.
  $B_i \leftarrow C_{i2} - C_{i1}$.
end
$N_3 \leftarrow \{G_i|A_i \leq B_i\}$.
$N_4 \leftarrow \{G_i|A_i > B_i\}$.
$S_3 \leftarrow$ Sort the groups in N_3 according to the SPT rule of A_i.
$S_4 \leftarrow$ Sort the groups in N_4 according to the LPT rule of B_i.
$\Pi \leftarrow [S_3, S_4]$ /* Π is the group sequence */

The following Lemma 2 gives the upper bound of the algorithm.

Lemma 2. *The above algorithm provides a bound of no more than 3 for the problem.*

Proof. Assume that the target value obtained by the above algorithm is C, and the optimal solution to this problem is C^*. Hence, the upper bound of C must be less than $\sum_{i=1}^{g} p_{i1} + \sum_{i=1}^{g} st_{i1} + \sum_{i=1}^{g} \sum_{j=1}^{n_i} (t) - t_2 + \sum_{i=1}^{g} p_{i2}$. In addition, we can see that C^* has the following three lower bounds:

$$LB_1 = \sum_{i=1}^{g} p_{i1} + \sum_{i=1}^{g} st_{i1} + t_1 + \min(p_{il2}), \tag{14}$$

$$LB_2 = \min(st_{ik}) + \min(p_{il1}) + t_1 + \sum_{i=1}^{g} p_{i2}, \tag{15}$$

$$LB_3 = \min(st_{i1}) + \min(p_{il1}) + (\sum_{i=1}^{n} \sum_{l=1}^{n_i} (t_1 + t_2)) - t_2 + \min(p_{il2}). \tag{16}$$

Therefore, the upper bound of the algorithm can be derived from the following equation.

$$\frac{C}{C^*} = \frac{3C}{3C^*} \leq \frac{3C}{LB_1 + LB_2 + LB_3} \leq \frac{3\sum\limits_{i=1}^{n} p_{i1} + 3((\sum\limits_{i=1}^{n} \sum\limits_{l=1}^{n_i} (t_1 + t_2)) - t_2) + 3\sum\limits_{i=1}^{n} p_{i2} + 3\sum\limits_{i=1}^{n} ST_i}{\sum\limits_{i=1}^{n} p_{i1} + \sum\limits_{i=1}^{n} p_{i2} + \sum\limits_{i=1}^{n} ST_i + (\sum\limits_{i=1}^{n} \sum\limits_{l=1}^{n_i} (t_1 + t_2)) - t_2} = 3 \tag{17}$$

□

6. Experimental Results and Discuss

In this section, computational experiments are presented to evaluate the performance of the proposed model and the heuristic algorithm. First, we use small-scale instances to verify the correctness of the model and the deviation between the algorithm and the optimal solution solved by model. Then, the algorithm was compared with the three lower bounds of the optimal solution using large-scale instances. The algorithm is implemented using Matlab language (Matlab R2015a), and the model is solved by CPLEX 12.10. The code-running environment is i5-12500H Intel CPU with 16.00 GB RAM hardware environment.

6.1. Experiment Design

As mentioned before, a difference exists between our studied problem and those in the literature, and no existing benchmark data can be used directly. Therefore, a number of test instances are generated based on the real situations from a large steel plant in China. The following combinations of g and n_i ($1 \leq i \leq g$) are set: $g \in \{3, 5, 10, 20, 50, 100, 150\}$ and $n_i \in \{3, 5, 10, 15\}$. Those data are divided into 6 small-scale classes ($g \in \{3, 5, 10\}$ and $n_i \in \{3, 5\}$) and 12 large-scale classes ($g \in \{20, 50, 100, 150\}$ and $n_i \in \{5, 10, 15\}$). One instance is generated for each combination, which results in 18 instances in total. Other production data for the instances are generated as follows: $p_{ilk} \in DU(5,30)$, $t_1, t_2 = DU[5,15]$; $st_{ik} = DU[5,10]$. Here, $DU(a,b)$ means a discrete uniform distribution between a and b.

6.2. Optimality Test

This section conducts experiments on the aforementioned six small-scale instances to verify the correctness of the model, and to observe the deviation of $C_{\max}$ obtained by our designed algorithm from the optimal one. For each instance, the time limit of CPLEX solver is set to 3600 s. The relative percentage increase (RPI) is used as the evaluation index; RPI is calculated by

$$\mathrm{RPI}(A) = (C_{\max}(A) - C^*_{\max}) \;/\; C^*_{\max} \times 100, \tag{18}$$

where $C_{\max}(A)$ is the objective value obtained by our algorithm, and $C^*_{\max}$ is the optimal target value obtained by CPLEX. The experimental results are shown in Table 1, where $LB_{\max}$ represents the maximum value of three lower bounds.

Table 1. Results for the model and designed algorithm.

$g \times n_i$	LB_{max}	$C_{max}(CPLEX)$	$C_{max}(A)$	RPI
3 × 3	217	222	222	0.000
3 × 5	298	298	298	0.000
5 × 3	434	451	455	0.887
5 × 5	528	539	542	0.557
10 × 3	610	612	619	0.814
10 × 5	915	917	931	1.086
Average	500	506	511	0.557

As shown in Table 1, when the problem scale is very small ($g = 3$ & $n_i = 3$), both CPLEX and our algorithm yield the same $C_{\max}$ value, confirming the correctness of the model. The $LB_{\max}$ values of the six instances are all smaller than the optimal $C_{\max}$ obtained by CPLEX, and the differences between them are extremely small, with an average deviation ratio of 1.2%. This indicates that the lower bound values are tight. Overall, the designed algorithm achieves a maximum RPI of 1.086% and an average RPI of 0.557%, which shows that the deviations in the solutions obtained by the algorithm from the optimal ones are very small. Therefore, we can conclude that our designed algorithm has a good ability to construct high-quality solutions for small-scale instances.

6.3. Results for Large-Scale Instances

To further validate the performance of our algorithm, we conducted experiments using the above 12 large-scale problem instances. Since these instances are beyond the solvability range of CPLEX, the $LB_{\max}$ is used as the benchmark for each instance. The results are shown in Table 2, where T represents the computing time of algorithms.

Table 2. Experimental results.

$g \times n_i$	LB_{max}	C	RPI	T
20 × 5	2307	2309	0.22	0.09
20 × 10	4673	4684	0.24	0.12
20 × 15	7254	7254	0.00	0.12
50 × 5	5263	5298	0.66	0.18
50 × 10	10,511	10,569	0.55	0.12
50 × 15	11,000	11,053	0.48	0.17
100 × 5	11,000	11,024	0.21	0.21
100 × 10	22,000	22,028	0.12	0.19
100 × 15	33,000	33,051	0.15	0.28
150 × 5	15,134	15,245	0.73	0.33
150 × 10	30,023	30,347	1.07	0.50
150 × 15	46,318	46,991	1.38	0.58
Average	16,543	16,654	0.48	0.24

It can be seen from Table 2 that, as the problem size increases, the RPI value also increases, indicating that the difficulty of solving the problem is positively related to the problem size. For the RPI indicator, there are 7 instances with RPI values less than 0.5%, and 10 instances with RPI values less than 1%. The maximum RPI value between the proposed algorithm and the maximum lower bound ($LB_{\max}$) is 1.38%, and the minimum RPI value is zero. Overall, the average RPI value for all instances is just 0.48%, which indicates that the solution obtained by our algorithm is very close to the lower bound of the optimal solution.

The average solution time of all instances for our algorithm is just 0.24 s. Even if the problem scales up to 150 × 15, it can be completed in 0.58 s, showing that the algorithm has high efficiency.

To analyze the performance of the algorithms in solving instances with different numbers of total jobs, a series of statistical analyses based on means and LSD intervals for IGD values are performed. The results are shown in Figure 3.

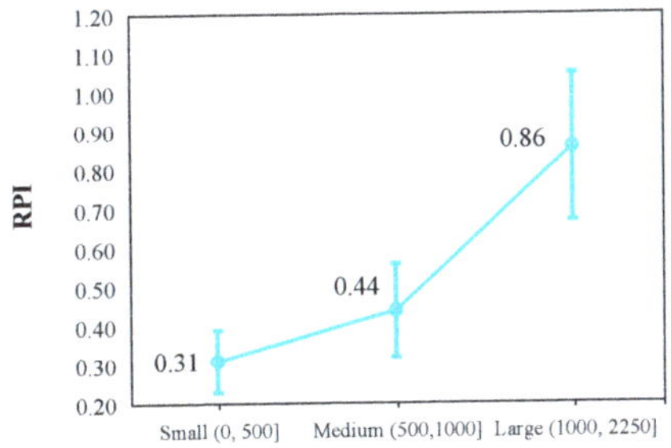

Figure 3. Results of RPI for different number of job sizes.

From Figure 3, we can observe that as the number of jobs increases, the RPI value of our algorithm shows a slight increase trend. Specifically, when the total number of jobs is in the small-scale range (0, 500], the overall RPI value is 0.31. It increases to 0.41 while the total number of jobs is in the medium-scale range (500, 1000], and further increased to 0.86 when the job size is in the large-scale range (1000, 2250]. The above results indicate that the number of jobs has a certain impact on the performance of the algorithm. No matter what the situation, the RPI value from our algorithm is always at a lower level, which confirms the effectiveness of our algorithm in solving the performance problem.

6.4. Comparison with a Real-World Heuristic

In the actual industrial production process, heuristic algorithms based on professional knowledge and human experience are usually used to solve the corresponding scheduling problems. For the problem studied in this work, the most commonly used method by enterprises is the largest processing time (LPT) rule, in which the job (group) with a longer processing time is given a higher priority. To be specific, the job scheduling sub-problem is solved first. For each group, sort the jobs within it in decreasing order of the total processing times on both the two machines ($p_{il1} + p_{il2}$), and generated a job sequence. Then, the completion time of each group should be calculated according to the job sequence within it; also, all of the groups should be arranged in decreasing order of their completion time.

The above heuristic (defined as A_1) is compared with our heuristic on the generated 12 instances. The experimental results are presented in Table 3. From Table 3, it can be seen that our algorithm achieves much better results than the real-world heuristic on all considered instances. The minimum RPI value between those two algorithms is 0.09%, the maximum value is 2.44%, and the average value is 0.74%, further confirming the effectiveness of our algorithm. The 0.74% improvement in makespan may seem modest, but it has a significant impact in industrial applications. It not only enhances production efficiency, but also facilitates energy conservation and emission reduction for energy-intensive manufacturing enterprises. In fact, our designed algorithm has been implemented in a large steel company in China, with satisfactory outcomes.

Table 3. Comparison for our algorithm and a real-world heuristic.

$g \times n_i$	A	A_1	$Gap(A_1 - A)$	RPI
20 × 5	2309	2333	24	1.04
20 × 10	4684	4739	55	1.17
20 × 15	7254	7267	13	0.18
50 × 5	5298	5320	22	0.42
50 × 10	10,569	10,827	258	2.44
50 × 15	11,053	11,064	11	0.10
100 × 5	11,024	11,115	91	0.83
100 × 10	22,028	22,053	25	0.11
100 × 15	33,051	33,088	37	0.11
150 × 5	15,245	15,404	159	1.04
150 × 10	30,347	30,375	28	0.09
150 × 15	46,991	47,613	622	1.32
Average	16,654	16,766	112	0.74

Therefore, it can be concluded that the designed heuristic algorithm is very effective in solving the studied problem.

7. Conclusions

In this work, a two-machine group scheduling problem arising from the real-world steel production is studied. This study makes both practical and theoretical contributions to the field by incorporating round-trip transportation times and limited transportation capacity constraints. To solve the problem, a mixed-integer programming formulation is first established to minimize the makespan. The problem's complexity is examined from two angles. First, when the number of transporters between machines is infinite, we demonstrate that the problem can be solved using a polynomial optimization algorithm. Second, in scenarios with only one transporter, it is proved that the problem is a strongly NP-hard problem. A two-stage heuristic algorithm with an upper bound of 3 is proposed. The proposed heuristic maintains solution quality within 1.38% of lower bounds for large problem instances. Overall, this study significantly advances our understanding of how to combine coordinated scheduling decisions with restricted material flows, which is essential to many multi-stage manufacturing settings. Practical implementations leveraging this research have the potential to yield reduced steel production timelines and improved just-in-time capabilities. From a theoretical perspective, the analysis and algorithms presented open rich avenues for better incorporating logistic realities like finite transporter into classical scheduling models.

Although this paper has made some progress, the following limitations remain. First, only a two-machine case is considered. However, there are often more than two machines in actual industrial environments. Second, the case of multiple transporters is not considered. Third, the two-stage heuristic algorithm designed in this work has certain limitations in the solution quality when solving some large-scale instances. Therefore, an area for further work is extending the problem to environments with more machines and transportation networks. Moreover, using intelligent optimization and reinforcement learning techniques to design more efficient algorithms is also an effective research direction.

Author Contributions: Conceptualization, Y.N. and S.D.; software, validation, investigation, and data curation, S.Y., B.W. and Z.Z.; methodology, formal analysis, and writing—original draft preparation, S.Y.; writing—review and editing and funding acquisition, Y.N. and S.D. All authors have read and agreed to the published version of the manuscript.

Funding: This research was funded by the National Natural Science Foundation of China, grant number 72301026, Ministry of education of Humanities and Social Science project, grant number 23YJA630090.

Data Availability Statement: The datasets used in the study are available from the corresponding author on reasonable request.

Conflicts of Interest: The authors declare no conflict of interest.

References

1. Özgür, A.; Uygun, Y.; Hütt, M. A review of planning and scheduling methods for hot rolling mills in steel production. *Comput. Ind. Eng.* **2021**, *151*, 106606. [CrossRef]
2. Soares, L.C.R.; Carvalho, M.A.M. Application of a hybrid evolutionary algorithm to resource-constrained parallel machine scheduling with setup times. *Comput. Oper. Res.* **2022**, *139*, 105637. [CrossRef]
3. Cao, J.; Pan, R.; Xia, X.; Shao, X.; Wang, X. An efficient scheduling approach for an iron-steel plant equipped with self-generation equipment under time-of-use electricity tariffs. *Swarm Evol. Comput.* **2021**, *60*, 100764. [CrossRef]
4. Chen, C.; Fathi, M.; Khakifirooz, M.; Wu, K. Hybrid tabu search algorithm for unrelated parallel machine scheduling in semiconductor fabs with setup times, job release, and expired times. *Comput. Ind. Eng.* **2022**, *165*, 107915. [CrossRef]
5. Bitar, A.; Dauzère-Pérès, S.; Yugma, C.; Roussel, R. A memetic algorithm to solve an unrelated parallel machine scheduling problem with auxiliary resources in semiconductor manufacturing. *J. Sched.* **2016**, *19*, 367–376. [CrossRef]
6. Tian, Z.; Zheng, L. Single machine parallel-batch scheduling under time-of-use electricity prices: New formulations and optimisation approaches. *Eur. J. Oper. Res.* **2024**, *312*, 512–524. [CrossRef]
7. Chen, L.; Cao, L.; Wen, Y.; Chen, H.; Jiang, S. A knowledge-based NSGA-II algorithm for multi-objective hot rolling production scheduling under flexible time-of-use electricity pricing. *J. Manuf. Syst.* **2023**, *69*, 255–270. [CrossRef]
8. Zhao, F.; Di, S.; Wang, L. A hyperheuristic with Q-learning for the multiobjective energy-efficient distributed blocking flow shop scheduling problem. *IEEE Trans. Cybern.* **2023**, *53*, 3337–3350. [CrossRef]
9. Tian, G.; Wang, W.; Zhang, H.; Zhou, X.; Zhang, C.; Li, Z. Multi-objective optimization of energy-efficient remanufacturing system scheduling problem with lot-streaming production mode. *Expert Syst. Appl.* **2024**, *237*, 121309. [CrossRef]
10. Dauzère-Pérès, S.; Ding, J.; Shen, L.; Tamssaouet, K. The flexible job shop scheduling problem: A review. *Eur. J. Oper. Res.* **2024**, *314*, 409–432. [CrossRef]
11. Strusevich, V.A. Complexity and approximation of open shop scheduling to minimize the makespan: A review of models and approaches. *Comput. Oper. Res.* **2022**, *144*, 105732. [CrossRef]
12. Lin, S.; Ying, K. Makespan optimization in a no-wait flowline manufacturing cell with sequence-dependent family setup times. *Comput. Ind. Eng.* **2019**, *128*, 1–7. [CrossRef]
13. Costa, A.; Cappadonna, F.V.; Fichera, S. Minimizing makespan in a flow shop sequence dependent group scheduling problem with blocking constraint. *Eng. Appl. Artif. Intell.* **2020**, *89*, 103413. [CrossRef]
14. Zhao, Z.; Liu, S.; Zhou, M.; Abusorrah, A. Dual-objective mixed integer linear program and memetic algorithm for an industrial group scheduling problem. *IEEE/CAA J. Autom. Sin.* **2021**, *8*, 1199–1209. [CrossRef]
15. Pan, Q.; Gao, L.; Wang, L. An effective cooperative co-evolutionary algorithm for distributed flowshop group scheduling problems. *IEEE Trans. Cybern.* **2022**, *52*, 5999–6012. [CrossRef]
16. Wang, Z.; Pan, Q.; Gao, L.; Wang, Y. An effective two-stage iterated greedy algorithm to minimize total tardiness for the distributed flowshop group scheduling problem. *Swarm Evol. Comput.* **2022**, *74*, 101143. [CrossRef]
17. Neufeld, J.S.; Gupta, J.N.D.; Buscher, U. A comprehensive review of flowshop group scheduling literature. *Comput. Oper. Res.* **2016**, *70*, 56–74. [CrossRef]
18. Liou, C.; Hsieh, Y. A hybrid algorithm for the multi-stage flow shop group scheduling with sequence-dependent setup and transportation times. *Int. J. Prod. Econ.* **2015**, *170*, 258–267. [CrossRef]

19. Ahmadizar, F.; Shahmaleki, P. Group-shop scheduling with sequence-dependent set-up and transportation times. *Appl. Math. Model.* **2014**, *38*, 5080–5091. [CrossRef]
20. Yuan, S.; Li, T.; Wang, B. A discrete differential evolution algorithm for flow shop group scheduling problem with sequence-dependent setup and transportation times. *J. Intell. Manuf.* **2020**, *32*, 427–439. [CrossRef]
21. Logendran, R.; Salmasi, N.; Sriskandarajah, C. Two-machine group scheduling problems in discrete parts manufacturing with sequence-dependent setups. *Comput. Oper. Res.* **2006**, *33*, 158–180. [CrossRef]

mathematics MDPI

Article

Fuzzy Multi-Item Newsvendor Problem: An Application to Inventory Management

João M. C. Sousa [1,*], Rodrigo Luís [1], Rui Mirra Santos [1], Luís Mendonça [2] and Susana M. Vieira [1]

1 IDMEC, Instituto Superior Técnico, Universidade de Lisboa, 1049-001 Lisboa, Portugal; rui.santos@tecnico.ulisboa.pt (R.M.S.); susana.vieira@tecnico.ulisboa.pt (S.M.V.)
2 IDMEC, Escola Superior Náutica Infante D. Henrique (ENIDH), 2770-058 Paço de Arcos, Portugal; luismendonca@enautica.pt
* Correspondence: jmsousa@tecnico.ulisboa.pt

Abstract: This paper proposes a novel approach to the fuzzy newsvendor problem for inventory management applications. The main contributions of the paper are the following: a new credibility estimation is proposed, to explore the neighborhood around the most impactful demand scenarios; a simulation procedure was designed for the different demand scenarios, which allows comparison of the proposed approach with classical and fuzzy multi-item newsvendor problems; a modified genetic algorithm (GA) is introduced to ameliorate previous genetic algorithms in both the generation and evaluation of solutions. The new formulation of the fuzzy newsvendor problem, together with the modified GA, were shown to improve the average profit by up to 55% in problems with low-budget scenarios.

Keywords: multi-item newsvendor problem; fuzzy newsvendor problem; inventory management; genetic algorithms; credibility estimation

MSC: 90B05; 90B90

1. Introduction

Every day, a newsvendor needs to buy journals based on an uncertain demand. Assuming that each journal has a fixed cost and selling price, if she/he asks for too many journals and the demand is insufficient, there is a reduction in the profit. On the other hand, if the demand is higher than the number of journals ordered, potential sales do not occur, resulting in "lost profits" [1]. This dilemma of buying more or less newspapers, which is known as the *newsvendor problem*, can be applied to any problem that deals with perishable goods, such as newspapers, magazines, fresh food, or holiday decorations, e.g., Christmas trees. This type of problem has one planning cycle of useful life with uncertain demand and can be modeled as an inventory management problem. Further, the framework of the newsvendor problem can also be applied to capacity investment problems, which can solve relevant societal challenges, such as medical capacity investments. One example is the establishment of epidemic diffusion models to characterize how transmission evolves with (and without) vaccination [2].

Several solutions can be found for solving various inventory management problems [1,3,4]. When multi-items are considered for perishable goods, one deals with a multi-item newsvendor problem (MINP). In this problem, it is important to consider the number of constraints and their type (cost, service level, etc.), the decision-making policies (e.g., optimizing expected profit, service level, etc.). Often, solutions are found using risk-averse techniques. Further, very often MINPs use probability density functions to model the uncertain demand [5–8].

However, the demanded probabilistic density functions are difficult to derive in real scenarios, especially for innovative and disruptive products, where there are not sufficient data to accurately predict the demand probability distribution. It is possible to mitigate these limitations by including additional information from human expertise using, e.g., fuzzy systems [9]. Fuzzy logic is a suitable tool for incorporating uncertain demands with a proven effectiveness in solving MINPs [9–11]. A fuzzy environment can use few data points to describe uncertainty through meaningful membership functions. Furthermore, fuzzy logic offers an ideal environment for describing the vagueness of human thinking through mathematical operations, defining linguistic terms such as "the demand of a product is around 2000" [12].

The first fuzzy solution to the newsvendor problem and inventory management with perishable goods dates back to 1996 [9]. Analytical analyses in a fuzzy environment are useful for specific cases, where it is possible to study a limited number of items in a well-isolated economic environment [13–16]. Problems arise when the number of items and their relations increase, leading to highly nonlinear problems, making analytical approaches hard to implement [17]. Most of the recent fuzzy [18–20] and non-fuzzy [21–25] solutions have focused on solving highly complex single-item problems, lacking generalization to multi-item problems.

Fuzzy MINP problems are usually solved using metaheuristic algorithms [10,11]. Inspired by real-world phenomena, metaheuristics use computational power to find solutions when the classical methods cannot, due to time and complexity. However, metaheuristics do not always guarantee that the solutions found are optimal. However, they can, at least, provide good results for highly complex optimization problems [26]. Shao proposed a genetic algorithm to solve the newsvendor problem with a fuzzy environment [10]. This paper extended the fuzzy objective functions proposed in [9], with the adoption of credibility theory concepts [27,28], namely using the concepts of possibility, necessity, and credibility of a fuzzy event, as well as the excepted value of a fuzzy variable [29] to derive objective functions for different decision-making policies. Further, in 2011, Taleizadeh [11] studied a variety of metaheuristic algorithms to solve a fuzzy single-period newsvendor problem and also proved the suitability of genetic algorithms for this problem.

This paper proposes the following contributions to the fuzzy multi-item newsvendor problem:

- A new credibility estimation is proposed to explore the neighborhood around the most impactful demand scenarios.
- A simulation procedure is designed for different demand scenarios, allowing the comparison of the different fuzzy MINP approaches.
- The genetic algorithm in [11] is modified to solve the fuzzy multi-item newsvendor problem, enhancing the work of [10] in both the generation and evaluation of solutions.

This paper is organized as follows. Section 2 describes classical and fuzzy multi-item newsvendor problems. The proposed hybrid algorithm used to solve fuzzy multi-item newsvendor problems is presented in Section 3. This section first describes a simulation procedure to generate the demand vectors. Then, the proposed credibility estimation is presented. Finally, the optimization architecture using a modified genetic algorithm with three novel mechanisms is described. Benchmark case studies are described in Section 4. Section 5 presents the obtained results, and the conclusions and future work are presented in Section 6.

2. Multi-Item Newsvendor Problem

This section introduces the formulation of the multi-item newsvendor problem. Section 2.1 presents the classical approach with probabilistic demand curves, and Section 2.2 explains the fundamentals of the fuzzy MINP approach.

2.1. Classical Multi-Item Newsvendor Problem

The newsvendor problem deals with situations where the demand for products or items is uncertain. Ordered items that are unsold or unused become obsolete, incurring a cost to dispose of them. However, when the initial amount of at least one of the items is too small, this causes loss of revenue. The classical formulation suggested in [30] uses a modified form of the original model proposed in 1964 [31]. The form in [30] minimizes the expected cost E, with this being minimization equivalent to maximizing an "expected profit" function. The model of the classical multi-item newsvendor problem is as follows:

$$\min\ E = \sum_{i=1}^{N} \left[c_i x_i + h_i \int_0^{x_i} (x_i - d_i) f_i(d_i) d(d_i) + v_i \int_{x_i}^{\infty} (d_i - x_i) f_i(d_i) d(d_i) \right], \tag{1}$$

subject to

$$\sum_{i=1}^{n} c_i x_i \leq B, \tag{2}$$

where the definition of the variables used in this classical multi-item newsvendor problem, which will be used throughout this paper, are the following:

E	expected cost
n	total number of items (products)
$i(=1,2,\ldots,n)$	an item index
c_i	cost per unit of item i
x_i	amount to be ordered of item i (stochastic variable)
h_i	cost incurred per item i for leftover
d_i	demand of item i
$f_i(d_i)$	probability density function of demand for item i
v_i	revenue per unit of item i
B	available budget.

This problem is commonly solved using a generic iterative method, by relaxing the problem constraint, applying the Leibniz rule, and using a Lagrangian optimization with a Lagrangian multiplier. This method is described in detail in [30], and is used for comparison purposes for the results, in Section 5. In order to generalize the uncertain demands, a fuzzy formulation of the MINP was introduced in the past [9] and will be described next.

2.2. Fuzzy Multi-Item Newsvendor Problem

This section describes the fuzzy multi-item newsvendor problem, which proved its effectiveness for solving MINP problems [9–11]. First, the definitions of possibility, necessity, credibility, and the expected value of a fuzzy demand are presented. Then, the estimation of possibility, necessity, and credibility is explained. Finally, the estimation of the expected profit, the key point of the fuzzy MINP, is described.

2.2.1. Definitions

The possibility, necessity, and credibility of a fuzzy event, presented in [27,28], are used in this paper. Let a fuzzy variable ξ have a membership function $\mu(u)$. The concepts of possibility, necessity, and credibility of a fuzzy event $(\xi \geq r)$ can be defined as:

$$\text{Pos}\{\xi \geq r\} = \sup \mu(u)\,,\ u \geq r \tag{3}$$

$$\text{Nec}\{\xi \geq r\} = 1 - \sup \mu(u)\,,\ u < r \tag{4}$$

$$\text{Cr}\{\xi \geq r\} = \frac{1}{2}[\text{Pos}\{\xi \geq r\} + \text{Nec}\{\xi \geq r\}] \tag{5}$$

where for our application ξ is a fuzzy demand with the membership function $\mu(u)$, u is the generic demand, and r is a profit value. Considering (3)–(5), the expected value of a fuzzy demand ξ is given by [27]:

$$E[\xi] = \int_0^{\infty} \text{Cr}\{\xi \geq r\}\, dr - \int_{-\infty}^{0} \text{Cr}\{\xi \leq r\}\, dr. \tag{6}$$

2.2.2. Formulation of the Fuzzy Multi-Item Newsvendor Problem

To formulate this problem, additional variables need to be defined:

r_i	retail price per unit $(r_i \geq c_i)$ of item i
s_i	salvage value per unit $(r_i \leq c_i)$ of item i
ξ_i	fuzzy demand of item i
$f(x_i, \xi_i)$	profit function for order quantity x_i and fuzzy demand ξ_i
$F(\mathbf{x}, \Xi)$	total profit for all items, in which $\mathbf{x} = (x_1, x_2, \ldots, x_n)$, $\Xi = (\xi_1, \xi_2, \ldots, \xi_n)$.

The profit function for ith item is given by

$$f(x_i, \xi_i) = \begin{cases} (r_i - c_i)x_i, & x_i \leq \xi_i \\ (r_i - s_i)\xi_i - (c_i - s_i)x_i, & x_i > \xi_i. \end{cases} \tag{7}$$

Then, the total profit of the newsvendor is as follows:

$$F(\mathbf{x}, \Xi) = \sum_{i=1}^{n} f(x_i, \xi_i), \tag{8}$$

subject to (2), as in the classical problem. The objective is to maximize the expected profit of the newsvendor, which can be formulated as follows:

$$\max \ E[F(\mathbf{x}, \Xi)] \tag{9}$$

subject to

$$B - \sum_{i=1}^{n} c_i x_i \geq 0, \tag{10}$$

$$x_i \geq 0, \tag{11}$$

3. Proposed Hybrid Algorithm

In order to solve the fuzzy multi-item newsvendor problem, it is necessary to define a simulation procedure that generates the demand vectors. The simulation procedure proposed to simulate the demand is presented in Section 3.1. A critical issue in the simulation procedure is to estimate the credibility, which is presented in Section 3.2. Afterwards, the proposed optimization architecture using a modified genetic algorithm is presented in Section 3.3.

3.1. Demand Simulation Procedure

This section presents a general simulation procedure for addressing fuzzy multi-item newsvendor problems. Let $\Xi = (\xi_1, \xi_2, \ldots, \xi_n)$ be the vector of fuzzy demands, for all n items. Let μ be the membership function of Ξ, and μ_i be the membership function of ξ_i, for $i = 1, \ldots, n$.

The simulation must generate a sufficiently large positive number for N demand vectors u_{ik}, with $i = 1, \ldots, n$, and $k = 1, \ldots, N$. This procedure simulates real scenarios by using a diverse range of demand vectors u_{ik}, with a greater emphasis on probable vectors, while still accounting for less likely ones. By computing the profit for each demand vector u_{ik} with a given solution, the average profit and profit standard deviation across all vectors can be determined.

Let one assume that $\mathbf{u}_k = (u_{i1}, u_{i2}, \ldots, u_{in})$ is a demand vector of n items. The estimated membership grade of the demand vector is given by

$$\mu(\mathbf{u}_k) = \mu(u_{1k}) \cap \mu(u_{2k}) \cap \cdots \cap \mu(u_{nk}) = \min(\mu(u_{1k}), \mu(u_{2k}), \ldots \mu(u_{nk})) \tag{12}$$

where $\mu(\mathbf{u}_k)$ is the estimated membership grade, and $\mu(u_{ik})$ is the membership grade associated with each order quantity of an item i, with $i = 1, 2, \ldots, n$.

The possibility and necessity estimations of multi-item solutions from the demand vectors $\mathbf{u}_k$ can now be estimated, respectively, in the following way:

$$\widetilde{\text{Pos}}\{R(x,\xi) \geq R_0\} = \max_{1 \leq k \leq N} \{\mu(u_k) | R(x, \mathbf{u}_k) \geq R_0\} \tag{13}$$

$$\widetilde{\text{Nec}}\{R(x,\xi) \geq R_0\} = 1 - \max_{1 \leq k \leq N} \{\mu(u_k) | R(x, \mathbf{u}_k) \leq R_0\} \tag{14}$$

where $R(x, \mathbf{u}_k)$ is the profit function, N is the total number of random demand vectors, and R_0 is a profit target. The estimation of the credibility is based on the previous estimations of possibility and necessity, as follows:

$$\widetilde{\text{Cr}}\{R(x,\xi) \geq R_0\} = \frac{1}{2}\left[\widetilde{\text{Pos}}\{R(x,\xi) \geq R_0\} + \widetilde{\text{Nec}}\{R(x,\xi) \geq R_0\}\right]. \tag{15}$$

This estimation is generic for a solution x and for the kth iteration. It is necessary to estimate the credibility for the complete simulation. The estimation proposed in this paper is described next.

3.2. Proposed Credibility Estimation

The proposed credibility estimation is presented in Algorithm 1. The main objective of this approach is to estimate the credibility of a solution x generating a profit higher than a profit target R_0. It repeats the estimation K times until it finds it. Estimations for different profit targets R_0 are further used to estimate the expected profit of the solution x.

The demand vector is randomly generated and considers quantities that have a membership grade higher than a α_{cut}, which are defined by 10% quantiles, and as so can have the following values:

$$\alpha_{cut} \in T(\alpha_{cut}) = [1.0^{-5},\ 0.1,\ 0.2,\ 0.3,\ 0.4,\ 0.5,\ 0.6,\ 0.7,\ 0.8,\ 0.9]. \tag{16}$$

Further, the α_{cut} is always equal or greater than the minimum value between the highest membership grades found for both possibility and necessity. The α_{cut} progressively increases the minimal membership grade of the randomly generated demand vectors. This is useful because the possibility estimation requires finding the demand vector with the highest membership grade that generates a profit higher than the profit target R_0, as defined in (13). In addition, the necessity estimation requires finding the demand vector with the highest membership grade that generates a profit lower than the profit target R_0, as defined in (14).

Note also that sometimes, due to the random generation, for low credibility solutions, the necessity estimation can be higher than the possibility estimation. These results are impossible, due to the nature of the problem, and therefore are automatically rejected by the algorithm.

The credibility is mandatory to estimate the expected profit of a solution x, with $x = (x_1, x_2, \ldots, x_n)$. To focus resources on plausible values, the profit targets are extracted from the interval defined by

$$\left[-\sum_{i=1}^{N} c_i x_i,\ \sum_{i=1}^{N} (v_i - c_i) x_i\right]. \tag{17}$$

On the one hand, the interval lower limit corresponds to the scenario where no sales are made. On the other hand, the upper limit corresponds to the scenario where all purchased items are sold.

Assuming that the total number of profit targets is given by S, the profit targets are equally distributed and the set of profit targets are defined by $r = (r_1, r_2, \ldots, r_S)$, where

$r_1 < r_2 < \ldots < r_S$. Equations (18)–(20) describe the necessary steps for estimating the expected profit E of a solution x:

$$E_1 = -\sum \widetilde{\mathrm{Cr}}\{R(x, \mathbf{u}_k) \leq r_j\}, \quad if\ r_j < 0 \tag{18}$$

$$E_2 = E_1 + \sum \widetilde{\mathrm{Cr}}\{R(x, \mathbf{u}_k) \geq r_j\}, \quad if\ r_j \geq 0 \tag{19}$$

$$E = E_2 \times \frac{(r_S - r_1)}{S} + \max(0, r_1) + \min(0, r_S) \tag{20}$$

The number of credibility samples S is a crucial variable in this estimation. This variable must be studied to obtain the best possible trade-off between computational time and accuracy.

Algorithm 1 Credibility Estimation

Require: x; R_0; $R(x, \mathbf{u}_k)$; $T(\alpha_{cut})$; K
  $\alpha_{cut} \leftarrow T(\alpha_{cut})$
  $\widetilde{\mathrm{Pos}} \leftarrow 0$; $\widetilde{\mathrm{Nec}} \leftarrow 0$; $l \leftarrow 0$; $stop \leftarrow False$
  while $stop = False$ **do**
    Compute random $\mathbf{u}_k$ with $\min(\mu(u_{1k}), \ldots, \mu(u_{nk})) \geq \alpha_{cut}$
    Compute $\mu(\mathbf{u}_k)$ using (12)

    ====== Possibility and Necessity Update ======
    if $R(x, \mathbf{u}_k) > R_0$ and $\mu(\mathbf{u}_k) > \widetilde{\mathrm{Pos}}$ **then**
      $\widetilde{\mathrm{Pos}} \leftarrow \mu(\mathbf{u}_k)$
    else if $R(x, \mathbf{u}_k) < R_0$ and $\mu(\mathbf{u}_k) > \widetilde{\mathrm{Nec}}$ **then**
      $\widetilde{\mathrm{Nec}} \leftarrow \mu(\mathbf{u}_k)$

    ===========Threshold Update ==========
    if $\min(\widetilde{\mathrm{Pos}}, \widetilde{\mathrm{Nec}}) > \alpha_{cut}$ **then**
      $\alpha_{cut} \leftarrow \min(\widetilde{\mathrm{Pos}}, \widetilde{\mathrm{Nec}})$ (soft threshold update)
    else if $l \geq K$ and $\alpha_{cut} \geq \max(T(\alpha_{cut}))$ **then**
      $stop \leftarrow True$ (finish execution)
    else if $l \geq K$ **then**
      $\alpha_{cut} \leftarrow \min(T(\alpha_{cut}) > \alpha_{cut})$ (hard threshold update)
      $l \leftarrow 0$
    else
      $l \leftarrow l + 1$

  =========== Finish Execution ==========
  $\widetilde{\mathrm{Nec}} \leftarrow 1 - \widetilde{\mathrm{Nec}}$
  if $\widetilde{\mathrm{Pos}} > \widetilde{\mathrm{Nec}}$ **then**
    Compute $\widetilde{\mathrm{Cr}}\{R(x, \xi) \geq R_0\}$ using (15)
  else
    $\widetilde{\mathrm{Cr}}\{R(x, \xi) \geq R_0\} = 0$ (solution rejected)

3.3. *Proposed Optimization Architecture*

The formulation of the fuzzy newsvendor problem allows its application to inventory problems. This is accomplished with an optimization architecture that combines a modified genetic algorithm (GA) and the expected profit estimation. Along with the common mechanisms of a genetic algorithm, crossover, mutation, and selection [32], novel problem-specific genetic mechanisms are introduced.

The proposed optimization architecture finds the solution $\mathbf{x} = (x_1, x_2, \ldots, x_n)$ with the highest expected profit, according to the fundamentals previously introduced in Section 2.

Algorithm 2 details the proposed genetic algorithm for maximizing the expected profit. This algorithm needs to estimate the credibility $\widetilde{\mathrm{Cr}}$, as proposed in Section 3.2 and Algorithm 1. The genetic algorithm used is the one in [10], using classic selection, crossover, and mutation operators. Further, the genetic algorithm also uses the novel problem-specific genetic mechanisms described in the next section.

Algorithm 2 Proposed Genetic Algorithm

Require: $G; i \leftarrow 0$
while $i < G$ **do**
    for each individual $\mathbf{x}$ of generation i **do**
        Compute profit interval using (17)
        Compute all profit targets r_j by equally sample profit interval
        Compute the credibility $\widetilde{Cr}\{R(x,\xi) \geq r_j\}$ for all j using Algorithm 1
        Compute expected profit $E[R(x,\xi)]$ using (18)–(20)
    Compute next population using novel GA mechanisms in Section 3.4
    $i \leftarrow i+1$
Select the individual x with the highest expected profit E.

3.4. *Novel Problem-Specific Genetic Mechanisms*

This section describes problem-specific mechanisms, which are implemented in the architecture proposed in Algorithm 2. These methods enhance the set of solutions by (1) discarding items in the initial population, (2) scaling chromosomes according to the available budget, and (3) introducing a problem-specific context to the crossover operator. This section thus proposes chromosome initialization, solution resizing, and chromosome normalization, which are described next.

3.4.1. Initialization with Zero Quantities

The initialization with zero quantities initializes chromosomes with a single non-zero ordering quantity x_i. After selecting a random item i for the non-zero ordering quantity, the chromosome is resized as explained in Section 3.4.2 to scale x_i to reach the available budget. If i is a profitable item, the chromosome is selected, because the expected profit is higher than chromosomes containing less profitable items. This mechanism aims to select (and further combine) only the most profitable items.

3.4.2. Solution Resizing

The solution resizing mechanism scales the chromosome ordering quantities x_i to use all the available budget. It scales the quantities up or down without changing the relative proportions between them. On the one hand, this mechanism can transform over-budget solutions into feasible solutions by scaling them down. On the other hand, it can scale up under-budget solutions to use all the available budget. To apply this mechanism, the ordering quantities x_i are resized to quantities x_{ri} by multiplying them by a resizing ratio, as follows:

$$x_{ri} = x_i \times \frac{B}{\sum_{i=1}^{N} c_i x_i} \tag{21}$$

3.4.3. Chromosome Normalization

This normalization makes the crossover independent of the absolute values in x, by normalizing them according to the items with the highest expected demand value. In this paper, the highest expected demand value comes from the item with the probabilistic density function $f_i(d_i)$, but it could also be the fuzzy value with the highest grade. To apply the chromosome normalization, first, the ordering quantities x_i must be normalized by applying the transformation:

$$x_{ni} = \frac{x_i}{u_i} \tag{22}$$

where x_i is the ordering quantity of item i, u_i is the expected demand value of the probabilistic distribution of item i, and x_{ni} is the normalized ordering quantity of item i. After the crossover has been applied, all normalized ordering quantities x_{ni} must be de-normalized by multiplying them by u_i.

4. Case Studies

The two benchmark case studies used in this paper were presented in [10,30,33]. The first numerical example is well known because it is simple (only six products) and it also shows that relaxing the non-negativity constraints sometimes leads to infeasible order quantities. The second example illustrates the application of the proposed approach for a large number of products, 17 in this case. This number is already similar to several real-world scenarios.

The optimization method presented in [30,33] is a generic iterative method (GIM) with two different use cases: one with exponential demand distributions, which is described in Section 4.1, and the other with normal demand distributions, described in Section 4.2.

4.1. Case Study 1: Exponential Demand Distribution

The first case study was proposed in [30] and used in [10], where the item demand is exponentially distributed. An exponential distribution for demand d_i with a mean value m_i is described in (23) and (24), defining its probability density function and cumulative distribution function, respectively.

$$f_i(d_i, m_i) = \begin{cases} 0, & d_i < m_i \\ \frac{1}{m_i} e^{-\frac{d_i}{m_i}}, & d_i \geq m_i \end{cases} \tag{23}$$

$$F_i(d_i, m_i) = \begin{cases} 0, & d_i < m_i \\ 1 - e^{-\frac{d_i}{m_i}}, & d_i \geq m_i. \end{cases} \tag{24}$$

In [10,30], the exponential demand distribution considered a problem with six items, as presented in Table 1, and a budget of 3500 currency units (CU).

Table 1. Data for Case Study 1: Revenue loss per unit, cost for leftover, cost per unit, and mean of demand for the six items.

Item	v_i (CU)	h_i (CU)	c_i (CU)	m_i
1	7	1	4	200
2	12	2	8	225
3	30	4	20	112.5
4	30	4	10	100
5	40	2	13	75
6	45	5	15	30

The GIM proposed in [30] solved this optimization problem by relaxing the problem constraint, applying the Leibniz rule and using a Lagrangian optimization with a Lagrangian multiplier. The obtained solution with the ordering quantities per item is presented in Table 2.

Table 2. Case Study 1: benchmark solution with ordering quantities per item.

Item	1	2	3	4	5	6
x_i	78.41	58.16	30.06	81.74	70.91	25.29

4.2. Case Study 2: Normal Demand Distribution

The second case study was proposed in [33] , and considers a normal distribution for demand d_i. A demand distribution d_i has the mean value m_i and the standard deviation σ_i, see (25) and (26), defining its probability density function and cumulative distribution function, respectively.

$$f_i(d_i, m_i) = \frac{1}{\sigma_i \sqrt{2\pi}} e^{-\frac{1}{2}(\frac{d_i - m_i}{\sigma_i})^2} \tag{25}$$

$$F_i(d_i, m_i) = \frac{1}{2}\left[1 + erf\left(\frac{d_i - m_i}{\sqrt{2}\sigma_i}\right)\right] \tag{26}$$

where

$$erf(x) = \frac{1}{\sqrt{\pi}} \int_{-x}^{x} e^{-t^2} dt. \tag{27}$$

This case study includes 17 items, as shown in Table 3, and an available budget of 2500 CU.

Table 3. Data for Case Study 2: Revenue loss per unit, cost for leftover, cost per unit, mean and standard deviation of demand for the 17 items.

Item	v_i (CU)	h_i (CU)	c_i (CU)	m_i	σ_i
1	7	1	4	102	51
2	12	2	8	73	18.3
3	30	4	19	123	30.8
4	30	4	17	95	23.8
5	40	2	23	62	15.5
6	45	5	15	129	43
7	16	1	10	69	34.5
8	21	2	10	83	41.5
9	42	3	40	120	30
10	34	5	20	89	22.3
11	20	3	10	115	38.3
12	15	5	7	91	30.3
13	10	3	4	52	17.3
14	20	3	12	76	38
15	47	2	33	66	16.5
16	35	4	21	147	36.8
17	22	1	11	104	34.7

The expected profit-maximizing solution proposed in [33] is presented in Table 4.

Table 4. Case Study 2: Benchmark solution with ordering quantities per item.

Item	x_i	Item	x_i
1	0	10	0
2	0	11	15.58
3	0	12	42.2
4	0	13	34.56
5	0	14	0
6	106.86	15	0
7	0	16	0
8	14.02	17	15.23
9	0		

4.3. Membership Functions for the Demand

The fuzzy MINP requires the definition of membership functions for the fuzzy demand. This paper considers trapezoidal and exponential membership functions, in order to compare two different types of membership functions.

A trapezoidal membership function is defined by four parameters (a, b, c, d) [34]. These four parameters define five different line segments alongside the complete universe of discourse. A definition of a trapezoidal membership function is given by:

$$\mu(x; a, b, c, d) = \max\left(\min\left(\frac{x-a}{b-a}, 1, \frac{d-x}{d-c}\right), 0\right). \tag{28}$$

An exponential membership function is defined, using as parameters the mean value m and the decay ratio d:

$$\mu(x; m, d) = \begin{cases} e^{d\frac{x-m}{m}}, & x \leq m \\ e^{-d\frac{x-m}{m}}, & x > m. \end{cases} \tag{29}$$

The membership function parameters for Case Study 1 were based on the ones presented in [10]. This paper adjusted them slightly in order to optimize the results, namely we used triangular membership functions that were revealed to be more suitable for the problem. The originals and the ones used in this paper are presented in Table 5.

Table 5. Membership functions for Case Study 1.

	From [10]		Proposed	
Item	**Type**	**Values**	**Type**	**Values**
1	Trapez.	(180, 190, 210, 220)	Triang.	(180, 200, 200, 220)
2	Trapez.	(210, 220, 230, 240)	Triang.	(210, 225, 225, 240)
3	Trapez.	(100, 110, 115, 125)	Triang.	(100, 112.5, 112.5, 125)
4	Trapez.	(80, 90, 110, 120)	Triang.	(80, 100, 100, 120)
5	Trapez.	(60, 70, 80, 90)	Triang.	(60, 75, 75, 90)
6	Trapez.	(20, 25, 35, 40)	Triang.	(20, 30, 30, 40)

For Case Study 2, trapezoidal and exponential membership functions were tested. The exponential ones gave slightly better results and were chosen for use. The membership functions for Case Study 2 are presented in Table 6.

Table 6. Membership functions selected for Case Study 2.

Proposed					
Item	**Type**	**Values**	**Item**	**Type**	**Values**
1	Exponential	(102, 6)	10	Exponential	(89, 6)
2	Exponential	(73, 6)	11	Exponential	(115, 6)
3	Exponential	(123, 6)	12	Exponential	(91, 6)
4	Exponential	(95, 6)	13	Exponential	(52, 6)
5	Exponential	(62, 6)	14	Exponential	(76, 6)
6	Exponential	(129, 6)	15	Exponential	(66, 6)
7	Exponential	(69, 6)	16	Exponential	(147, 6)
8	Exponential	(83, 6)	17	Exponential	(104, 6)
9	Exponential	(120, 6)			

5. Results

This section presents the results using the hybrid algorithm proposed in Section 3. The results are compared with previous classical and fuzzy newsvendor problems. The case studies presented in Section 4 were used to asses the performance of the hybrid algorithm proposed in this paper. These comparisons intend to understand if a more flexible framework—with the ability to incorporate complex profit functions and human expertise—can obtain better results than previous classical and fuzzy approaches that lacked this kind of flexibility.

5.1. Impact of the Genetic Algorithm Parameters

First, the parameters of the genetic algorithm are properly tuned. The first parameters to be explored were the number of generations, which are presented in Table 7. We tested population sizes between 10 and 100 individuals. We used 20 generations to assure some convergence of the algorithm. The population size that obtained the best fitness for Case Study 1 was 75, and for Case Study 2 it was 50. These parameters were thus fixed to these values.

Table 7. Tuning of population size. The line in bold is the one with the best fitness.

Case Study	Generat.	Popul. Size	Fitness	Time [s]
1	20	10	4535 ± 210	105
1	20	25	4882 ± 111	156
1	20	50	4918 ± 99	312
1	**20**	**75**	$\mathbf{5061 \pm 23}$	**372**
1	20	100	4928 ± 129	510
2	20	10	1948 ± 285	198
2	20	25	2915 ± 49	234
2	**20**	**50**	$\mathbf{3015 \pm 66}$	**472**
2	20	75	2959 ± 66	590
2	20	100	3031 ± 49	848

Table 8 presents the test performed in both case studies to find the best number of generations for the genetic algorithm. The problem did not require a large number of generations to converge. Values between 5 and 30 were tested. It was found out that for Case Study 1, 20 iterations gave the best fitness, while 15 generations were the best for Case Study 2.

Table 8. Tuning of the number of generations. The line in bold is the one with the best fitness.

Case Study	Generat.	Popul. Size	Fitness	Time [s]
1	5	75	4935 ± 104	28
1	10	75	5027 ± 53	53
1	15	75	4930 ± 128	128
1	**20**	**75**	$\mathbf{5064 \pm 23}$	**230**
1	30	75	4888 ± 103	367
2	5	50	3011 ± 92	153
2	10	50	2994 ± 39	259
2	**15**	**50**	$\mathbf{3045 \pm 57}$	**471**
2	20	50	3022 ± 66	593
2	30	50	3014 ± 47	710

The tuning of the crossover probability is presented in Table 9. We tested values from 10% to 90%. For both case studies, the value of 80% was found to give the best results. This is interesting, as this is a very common value chosen for this parameter in genetic algorithms.

Table 9. Tuning of the crossover probability. The line in bold is the one with the best fitness.

Case Study	Crossover Probab.	Fitness
1	0.1	48923 ± 160
1	0.3	4883 ± 69
1	0.5	4950 ± 126
1	0.7	4988 ± 103
1	**0.8**	**5107 ± 57**
1	0.9	5067 ± 61
2	0.1	3465 ± 158
2	0.3	3645 ± 89
2	0.5	3650 ± 21
2	0.7	3657 ± 16
2	**0.8**	**3742 ± 44**
2	0.9	3725 ± 41

Last but not the least, we tested the best value for the probability of mutation in the chromosomes, see Table 10. We tested values from 5% to 90%. Please note that very high values (above 70%) can be considered as a random search. The value of 20% was found to be the best value of mutation for both case studies.

Once the usual parameters of the GA had been selected, it was possible to test the impact of the novel problem-specific mechanisms proposed in this paper. This analysis is given next.

Table 10. Tuning of the mutation probability. The lines in bold are the ones with the best fitnesses.

Case Study	Mutation Probab.	Fitness
1	0.05	4987 ± 98
1	0.1	4924 ± 105
1	**0.2**	**5107 ± 57**
1	0.3	4893 ± 64
1	0.4	5002 ± 101
1	0.5	5100 ± 22
1	0.7	4967 ± 135
1	0.9	5016 ± 69
2	0.05	3693 ± 28
2	0.1	3698 ± 34
2	**0.2**	**3742 ± 44**
2	0.3	3716 ± 41
2	0.5	3728 ± 28
2	0.7	3701 ± 68
2	0.9	3701 ± 45

5.2. Impact of the Novel Problem-Specific Mechanisms

This section evaluates the impact of the specific features proposed in this paper on the performance of the optimization. Each of the introduced problem-specific generic mechanisms presented in Section 3.4, namely: initialization with zero quantities, solution resizing and chromosome normalization are analyzed separately.

First, Table 11 presents the influence of the initialization with zero quantities, introduced in Section 3.4.1. This mechanism proved to be advantageous for Case Study 2. However, it proved to be highly disadvantageous in Case Study 1. Therefore, the effect of this initialization varied significantly between the case studies. This mechanism must then be tested, and used only if it leads to better results.

Table 11. Results using initialization with zero quantities. Lines in bold are the ones with the best fitness.

Case Study	Init. with Zero Quantities	Fitness	Simulated Profit
1	Yes	4167.9	2860.3
1	**No**	**4940.9**	**2853.0**
2	**Yes**	**3741.9**	**3797.3**
2	No	2229.9	2446.6

The effect of the solution resizing introduced in Section 3.4.2 is shown in Table 12. The solution resizing was primarily implemented to eliminate unfeasible solutions. This effect is emphasized in the table; the number of unfeasible solutions is zero, as expected. But beyond this, it had the effect of increasing the fitness and the profit. Therefore, this feature was always used in the genetic algorithm.

Table 12. Results using solution resizing. Lines in bold are the ones with the best fitness.

Case Study	Sol. Resizing	Fitness	Unfeasible Sol.	Simulated Profit
1	**Yes**	**4167.9**	**0**	**2860.3**
1	No	3945.1	250.4	2293.2
2	**Yes**	**3741.9**	**0**	**3797.3**
2	No	2208.8	122.2	2305.6

The last modification proposed for introduction in the GA, normalization of the chromosome (which was described in Section 3.4.3), had the results presented in Table 13. It can be observed that the performance in terms of fitness and simulated profit was slightly reduced. However, it is recommended to always try this mechanism in different case studies, because it leads to a smaller computational effort (about a 5 to 10% reduction).

Table 13. Results using chromosome normalization. Lines in bold are the ones with the best fitness.

Case Study	Chromosome Norm.	Fitness	Simulated Profit
1	Yes	4889.5	2827.4
1	**No**	**4940.9**	**2853.0**
2	Yes	3713.7	3755.7
2	**No**	**3741.9**	**3797.3**

5.3. Computational Performance

Scalability is crucial when designing industrial solutions. It is common for real-world inventory management problems to increase the number of items, and thus the number of decision variables. A problem can become impossible to solve in real time when the computational power does not keep up with this increase in dimensions. Thus, computational efficiency is a critical aspect when implementing iterative optimization algorithms, such as genetic algorithms [35,36].

Genetic algorithms are excellent candidates for applying parallel computing. They have several steps where they perform multiple independent tasks, such as fitness evaluation or creation of a population. We used parallelism in the fitness evaluation procedure, since this is the phase with the highest computational cost. The parallel computation was implemented in a cloud environment.

Every program running in the cloud has an environment previously defined by the user. This environment is called a container. The container has all the necessary packages, as well as the source code to be executed. Additionally, the container receives all required variables (in the MINP, the crossover probability, population size, etc.) as environment variables. This results in an isolated and constant environment that allows running a given program for different input variables. With the container defined, it is possible to pass its image to a machine of choice. The device will then execute the tasks described in the source code. Moreover, given a well-defined environment, there will not be any operating incompatibilities during execution. Figure 1 illustrates the overall containerization life cycle.

The ability to perform the same tasks in different machines without altering the source code or conditions is an advantage of containerization. Table 14 presents the characteristics of the set of cloud virtual machines used in this paper. We wanted to find the set exhibiting the best ratio between computational power and performance.

The proposed algorithm was run for both case studies using exponentially distributed demands, considering the different machines in Table 14 and applying parallel computing. Figure 2 shows the relation between the number of virtual CPUs and the run time. For Case Study 2, the more demanding case, Machine 1 had a running time of 9216 s, while Machine 5, the one with the best ratio between power and performance, needed only 340 s to complete the job. The running time reduction between these machines was 96%.

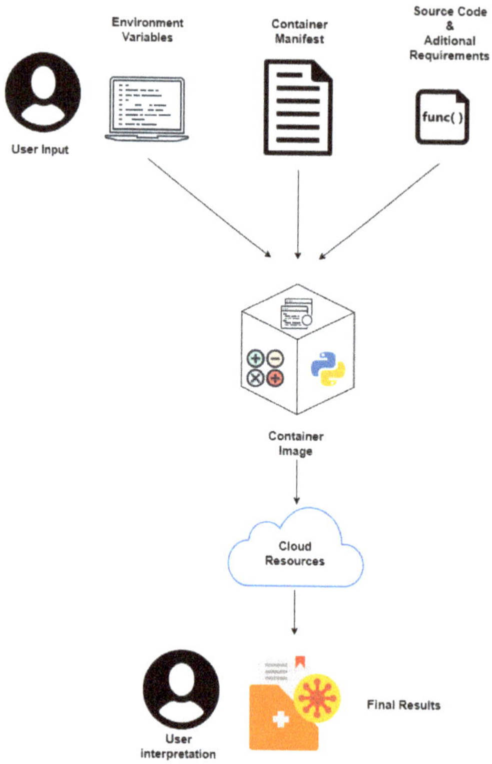

Figure 1. Containerization life cycle.

Table 14. Properties of the virtual machines.

	vCPU	Memory [GB]
Machine 1	2	8
Machine 2	4	16
Machine 3	8	32
Machine 4	16	64
Machine 5	48	192
Machine 6	96	384

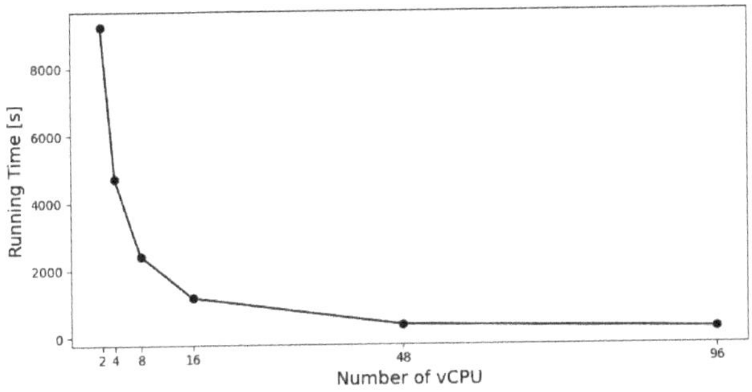

Figure 2. Number of vCPU per machine and running time used in Case Study 2.

Table 15 shows the running time with and without parallelism, both using Machine 5. Without parallel computing, the use of powerful machines becomes irrelevant. Using the integration of parallel computing and cloud resources reduced the computation time by 98.3% (from 5.6 h to less than 6 min). This drastic reduction made problems feasible that were almost impossible to solve due to time constraints. The results obtained in the next section used Machine 5 in a cloud environment with parallelism. The maximum running time was about 8 minutes.

Table 15. Machine 5: Performance with and without parallelism.

	Parallel Execution	Running Time [s]
Machine 5	Yes	340
Machine 5	No	20,342

5.4. Main Results

In this section, we present the main results of our study. It compares the performance of three different methods for solving the case studies in Section 4. The first method is the classical approach, introduced in Section 2.1, the second methods is the fuzzy genetic algorithm proposed in [10], and the third is the hybrid algorithm proposed in this paper in Section 3.

Table 16 presents the obtained results. The GA was run 50 times, and the results show the average and the standard deviation of the obtained profit. It is clear for both case studies that the proposed hybrid algorithm outperformed the other two approaches in terms of profit. In Case Study 1, the simplest case, it was only slightly better than the other approaches. However, in Case Study 2, it significantly outperformed the previous fuzzy approach in [10]. Moreover, it also slightly outperformed the classical approach.

Table 16. Simulation results in terms of average profit and standard deviation of the profit.

Case Study	Method	Profit
1	Classical approach	2877.1 ± 2.0
1	Fuzzy GA from [10]	2889.8 ± 1.2
1	Proposed hybrid algorithm	2914.7 ± 1.5
2	Classical approach	3869.4 ± 0.5
2	Fuzzy GA from [10]	2833.6 ± 0.2
2	Proposed hybrid algorithm	3878.7 ± 0.8

The standard deviation of all approaches was relatively small, showing the effectiveness of the genetic algorithm. For Case Study 1, the proposed algorithm had a smaller standard deviation than the classical approach, but slightly larger than the fuzzy MINP optimized with GA in [10]. In Case Study 2, the proposed algorithm presented a slightly larger standard deviation than the other two approaches, but without affecting the excellent result obtained for the profit.

Summarizing, the proposed hybrid algorithm was able to significantly improve on the previous fuzzy approach and it also slightly improved on the classical approach. The main drawback was its computational demand.

6. Conclusions

A novel approach to the fuzzy newsvendor problem for inventory management applications was proposed in this paper. A hybrid algorithm was proposed to solve fuzzy multi-item newsvendor problems by introducing a simulation procedure to generate the demand vectors. One of the main contributions of this work was the redesigning of a mandatory variable in the simulation procedure, the credibility estimation, which introduced a dynamic adjustment of an α_{cut} threshold to generate meaningful demand vectors, instead of using a purely random vector generation. Further, a modified genetic algorithm that discards some products in the initial population, scales the chromosomes according to the available budget, and makes the crossover operator independent of the absolute values of the solutions.

The proposed hybrid algorithm was compared to other classical and fuzzy approaches in two benchmark case studies, and it slightly outperformed the classical approach. However, it clearly outperformed the previous fuzzy approach. In the most complex case, Case Study 2, it improved the profit by 55%. This performance increase was the result of introducing a new initialization with null values, which proved to be a valuable mechanism in low-budget scenarios, where there is the need for rejecting less profitable items. Please note that Case Study 2 already has a high dimension and it is similar to a large number of real-world problems in inventory management. The main limitation of the proposed approach was the computational effort of the algorithm. Using a cloud environment and parallel computing led to low computational times (about 8 min), which is very acceptable. However, these resources can be expensive.

The proposed hybrid algorithm is very flexible. Despite using fixed costs to prove its effectiveness against analytical approaches, this solution can work with nonlinear pricing models. To perform this, one only needs to integrate the pricing information when calculating profits in the credibility estimation. This is suggested for future work. Moreover, there is the possibility of changing performance measures. Profit was used to prove the effectiveness against analytical approaches, but the algorithm could prioritize the solutions that most satisfied possible customer demand, by replacing the profit calculation with a service-level calculation, for instance. We used perhaps the most usual version of a fuzzy number. However, other fuzzy numbers such as Z–numbers [37], G–numbers [38], or R–numbers [39] could be used. This is another avenue of future research. Last but not the least, in the near future, we are going to implement the fuzzy MINP in a model of medical capacity investment, to evaluate the impact of health public policies in terms of infant mortality rates.

Author Contributions: Methodology, J.M.C.S., R.L., R.M.S., L.M. and S.M.V.; software, R.L. and R.M.S.; validation, J.M.C.S., R.L., R.M.S., L.M. and S.M.V.; formal analysis, L.M. and S.M.V.; investigation, J.M.C.S., R.L., L.M. and S.M.V.; writing—original draft, R.L.; writing—review and editing, J.M.C.S., L.M. and S.M.V.; supervision, J.M.C.S. and R.M.S. All authors have read and agreed to the published version of the manuscript.

Funding: This work was supported by the Fundação para a Ciência e para a Tecnologia (FCT), by the project AI4Life, DSAIPA/DS/0054/2019. The authors also acknowledge FCT for its financial support via the projects LAETA Base Funding (DOI: 10.54499/UIDB/50022/2020) and LAETA Programatic Funding (DOI: 10.54499/UIDP/50022/2020).

Data Availability Statement: Data are contained within the article.

Conflicts of Interest: The authors declare no conflict of interest.

References

1. Choi, T.M. *Handbook of Newsvendor Problems. International Series in Operations Research & Management Science*; Springer: Berlin/Heidelberg, Germany, 2012. [CrossRef]
2. Chen, X.; Dong, Y.; Wu, M. Medical capacity investment for epidemic disease: The effects of policymaker's confidence and public trust. *Risk Anal.* **2023**, *43*, 1187–1211. [CrossRef] [PubMed]
3. Wilson, E.B. The Mathematical Theory of Investment. *Science* **1888**, *42*, 248–249. [CrossRef]
4. Mu, M.; Chen, J.; Yang, Y.; Guo, J. The Multi–product Newsvendor Problem: Review and Extensions. In Proceedings of the 2019 6th International Conference on Behavioral, Economic and Socio-Cultural Computing, Beijing, China, 28–30 October 2019; pp. 6–9.
5. Lau, H.S.; Lau, A.H.L. The multi-product multi-constraint newsboy problem: Applications, formulation and solution. *J. Oper. Manag.* **1995**, *13*, 153–162. [CrossRef]
6. Lau, H.S.; Lau, A.H.L. The newsstand problem: A capacitated multiple-product single-period inventory problem. *Eur. J. Oper. Res.* **1996**, *94*, 29–42. [CrossRef]
7. Shi, J.; Zhang, G.; Sha, J. Jointly pricing and ordering for a multi–product multi–constraint newsvendor problem with supplier quantity discounts. *Appl. Math. Model.* **2011**, *35*, 3001–3011. [CrossRef]
8. Shi, J.; Bao, Y. Multiproduct multiperiod newsvendor problem with dynamic market efforts. *Discret. Dyn. Nat. Soc.* **2016**, *2016*, 7674027. [CrossRef]
9. Petrović, D.; Petrović, R.; Vujošević, M. Fuzzy models for the newsboy problem. *Int. J. Prod. Econ.* **1996**, *45*, 435–441. [CrossRef]
10. Shao, Z.; Ji, X. Fuzzy multi–product constraint newsboy problem. *Appl. Math. Comput.* **2006**, *180*, 7–15. [CrossRef]
11. Taleizadeh, A.A.; Barzinpour, F.; Wee, H.M. Meta-heuristic algorithms for solving a fuzzy single-period problem. *Math. Comput. Model.* **2011**, *54*, 1273–1285. [CrossRef]
12. Sousa, J.M.C.; Kaymak, U. *Fuzzy Decision Making in Modeling and Control*; World Scientific Inc.: Singapore, 2002.
13. Ishii, H.; Konno, T. A stochastic inventory problem with fuzzy shortage cost. *Eur. J. Oper. Res.* **1998**, *106*, 90–94. [CrossRef]
14. Li, L.; Kabadi, S.N.; Nair, K.P. Fuzzy models for single-period inventory problem. *Fuzzy Sets Syst.* **2002**, *132*, 273–289. [CrossRef]
15. Dutta, P.; Chakraborty, D.; Roy, A.R. A single-period inventory model with fuzzy random variable demand. *Math. Comput. Model.* **2005**, *41*, 915–922. [CrossRef]
16. Dutta, P.; Chakraborty, D.; Roy, A.R. An inventory model for single-period products with reordering opportunities under fuzzy demand. *Comput. Math. Appl.* **2007**, *53*, 1502–1517. [CrossRef]
17. Shekarian, E.; Kazemi, N.; Abdul-Rashid, S.H.; Olugu, E.U. Fuzzy inventory models: A comprehensive review. *Appl. Soft Comput.* **2017**, *55*, 588–621. [CrossRef]
18. Adhikary, K.; Roy, J.; Kar, S. A distribution-free newsboy problem with fuzzy-random demand. *Int. J. Manag. Sci. Eng. Manag.* **2018**, *13*, 200–208. [CrossRef]
19. Bhosale, M.R.; Latpate, R.V. Single stage fuzzy supply chain model with Weibull distributed demand for milk commodities. *Granul. Comput.* **2021**, *6*, 255–266. [CrossRef]
20. Latpate, R.V.; Bhosale, M.R. Single cycle supply chain coordination model for fuzzy stochastic demand of perishable items. *Iran. J. Fuzzy Syst.* **2020**, *17*, 39–48.
21. Kouvelis, P.; Zhao, W. Supply chain contract design under financial constraints and bankruptcy costs. *Manag. Sci.* **2016**, *62*, 2341–2357. [CrossRef]
22. Cohen, M.C.; Lobel, R.; Perakis, G. The impact of demand uncertainty on consumer subsidies for green technology adoption. *Manag. Sci.* **2016**, *62*, 1235–1258. [CrossRef]
23. Ban, G.Y.; Rudin, C. The big Data newsvendor: Practical insights from machine learning. *Oper. Res.* **2019**, *67*, 90–108. [CrossRef]
24. Levine, S.D.; Chen, K.Y. Neural Network Modeling of Gist and Verbatim in Business Decision Making. In Proceedings of the International Joint Conference on Neural Networks (IJCNN), Rio de Janeiro, Brazil, 8–13 July 2018; pp. 1–8.
25. Kouvelis, P.; Zhao, W. Who should finance the supply chain? Impact of credit ratings on supply chain decisions. *Manuf. Serv. Oper. Manag.* **2018**, *20*, 19–35. [CrossRef]
26. Quintero-Duran, M.; Candelo, J.E.; Sousa, V. Recent trends of the most used metaheuristic techniques for distribution network reconfiguration. *J. Eng. Sci. Technol. Rev.* **2017**, *10*, 159–173. [CrossRef]
27. Liu, B. *Theory and Practice of Uncertain Programming. Studies in Fuzziness and Soft Computing*; Springer: Berlin/Heidelberg, Germany, 2002; Volume 4, pp. 57–71. [CrossRef]
28. Liu, B. *Uncertainty Theory. Studies in Fuzziness and Soft Computing*; Springer: Berlin/Heidelberg, Germany, 2004. [CrossRef]
29. Liu, B.; Liu, Y.K. Expected value of fuzzy variable and fuzzy expected value models. *IEEE Trans. Fuzzy Syst.* **2002**, *10*, 445–450. [CrossRef]
30. Abdel-Malek, L.; Montanari, R.; Morales, L.C. Exact, approximate, and generic iterative models for the multi-product Newsboy problem with budget constraint. *Int. J. Prod. Econ.* **2004**, *91*, 189–198. [CrossRef]
31. Hadley, G.; Whitin, T.M. Analysis of Inventory Systems. *J. Am. Stat. Assoc.* **1964**, *59*, 283–285. [CrossRef]
32. Holland, J.H. Outline for a Logical Theory of Adaptive Systems. *J. ACM (JACM)* **1962**, *9*, 297–314. [CrossRef]
33. Abdel-Malek, L.L.; Montanari, R. An analysis of the multi-product newsboy problem with a budget constraint. *Int. J. Prod. Econ.* **2005**, *97*, 296–307. [CrossRef]

34. Jang, J.; Sun, C.; Mizutani, E. *Neuro-Fuzzy and Soft Computing-A Computational Approach to Learning and Machine Intelligence*; Prentice Hall: Saddle River, NJ, USA, 1997. [CrossRef]
35. Oral, M.; Kettani, O. Reformulating nonlinear combinatorial optimization problems for higher computational efficiency. *Eur. J. Oper. Res.* **1992**, *58*, 236–249. [CrossRef]
36. Andrianov, A.N.; Anikin, A.S.; Bychkov, I.V.; Gornov, A.Y. Numerical solution of huge-scale quasiseparable optimization problems. *Lobachevskii J. Math.* **2017**, *38*, 870–873. [CrossRef]
37. Zadeh, L.A. A note on Z–numbers. *Inf. Sci.* **2011**, *181*, 2923–2932. [CrossRef]
38. Ghoushchi, S.J.; Khazaeili, M. G-Numbers: Importance-necessity concept in uncertain environment. *Int. J. Manag. Fuzzy Syst.* **2019**, *5*, 27–32. [CrossRef]
39. Seiti, H.; Hafezalkotob, A.; Martínez, L. R-numbers, a new risk modeling associated with fuzzy numbers and its application to decision making. *Inf. Sci.* **2019**, *483*, 206–231. [CrossRef]

MDPI AG
Grosspeteranlage 5
4052 Basel
Switzerland
Tel.: +41 61 683 77 34

Mathematics Editorial Office
E-mail: mathematics@mdpi.com
www.mdpi.com/journal/mathematics

www.ingramcontent.com/pod-product-compliance
Lightning Source LLC
Chambersburg PA
CBHW061623210926
51850CB00009B/2419
* 9 7 8 3 7 2 5 8 4 3 6 7 1 *